CAPITALISM, SOCIALISM AND KNOWLEDGE

ASSOCIAZIONE SIGISMONDO MALATESTA

The Associazione Sigismondo Malatesta is a private cultural Association founded in 1988 and run by a group of scholars working in different fields and coming from different Italian universities: Naples, Rome, Venice and Bari.

The Association promotes meetings, conferences and seminars in the fields of economics, history of ideas, comparative literature and history of theatre. The home of the Association is the Rocca Malatestiana in Sant'Arcangelo di Romagna – Rimini.

Capitalism, Socialism and Knowledge

The Economics of F.A. Hayek
Volume II

Edited by

M. Colonna

Università degli Studi di Napoli
Italy

H. Hagemann

Universität Hohenheim
Stuttgart, Germany

O.F. Hamouda

Glendon College, York University
Toronto, Canada

Edward Elgar

Published by
Edward Elgar Publishing Limited
Gower House
Croft Road
Aldershot
Hants GU11 3HR
England

Edward Elgar Publishing Company
Old Post Road
Brookfield
Vermont 05036
USA

Printed in Great Britain at the University Press, Cambridge

British Library Cataloguing in Publication Data
Economics of F.A. Hayek. – Vol.2:
Capitalism, Socialism and Knowledge
  I. Colonna, M.
  330.1

Library of Congress Cataloguing in Publication Data
The Economics of F.A. Hayek / edited by M. Colonna, H. Hagemann.
    Includes index.
    Contents: v. 1. Money and business cycles — v. 2. Capitalism,
  socialism, and knowledge / edited by M. Colonna, H. Hagemann, O.Hamouda.
    1. Money.   2. Business cycles.   3. Capitalism.   4. Socialism.
  5. Economic man.   6. Hayek, Friedrich A. von (Friedrich August),
  1899–1992.   I. Hayek, Friedrich A. von (Friedrich August), 1899–1992.
  II. Colonna, M. (Marina)   III. Hagemann, Harald.   IV. Hamouda, O.F.
  HG221.E254   1994   93–42575
  330.1–dc20   CIP
                                                                      r 94

ISBN 1 85898 011 9 (Volume I)
     1 85898 012 7 (Volume II)
     1 85278 545 4 (2 volume set)

Contents

Contributors

Riccardo Bellofiore, Università degli Studi di Bergamo, Italy
Jack Birner, Rijksuniversiteit Limburg, Maastricht, Netherlands
Stephan Böhm, Universität Graz, Austria
Bruce J. Caldwell, University of North Carolina, Greensboro, USA
Omar F. Hamouda, Glendon College, York University, Toronto, Canada
Bruno Jossa, Università degli Studi di Napoli, Italy
Tony Lawson, University of Cambridge, UK
Ferdinando Meacci, Università degli Studi di Padova, Italy
Laurence S. Moss, Babson College, Babson Park, Mass., USA
Robin Rowley, McGill University, Montreal, Canada
Andrea Salanti, Università degli Studi di Bergamo, Italy
Ian Steedman, University of Manchester, UK
Erich W. Streissler, Universität Wien, Austria
Carlo Zappia, Università degli Studi di Siena, Italy

Introduction

Friedrich August von Hayek was born in Vienna on 8 May 1899 and died in Freiburg on 23 March 1992. Hayek was a leading figure both in the tradition of classical liberalism and in Austrian economics. His scientific work covered seven decades, and it explored several academic disciplines, including economics, philosophy, political science, history of thought, jurisprudence, epistemology and theoretical psychology. Examination of the most important aspects of his extraordinarily intensive activity shows quite clearly that all were focused on the ultimate goal of explaining the spontaneous order of a free market society and the ways to preserve it. In recent reappraisals of Hayek's life work, the great variety of his contributions has been sometimes seen as a complex system of ideas of such coherence that it seems to have sprung from an ambitious architectonic programme.

Over seven decades, undeterred by sharp fluctuations in the relative acceptance of his thought, Hayek was a prolific promoter of his ideas. As a young scholar he drew tremendous attention from his academic peers after his arrival at the London School of Economics. Subsequently, he lost ground over his abrasive clash with Keynes and the Cambridge school, and his early promise seemed overshadowed in the period immediately following World War II. With the onset of the cold war, however, as other economists focused their attention on the optimism of growth and the stimulus or stabilization of effective macroeconomic demand, economic developments in communist countries presented Hayek with a platform from which to reissue his pessimistic warnings of the dangers and inefficiencies of centralized planning. Later, in the 1970s, when industrialized nations suffered both financial instability and high rates of inflation, the time was ripe for an alternative voice. First, monetarism became attractive as a rival to Keynesian remedies. Then, as new conservative governments took power, politicians and their officials increasingly sought the advice of Hayek and his disciples. For many observers, the decade of the 1980s can be characterized by the revival of Hayek's influence on economic policy, by the promotion of individual enterprise and by the desire to remove many trappings of the interventionist era – although Hayek enjoyed only a quite modest support among academic economists. Finally, in recent academic debates on trade cycle, money and equilibrium, economists of several different schools of thought have begun to refer to Hayek's early contributions, despite the fact that substantial disagreements remain as to their interpretation and merit.

When Hayek was a student at the University of Vienna, attending courses in law, economics and psychology, his interest in economics had already been stimulated by some early reading (before and during the war) in philosophy, methodology and economic planning. From the very beginning the need to understand economics was seen by Hayek as a necessary step in the understanding of wider problems of the political order and the organization of society. At the university Hayek got his main general introduction to economics from the last lectures of Friedrich von Wieser and from reading Carl Menger's *Grundsätze der Volkswirtschaftslehre*. But the research programme which led him to become first an economist, and later a social and political philosopher, was originally conceived under the influence of Ludwig von Mises who introduced Hayek to two of the topics which would become a prominent part of the first stage of that programme: monetary and trade cycle theory and what at that time was called economic calculation under socialism. Hayek met Mises at the Österreichische Abrechnungsmat (a government office for settling prewar debts) where he was appointed to a temporary job in 1921, and at the Miseskreis of which he was a member from 1924 to 1931. In 1927 they both founded the Österreichisches Institut für Konjunkturforschung.

From 1924 to 1942 Hayek made important contributions to price theory, monetary theory and capital theory. But the ultimate aim of his work in each of these fields was to integrate them into a unified theory which could explain industrial fluctuations. This aim originated in Hayek's discontent both with static general equilibrium theory and its evident inability to explain recurrent trade cycle, and with the then dominant monetary trade cycle theories and their exclusive focus on general price level.

According to Hayek the proper task of monetary theory was not to investigate the relation between the quantity of money and the general price level, but the relation between the variations in the quantity of money and their impact on relative prices. The integration of monetary and price theory was attempted in his first important theoretical essay in 1928: 'Das intertemporale Gleichgewichtssystem der Preise und die Bewegungen des "Geldwertes"' (translated into English in 1984) and became the basis of his 1929 *Geldtheorie und Konjunkturtheorie* (translated into English in 1933), where he gave a detailed methodological explanation of what should be a proper starting point for a satisfactory monetary theory of the trade cycle. Hayek's thesis was that money, when it is present, loosens the close interrelationships which are described by pure theory under the assumption of barter and creates the possibility that the price mechanism will not operate according to the self-regulating principles of price theory. Hayek claimed that any change in the volume of money formed the 'necessary and sufficient' condition for the emergence of the trade cycle. From the start, Hayek's trade cycle theory was unique: it differed from the monetary theories of the trade cycle then prevailing in the Anglo-Saxon world because of its rejection of even the notion of the general price level and its insistence on the influence of money on relative prices and real quantities. But it differed also from the real trade cycle theories then prevailing in continental Europe by its exclusive focus on money as *the* causal factor, explicitly refuting any causal role to changes in real data.

Hayek's next step in the working out of his trade cycle theory came two years later, when he was invited by Lionel Robbins to give four lectures at the London School of Economics. The content of those lectures was published in 1931 under the title *Prices and Production*. In the present revival of Hayek's work, the hostility of Keynes and Sraffa to that little book of 112 pages has become well known again.

In *Prices and Production* Hayek's main concern was with the changes in capital structure brought about by changes in the volume of money, in particular describing the self-reversing real effects of credit expansion. The burden of his theory was that all new capital goods which are created with the help of a credit expansion ('voluntary' savings being constant) will be destroyed during the crisis which necessarily follows the upward phase of the cycle. In other words, in a free market society newly created money can never take the place of true voluntary savings: money expansions do have temporary distorting effects on the price system and on the directions of production, but because these effects are not in harmony with the free choices of the consumers, money will never be able to change permanently the relative scarcity of capital. It is here that is to be found Hayek's first positive attempt at integrating monetary and capital theory, a line of research which Hayek himself regarded as an evolution of Wicksell's and Mises's contributions to monetary theory.

Although Hayek never repudiated the core of the trade cycle theory expounded in *Prices and Production*, he very soon came to realize some 'irremediable defects' of that 'exposition'. As he explicitly stated in the preface to the 1935 edition of *Prices and Production*, those defects were partly due to some highly simplified assumptions and, more importantly, to the fact that he had based his whole argument on the main propositions of the Austrian theory of capital before having developed it in greater detail and adapted it to the complex phenomena to which it was applied.

Under pressure from the criticisms of many contemporaries, Hayek wrote several articles in order to clarify, improve and defend specific aspects of his trade cycle theory. Among those articles, the two essays, 'Profits, Interest, and Investment' (1939) and 'The Ricardo Effect' (1942) can perhaps be regarded as the most relevant. At the same time, faithful to his original plan, he undertook the more fundamental task of recasting the Jevons–Böhm-Bawerk–Wicksell position in the field of capital theory in order to provide a

satisfactory integrated theoretical foundation for his explanation of more
complex phenomena. The publication in 1941 of his *The Pure Theory of
Capital* was in fact only a partial answer to all the questions raised by his
trade cycle theory: in the first chapter Hayek warns the reader that the content
of the book is only an 'introduction' to a more comprehensive and more
realistic study of the phenomena of capitalistic production – the full treatment of the economic process as it proceeds in time, and the monetary
problems that are connected with this process being outside the compass of
the book. Thus, in *The Pure Theory of Capital* Hayek confined himself to the
limited, although extremely complicated study of what type of productive
equipment is the more profitable to be created under various conditions, and
how the different parts of productive capacity are made to fit together in any
given moment of time. From the methodological point of view Hayek's
approach, which entailed a detailed description of all capital goods in terms
of their multifaceted characteristics (complementarity, reproducibility, sub-
stitutability, durability and specificity), marked an important change in the
development of capital theory. According to Hayek, his new research in that
field had the important advantage of putting capital theory 'in a form which
would prove useful for the study of industrial fluctuations'. Within that
approach, it was a matter of primary importance for Hayek both to reject the
commonly used notion of capital as a homogeneous substance the quantity of
which could be regarded as a datum, and to abandon one of the most inappropriate simplifications which he himself was responsible for in *Prices and
Production*, namely the use of the notion of an average period of production.
It could be interesting to remark that as early as in his 1927 essay 'Zur
Problemstellung der Zinstheorie' (translated into English in 1984), Hayek
criticized Böhm-Bawerk for having regarded the given structure of production in general as a datum. Quite surprisingly he even concluded that as long
as this assumption was a necessary one, it 'would imply nothing less than a
declaration of bankruptcy of the entire theory of value' (1984, pp. 61, 68).
Hayek's first attempt at abandoning the oversimplified notion of the average
period of production can be traced back to his 1934 essay 'On the Relationship between Investment and Output'.

The early 1940s marked the end of Hayek's first stage of research on
formal economics, and the beginning of his commitment in two adjacent
fields: social sciences methodology and the interweaving of the philosophy,
jurisprudence and economics of freedom. Apart from several important articles, some of which have been reprinted in *New Studies in Philosophy,
Politics, Economics, and the History of Ideas* (1978), his major works are:
The Road to Serfdom (1944), *Individualism and Economic Order* (1949), *The
Counter-Revolution of Science. Studies on the Abuse of Reason* (1952), *The
Sensory Order. An Inquiry into the Foundations of Theoretical Psychology*

(1952), *The Constitution of Liberty* (1960), *Studies in Philosophy, Politics, and Economics* (1967), *Law, Legislation and Liberty* (1973–79), and *The Fatal Conceit. The Errors of Socialism* (1988).

This new line of research had roots in Hayek's previous work. Hayek's trade cycle theory, with all its monetary and capital theoretical implications, had the explicit role of providing a 'scientific' proof of the harmful effects resulting from the price stabilization policies which since the 1920s had gained almost general approval. By contrasting the smooth working of a free market economy with its hampered movements due to government interference, Hayek soon realized the 'contradiction' between the economic events described by all trade cycle theories and the fundamental principles of the equilibrium theory which they had to utilize in order to explain those events. According to Hayek this problem stemmed from the fact that the then prevailing 'elementary' general equilibrium models were far from clear on how the state of equilibrium was achieved, and how prices could perform their task of coordinating the production and consumption plans of individual economic actors in the real world. Hayek's first attempt at clarifying this point within a general equilibrium context was in his 1928 essay on intertemporal equilibrium (mentioned above) by introducing time and money under the assumption of perfect foresight. The problem was then tackled again in a series of writings whose innovative methodological content has been recognized only recently. Following this new line of research Hayek began to inquire into the nature of the market system, that is into the problem of what sort of information market prices transmit, and why the contribution of the price system to the social well-being is irreplaceable. Hayek's notion of prices as 'signals', of the 'division of knowledge' and of spontaneous order' are the most innovative offsprings of his research.

The earliest contributions to the topic ran parallel with his writings on trade cycle theory and originated from his involvement, together with Ludwig von Mises, in the debate over economic calculation under socialism. Hayek wrote three articles on this topic: 'The Nature and History of the Problem' (1935a), 'The Present State of the Debate' (1935b), both published in the book *Collectivist Economic Planning* he edited, and 'Socialist Calculation: The Competitive "Solution"' (1940). The articles were a response to H.D. Dickinson, O. Lange and A. Lerner, and more specifically to O. Lange's neoclassical economic theory of market socialism, where the pricing problem was supposed to be solved by a true market process for consumer goods, and by a central planning board through the trial and error process for the communally owned resources, while managers were supposed to act so as to equal the marginal cost of any product to its price and the price of any resource to its marginal value product. Hayek's rejection of the claim that market socialism would be morally superior and more efficient than capitalism started by pointing out Socialists' misunderstanding of the nature of the market economy and the complexity of the problems which the price mechanism solves by interacting with the spontaneous actions of the market participants. At the heart of his demonstration of the practical impossibility of conveying to a central board all the information which makes the free market society as efficient as it is there was a theoretical argument which Hayek would develop later: knowledge is a discovery process carried out by the individual participants in the market. Technical knowledge 'consists in a technique of thought which enables the individual to find new solutions rapidly as soon as he is confronted with new constellations of circumstances' (a similar argument would apply to the knowledge of consumers about their preferences). Thus, according to Hayek, because knowledge is dispersed among myriads of people and is in a continuous process of creation and revision, the advantage of the free market in 'decentralizing' the task of collecting all kinds of data by entrusting it to the price mechanism must be seen in its ability 'to react to some extent to all ... small changes and differences'. Only under such conditions is it possible to take a 'rational decision' even in questions of detail, a circumstance which in the aggregate decides the success of productive effort (1935b, pp. 210–13).

The challenge thrown down by market socialism forced Hayek to deepen his understanding of the functioning of a free market society and, in so doing, to undertake the systematic study which led him to write his first most important contributions to the problem of economic knowledge: 'Economics and Knowledge' (1937), 'The Use of Knowledge in Society' (1945), and 'The Meaning of Competition' (1946), all reprinted in *Individualism and Economic Order*.

The extensive literature generated by Hayek's ideas during the 60 years of his intense intellectual activity and after his death reveals a marked change of attitude by the profession. While during the 1930s a polite scepticism pervaded the comments of even those economists who were in the same camp as Hayek, nowadays the recognition of the significance of Hayek's work and of its attractions as a system of thought have become typical even among scholars basically out of sympathy with Hayek.

During the 1930s and early 1940s the most hostile criticisms of Hayek were concentrated on what was the most important, but also one of the most difficult points in Hayek's theory, namely his claim that any 'transition to more roundabout methods of production', or any 'lengthening of the structure of production' brought about by a credit expansion (which manifests itself during the upward phase of the cycle) contains the seeds of its own destruction, i.e. brings with it an inevitable crisis. Both the monetary theory and the capital theory embedded in Hayek's trade cycle analysis were put under severe scrutiny by a large number of scholars, either to show that there was no difference between such a transition being brought about by monetary expansion or by true voluntary saving, or that the crisis was not at all inevitable, or that monetary expansion was not the only, and not even the most important cause of the trade cycle, or that – under Hayek's assumptions of full employment and flexible prices – the cyclical movements described by him could not even exist. Nevertheless, in the early 1940s, because of the increasing interest in Keynes's *General Theory* and its economic policy implications, the debate on Hayek's trade cycle theory, and on trade cycle theories in general, died out. For 40 years it was almost forgotten that in the 1930s Hayek was the principal rival of Keynes.

The greater interest in Hayek's work reemerged in the late 1970s. This seems due not so much to the fact that Hayek was awarded the Nobel Prize for Economics in 1974, but more to the fact that Hayek's contributions after the early 1940s dealt with much wider topics than pure economic theory, thus raising and stimulating interest and debates in a large audience, which includes economists, but which has involved those interested in methodological issues and in analytical yet comprehensive explanations of the working of a capitalist society.

Part of this new work on Hayek has been devoted to a reappraisal of his trade cycle theory. Lucas's appeal to Hayek as the ancestor of his own business cycle theory has in fact provoked a considerable number of essays on whether, or within which limits this descent holds. Other authors have pointed out some misunderstandings of Hayek's theory by his early critics. Although there have been some authors who supported Hayek's trade cycle theory even on technical grounds, most of the present debate on his economics seems to be concerned mainly with his ability to inspire new research, and with his far-reaching insights into methodological issues.

The present collection of essays originated in the conference 'The Economics of Hayek', conceived by the editors in April 1990 in Cambridge, England and held in July 1992 at the Rocca Malatestiana in Sant'Arcangelo di Romagna (Rimini, Italy) under the generous auspices of the cultural organization Associazione Sigismondo Malatesta. While the conference and the essays are the consequence of the recent revival of interest in Hayek's work, several of them take up the ideas that engaged economists during the 1930s and early 1940s on Hayek's early work. This has entailed a twofold reevaluation. On the one hand, the essays examine the merits of arguments raised during that early debate; on the other hand they return directly to Hayek's early work that focused especially on capital, money and dynamics. They have been collected into two volumes, *Money and Business Cycles*, and *Capitalism, Socialism and Knowledge*.

Volume I, *Money and Business Cycles*, is devoted almost entirely to Hayek's trade cycle theory and the related dynamic economics. It contains three sections entitled: 'Money and the Trade Cycle', 'Hayek and Structural Theories of the Business Cycle' and 'Hayek and Equilibrium Business Cycle Theories'.

Part I contains the papers by David Laidler, Marina Colonna, Mario Seccareccia, Hans-Michael Trautwein, and John Eatwell and Murray Milgate, each of which, from a different point of view, assesses the role of money and monetary theory in Hayek's business cycle analysis. In 'Hayek on neutral money and the cycle', David Laidler describes and places in their historical context Hayek's contributions to macroeconomics in the 1920s and 1930s. He also appraises their importance relative to contemporary as well as to later work. Marina Colonna in her 'Hayek's trade cycle theory and its contemporary critics' sets Hayek's contribution to trade cycle theory in the context of past attempts to explore the relationships between economic instability and monetary policy. The paper attempts to clarify the important aspects of Hayek's analysis in order to show if and in what sense Hayek's theory is unique.

Also in Part I, Mario Seccareccia's 'Credit money and cyclical crises: the views of Hayek and Fisher compared' is a review of Hayek's and Fisher's versions of the monetary overinvestment cycle theory. It examines Fisher's favouring the 'nationalization' of money and Hayek's advocating of the contrary during the 1970s. In his contribution 'Hayek's double failure in business cycle theory: a note' Hans-Michael Trautwein identifies two fundamental flaws in Hayek's account of money and the trade cycle. The first flaw is a logical gap between Hayek's non-monetary equilibrium benchmark and the credit cycle; the second is his somewhat schizophrenic treatment of the banking system as endogenous and exogenous cause of cyclical fluctuations. John Eatwell and Murray Milgate argue that although Hayek's theory of competition and his attack on the orthodox concept of perfect competition are attractive and persuasive, his argument, nonetheless, contains an internal contradiction. A brief comment by Giancarlo de Vivo has also been included at the end of Part I.

Part II includes contributions by Harald Hagemann, and Meghnad Desai and Paul Redfern, in which the issue of the real nature of production is emphasized. In 'Hayek and the Kiel school: some reflections on the German debate on business cycles in the late 1920s and early 1930s' Harald Hagemann focuses first on the causal endogenous factors of money, credit and technological change found in Hayek's and Lowe's theories of the trade cycle. He then analyses the vertical and horizontal nature underlying their respective structures of production. Meghnad Desai and Paul Redfern in their paper, 'Trade cycle as a frustrated traverse' give an analytical reconstruction of Hayek's argument in *Prices and Production*. They construct a simple numerical account of the equilibrium traverse of a growing economy in order to clarify the analytical anatomy of Hayek's famous triangle diagrams.

Finally, in Part III, Gilles Dostaler in 'The formation and evolution of Hayek's trade cycle theory' examines the genesis and the evolution of Hayek's theory of business cycles in the 1920s and 1930s. Dostaler highlights the richness and the complexities of Hayek's theory even though, he claims, one can reject both his premises and his practical conclusions. Christof Rühl in 'The transformation of business cycle theory: Hayek, Lucas, and a change in the notion of equilibrium' investigates and challenges the claim that Hayek was one of the forerunners of modern equilibrium business cycle theory by analysing his contribution to the interwar business cycle debate and his technical approach in the light of today's new classical mode of analysis. In 'Hayek and modern business cycle theory' Richard Arena argues that even though there are specific common features in both Hayek and the new classical theory that would make them part of the same tradition, they also present striking differences that make the two conflict.

Volume II, *Capitalism, Socialism and Knowledge*, contains chapters that focus on three particular issues, 'Capital', 'Socialist calculation' and 'Methodology', topics less discussed by economists and related to Hayek's methodological and philosophical contributions.

Part I, the set of essays dedicated to Hayek's theory of capital, includes the papers by Ian Steedman and Ferdinando Meacci which both address Hayek's pure theory of capital. Ian Steedman focuses his analysis solely on Hayek's difficult book *The Pure Theory of Capital*. He briefly explains Hayek's objective: to correct and improve the theory of capital in the tradition of Jevons, Böhm-Bawerk and Wicksell. He then concentrates on the critical aspect of Hayek's own contribution. Steedman reviews the entire book section by section and shows how despite Hayek's caution and often his rejection of traditional tools, Hayek retained the conclusion his predecessors had built specifically on premises he rejected. Ferdinando Meacci in his 'Hayek and the deepening of capital' is concerned with the nature and role of time-consuming methods of production in a dynamic economy. His discussion concentrates on the concertina effect, the Ricardo effect and the input and output functions. He explains Hayek's weaknesses in attempting to grasp the dynamics of both effects, thus limiting considerably his input and output functions.

Part II contains chapters by Erich Streissler, Bruno Jossa and Laurence Moss that deal with the widely debated topic of Hayek's socialist calculation, a subject that occupied most of Hayek's attention. Erich Streissler in his erudite 'Hayek on information and socialism' not only situates Hayek's ideas in relation to those of Adam Smith and the Austrians and in contrast to those of Lange and Lerner; he also explains Hayek's analysis of information in planning and its implication for policy. In 'Hayek and market socialism' Bruno Jossa, on the other hand, uses Lange's notion of market socialism as a reference to discuss and analyse Hayek's market economy. Jossa makes a distinction between centrally planned economies and market socialism with autonomous firms. He argues that Hayek's attack on the latter is inappropriate. Laurence Moss considers in 'Hayek and the several faces of socialism' the impact that Hayek's attacks on certain variants of socialist thought had on the evolution of his economic ideas. The lesson one can draw, Moss maintains, is not that Hayek gave up economics, as his critics have asserted, but that he simply changed his emphasis from the study of the management of a household in an 'ordered structure' into the study of the 'catallaxy'. This explains the importance of his insistence on the notions of law, order and market structure.

Part III deals with various philosophical and methodological aspects of Hayek's thought, Hayekian issues far less discussed by economists than by other scholars; its four essays are by Bruce Caldwell, Tony Lawson, Stephan Böhm and by Omar Hamouda and Robin Rowley jointly. Bruce Caldwell begins his essay by placing Hayek's theory in the context of the development of Austrian methodological thinking. He then proceeds in his 'Four theses on Hayek' to discuss how Hayek's transformation involved a move away from equilibrium theory, how with a shift of emphasis from economics to more sociological and philosophical issues, Hayek set the stage for his methodology in his 'Scientism' essay, and finally how Popper had little influence on Hayek's methodology. In contrast Tony Lawson questions Terence Hutchison's and Caldwell's claim that Hayek's early changes in his methodology were significant. In 'Realism and Hayek: a case of continuing transformation', he maintains that Hayek struggled all along to overcome methodological difficulties, with the results of his struggle becoming only recently apparent in his 'Scientism'. From a realist perspective, Lawson relates Hayek's ontological presuppositions to the nature of the objects of natural and social science.

In the third essay of this final part, 'Hayek and knowledge: some question marks' Stephan Böhm has a twofold aim: first to draw attention to the profound differences between Hayek's notions of knowledge and the concept of information as usually understood in the recent economics of information and search, and second to explore some of the philosophical underpinnings and ramifications of the role of knowledge in economics as understood by Hayek. Omar Hamouda and Robin Rowley, for their part, are concerned with the role of information in 'Rational processes: markets, knowledge and uncertainty'. In their analysis of Hayek's rational processes, Hamouda and Rowley focus on the pertinence of Hayek's thinking on prediction and explanation, data and testing, and the reappraisal by economists of information sharing and the value of competition. They argue that Hayek's individualism and spontaneous order do not establish the only information system that yields efficient economic results. Brief comments by Riccardo Bellofiore,

Jack Birner, Andrea Salanti and Carlo Zappia have also been included at the end of Volume II.

The editors, as the organizing committee of the conference, 'The Economics of Hayek', wish to express their thanks not only to the contributors of papers, but also to the more than 60 participants in the conference. We would also like to thank Erich Streissler for his memorable dinner speech. Financial support came from Assessorato alla Cultura della Regione Emilia Romagna, the Banco di Napoli, and the Associazione Sigismondo Malatesta. Finally we would like to express our thanks to our publisher, Edward Elgar, for his interest and patience.

Marina Colonna
Harald Hagemann
Omar F. Hamouda

PART I

CAPITAL

1   On *The Pure Theory of Capital* by F.A. Hayek

*Ian Steedman**

Hayek opened the Preface to his work *The Pure Theory of Capital* with these words: 'This highly abstract study of a problem of pure economic theory has grown out of the concern with one of the most practical and pressing questions which economists have to face, the problem of the causes of industrial fluctuations' (1941, p. v; the Preface is dated June, 1940). And he went on to explain that, the urgent and concrete nature of these questions notwithstanding, 'it seemed imperative ... to turn back to the revision of the fundamentals and to work out a theory of capitalist production which would prove adequate for the analysis of dynamic changes ... I have become definitely convinced that nothing holds up real progress so much as ... impatience which disregards the necessity of first getting the foundations clearly laid out' (pp. v–vi). As is well known, Hayek found those foundations in the work of Jevons, Böhm-Bawerk and Wicksell but, as he clearly acknowledged, he also found that he had to do far more than to provide 'a systematic exposition of ... a fairly complete body of doctrine' (p. vi). To the contrary, Hayek discovered that 'some of the simplifications employed by the earlier writers had such far-reaching consequences as to make their conceptual tools almost useless in the analysis of more complicated situations' (p. vi). Thus, 'it is precisely further analysis which the theory of capital requires' (p. vii).

In very general terms it is, then, clear enough what objective Hayek set for himself in *The Pure Theory of Capital*; he was to expound a corrected and improved version of a pure capital theory, in the tradition of Jevons, Böhm-Bawerk and Wicksell, which would eventually serve as the foundation for a study of industrial fluctuations. As Hayek put it on the first page of Chapter I, 'The Scope of the Inquiry', *The Pure Theory of Capital* could be 'appropriately described as an Introduction to the Dynamics of Capitalistic Production, provided the emphasis were laid on the word Introduction, and provided that it were clearly understood that it deals only with a part of the wider subject to which it is merely a preliminary. The whole of the present discussion is essentially preparatory' (p. 3). Just 350 pages later, in introducing Part IV, 'The Rate of Interest in a Money Economy', Hayek remarks that, 'The

*I wish to thank S. Böhm, J.M. Currie, A. Jarvis, H.D. Kurz and S. Parrinello for assistance of various kinds.

task of the first three Parts of this book has been to show ... why there will be certain differences between the prices of the factors of production and the expected prices of the products, and why these differences will stand in a certain uniform relationship to the time intervals which separate the dates when these prices are paid' (p. 353). The modest nature of the cited claims with which Hayek 'brackets' the first three Parts of *The Pure Theory of Capital* (on pp. 3 and 353), in conjunction with the considerable length of these Parts, might lead one to ask for a more detailed account of what it is that Hayek attempts therein.

In assessing Hayek's contribution to economics, Machlup wrote, 'If I had to single out the area in which Hayek's contributions were the most fundamental and pathbreaking, I would cast my vote for the theory of capital' (1977, p. 50) and he then repeated his previous assessment of the work, that it is his 'sincere conviction that this work contains some of the most penetrating thoughts on the subject that have ever been published' (1977, p. 29). Machlup's quite long list of 'the themes to which this book *The Pure Theory of Capital* has made most significant contributions' has – at least – one interesting feature: it consists of ways of thinking about capital-theoretic matters, rather than of specific results of the form $(dx_j/dz_i) < 0$ (1977, pp. 29–30). Machlup's view, originally published in 1974, may remind one somewhat of the position adopted by Hicks in his review of Austrian capital theory, published one year earlier. Having noted that the period of production and 'roundaboutness' must be abandoned in the presence of fixed capital, he asks 'is there anything left?' and answers that, 'The chief things, I am going to maintain, are left' (1973a, p. 193). According to Hicks, the 'true insights' of 'Austrian' capital theory lie in the recognition that 'Production is a process, a process in time ... the characteristic form of production is a sequence, in which inputs are followed by outputs. Capital is an expression of sequential production. Production has a time-structure, so capital has a time-structure' (1973a, pp. 193–4). While Hicks is not referring explicitly to *The Pure Theory of Capital* here, he does remark that he is considering the theory 'in the form I learned it myself from Professor Hayek ... [in] 1931–5' (1973a, p. 190), so that it is of some interest to us that Hicks's characterization of the true insights of this kind of theory again refers to ways of seeing production and not to specific results. A third commentator – again sympathetic to Hayek's work – who may help us in grasping the nature of *The Pure Theory of Capital* is Shackle. In a paper originally published in 1981, Shackle describes the book as 'a final report on Böhm-Bawerk's proposal', this report being the product of 'an intense and sustained effort nothing short of heroic' (1988, p. 173). The 'huge effort' is referred to again on p. 180, where Shackle writes: 'That such an effort was needed, that Hayek encountered numberless and daunting troubles, that so long a book was required to contain the implications of an ostensibly incisive idea – capital is the working of time-lapse in production – suggests inevitably that too much was expected of a tool which had, at first sight, so brilliant a glow of promise' (1988, p. 180). Hayek's thoroughness and intellectual honesty, Shackle suggests, 'had the opposite effect of the presumably intended one. In his prodigious effort at final vindication of the Jevons–Böhm-Bawerk–Wicksell idea, Hayek … explains in detail why [time-lapse] cannot be reduced to an *average period of production*' (1988, p. 180). (Shackle's picture of the book as a heroic failure is consistent with Lachmann's pithy observation – not directed specifically at Hayek's work – that 'to reduce the whole complex of relationships among capital resources … to the single dimension of time is a bold idea … but not a very good one' (1976, p. 146)).

If three sympathetic commentators can encourage us to find in Hayek's book a way of seeing capital and production, together with the rejection of some specific results previously derived from that vision – rather than to find specific results, new or old – that certainly suggests that definite, precise results are not a central feature of *The Pure Theory of Capital*. Even while it is true that there are some 'traditional propositions' to be found in that work (see below), elucidation and, where necessary, criticism of '$(dx_j/dz_i) < 0$' results in the book would not prove to be a very satisfying activity, for at least three reasons. The first is that such results are indeed not prominent or central in the work and the second reason is that such critical assessment would today be better directed to more recent theory, such as that embodied in Hicks's *Capital and Time* (1973b) or even, following Burmeister's suggestion (1974), in a von Neumann-like presentation of 'Austrian' capital theory. The third reason is that Hayek himself, in *The Pure Theory of Capital*, is frequently cautious about the whole exercise, expresses doubts about the relation of simple theoretical cases to reality and several times breaks off a line of argument, urging that it is not worthwhile to push on into further complexity. In Chapter III, 'The Significance of Analysis in Real Terms', for example, Hayek writes: 'The fact that almost this entire volume is devoted to the equilibrium or "real" aspects of our problem must not be taken to mean that we attach excessive importance to these aspects. The idea is rather to emphasise the width of the gulf which separates this exercise in economic logic from any attempt directly to explain the processes of the real world' (p. 39). In Chapter VI, 'The Duration of the Process of Production and the Durability of Goods: Some Definitions', Hayek refers to the continuous input–point output and point input–continuous output cases (pp. 66–7) and then observes that 'it is almost impossible in real life to find cases where time elapses between the application of the factors and the enjoyment of the results in only one of these ways' (p. 67). It is 'almost always' the continuous input–continuous output case which is relevant in practice and the input–output 'relationships are so completely intertwined that it is extremely difficult to disentangle them' (p. 68). Hayek concludes that it is therefore 'so much the more necessary' to analyse the extreme cases but this is clearly a case of making the best of a bad job. Again, in Chapter XVI, 'The Marginal Value Product of Investment: The Problem of Attribution (Imputation)', after analysing some simple cases Hayek notes that his analysis should be extended to the continuous input–continuous output case involving durable goods and to certain cases involving durable goods which require cooperating factors in order to produce (pp. 210–11). He writes: 'Although these cases present no really new problems, their actual analysis is so complicated that it is hardly possible to give it in any detail without resorting to an elaborate mathematical apparatus, and they are consequently best left to more specialised studies' (p. 211).[1]

Rather than pursue specific, constructive results in *The Pure Theory of Capital*, then, we shall seek to consider a number of the more general and/or negative lessons which emerge fairly clearly from this long and complex work, in part with an eye to the history of economic thought. Before we begin that consideration, however, it may be helpful to the reader to recall the general structure of the book. Part I, 'Introductory', is over 90 pages long and is by no means 'merely' introductory. Part II, 'Investment in a Simple Economy', some 150 pages in length, considers capital-theoretic problems in the highly simplified context of a 'communist' economy planned by a unique dictator; the emphasis is determinedly on the 'productivity' aspect, with time-preference being introduced only in the last 30 pages. Part III, 'Capitalistic Production in a Competitive Community', of just over 100 pages, extends the analysis to a market economy with many agents. Part IV, 'The Rate of Interest in a Money Economy', is less than 60 pages in length and hardly adequate to its topic. Only passing reference will be made below to Part IV which, as Hayek himself notes, is 'rather more condensed and sketchy than I had intended' (p. viii), as a result of wartime pressures. While Lutz wrote that the 'second half of Hayek's study ... is in my opinion excellent' (1943, p. 302), Smithies considered that Hayek's Part IV 'almost gives the impression of having been included as an afterthought' (1941, p. 778). Hawtrey, rather less harshly, suggested that, 'Unfortunately the intrusion of the war and its preoccupations prevented him from fully developing this Part [IV]. As it stands it by no means fills the gaps' (1941, p. 290). There are also three appendices and a long bibliography, by no means all of the entries in the latter being explicitly referred to elsewhere in *The Pure Theory of Capital*.

Stationary states, equilibrium and expectations

When Hayek describes *The Pure Theory of Capital* as 'an Introduction to the Dynamics of Capitalistic Production' (p. 3), it is not to be expected that he refers to a 'quasi stationary state' dynamics in which the scale of the economy changes but all proportions are time-invariant. Nor does he. Opening Chapter II, 'Equilibrium Analysis and the Capital Problem', Hayek refers to 'a stationary state, where most of the interesting and important capital problems are absent' (p. 14; see also p. 87) and much later in the book, in Chapter XIX, 'The General Conditions of Equilibrium', he urges 'the difficulty of saying much that is useful about the general theory of capital so long as we confine ourselves to the analysis of the stationary state' (p. 265). Hayek's method of analysis, indeed, almost ensures that a stationary state will not obtain. For, in both Part II and Part III, he considers what happens after some arbitrary point in time which is immediately preceded by some kind of shock to the economic system. Consequently, as Hayek points out with reference to the Part II analysis, the consumption vector will not be of constant composition over time and, in principle, the necessary changes will continue for ever, albeit diminishing in size as time wears on; relative values will thus also change over time, perhaps considerably so in the initial stages (pp. 166–7). As Lutz points out, still with reference to Part II, it follows that the output and capital stock vectors will also change through time – 'we have to deal with a process of continuous change. The system will approach a stationary state, but, according to Hayek will, in principle, never reach it' (1943, p. 308). The same is true of the Part III analysis for the 'Competitive Community'. Because of the change in conditions just prior to the starting date of the analysis, some machines may not be replaced, having become obsolescent; there will be a gradual shift to 'a new and different investment structure' and 'the system will make only an asymptotic approach to the position of an ideal final equilibrium', even if no further changes in the data intrude (1941, pp. 262–4; cf. Hayek's much earlier dismissal of stationary equilibrium, p. 16, on the grounds that it 'could be reached only after the lapse of a very long time').

Our reference to obsolescence draws attention to one of the (several) reasons why stationary states are of limited interest to Hayek in *The Pure Theory of Capital*, namely that he is very conscious of the importance of technical change, invention and the (probably) resulting obsolescence of old machines. The whole of Chapter XXIII is devoted to 'The Effects of Unforeseen Changes and in particular of Inventions', while the preceding chapter contains two full pages on obsolescence and rejects as 'baseless' any suggestion that physical depletion through wear and tear is in any sense more fundamental than 'mere' obsolescence, i.e. loss of value without physical change (p. 301). (Hayek reiterates this rejection in his subsequent reply to Pigou on the subject of maintaining capital intact; 1941a, pp. 276–7.) Somewhat ironically, Smithies was soon to turn these considerations against Hayek, to some extent; in objecting to Hayek's emphasis on circulating capital and his portrayal of non-permanence as *the* essential feature of capital goods, Smithies simply invited the reader to consider the case of machines with unlimited physical lives in the presence of technical advance! (1941, p. 777)

A further reason why Hayek is not concerned with stationary states is that he rightly recognizes the presence, within his category of 'non-permanent' resources, of 'natural resources in so far as they are "wasting assets"' (1941 p. 57).[2]

What should the capital theorist study, then, if not stationary states? There is no doubt as to what Hayek, in *The Pure Theory of Capital*, regards as the true goal: 'an explanation of the economic process as it proceeds in time, an explanation in terms of causation which must necessarily be treated as a chain of historical sequences ... a unilateral dependence of the succeeding event on the preceding one. This kind of causal explanation of the process in time is of course the ultimate goal of all economic analysis' (p. 17). Equally certain, however, is the fact that Hayek neither achieves this goal in the book, nor has any illusions about having done so. His analysis is based rather in the 'intermediate field', 'preparatory' to a full causal analysis, of an equilibrium in which 'the plans of different members of a society ... are fully adjusted to one another' (pp. 17–18; clearly the Part II discussion of the one-dictator economy is merely a prolegomenon with respect to such analysis). Such an equilibrium does not entail stationarity (nor, of course, exclude it) but in- volves, rather, mutually consistent expectations held by the various agents. 'It is in this sphere alone that we can usefully discuss equilibrium relations extending over time, and in which consequently the pure theory of capital mainly falls' (p. 19; see also pp. 244, 247, 397). Much later, Hayek remarks that 'the assumption of certainty about the more distant future, although we have so far based our argument on it, is not really essential for our concept of equilibrium' (p. 357), the idea – apparently – being that agents' plans need only be strictly compatible in so far as they are definite, those agents holding money against the more uncertain aspects of the future.

Lutz (1943, p. 309) captures Hayek's method rather well when he remarks that, 'Whereas the analysis of Wicksell and Böhm-Bawerk was purely static, Hayek's approach is dynamic ... a step in the direction of period analysis' and notes that, in principle, Hayek abandons statics, even if 'his analysis very often retains the characteristics of statics'. Smithies, probably less accurately, describes Hayek as following the method of 'modern business cycle analysis ... although he never seems quite to realize it' (1941, p. 772). Such *apparently* different assessments are perhaps not that surprising given that Hayek was, knowingly, not carrying out the type of analysis he would really have wished to perform but only providing 'a kind of foil' such that, by seeing how expectations are in fact disappointed one builds a bridge from equilib- rium analysis towards a causal sequence explanation (p. 23; but see also the cautionary p. 23, n. 1).[3] Much more could, of course, be said about expectations in *The Pure Theory of Capital* (see, for example, pp. 156 n. 1, 239–40, 304, 331, 335, 343, 357) but we confine ourselves to the remarks of one commentator, generally sympathetic to Hayek, on the latter's concept of consistent plans equilibrium. Shackle writes: Hayek 'abstracts from … uncertainty. How can time as a field of choice (time-to-come) be discussed in any meaningful abstraction from uncertainty?' (1988, p. 176). Shackle does not refer to Hayek's claim that certainty is not essential but it seems improbable that he would have been fully appeased by it. Even more sharply, Shackle simply refuses the idea of the mutual compatibility of the expectations and intentions of different agents: 'Individuals will not necessarily surrender the freedom of imagination, of enterprise, of attempted exploitation of the void of time-to-come, in order to try to reconcile their ambitions with those of all other individuals. The seething cauldron of history mocks such a notion' (1988, p. 183). Even if one takes this to be 'merely' a dramatic statement about reality, and not a demonstration of the internal logical incoherence of the concept of a mutually consistent plans equilibrium, one may well bear it in mind as a reminder of the decidedly incomplete nature of Hayek's analysis in *The Pure Theory of Capital*.

Capital theory, interest theory and the rate of profit

Stationary state analysis often involves a single, uniform rate of profit, while intertemporal general equilibrium analysis often appears to lead to a plethora of distinct own rates of interest; what does Hayek, in his book, have to say about such matters? Before considering this question, we should perhaps ask whether the book should be viewed primarily as a work on interest theory or one on capital theory. That the distinction may not be an idle one is suggested by, for example, Lachmann's statement – apparently with reference to (Mengerian?) 'Austrian' theorists in general – that, 'Our capital theory, unlike Böhm-Bawerk's, is not devised to serve as a basis for an interest theory. Its purpose is to make the shape, order, and coherence of the capital structure intelligible in terms of human action' (1976, p. 147). Lutz, of course, entitled his 1943 review article on *The Pure Theory of Capital* 'Professor Hayek's Theory of Interest' and Hayek, in his admittedly very brief 'Comment' thereon, did not demur. Within the book, however, Hayek can be read as emphasizing the capital theory rather than the interest theory aspect, *à la* Lachmann. On the very first page of the text he states that his 'main concern' will be with the choice of what equipment to make and of how to utilize existing equipment, 'rather than to explain the factors which determined the value of a given stock of productive equipment and of the income that will be derived from it' (p. 3). And Hayek quickly becomes even more explicit, insisting that capital-theoretic problems 'have hardly ever been studied for their own sake and importance... Such analysis as they have received has been almost entirely subordinate to another problem, the problem of explaining interest. And the treatment of the theory of capital as an adjunct to the theory of interest has had somewhat unfortunate effects on its development' (pp. 4–5). The point is put more positively later on, when Hayek writes that 'the explanation of interest will not be the sole or central purpose of the present study ... [It] will be an incidental though necessary result of an attempt to analyse the forces which determine the use made of the productive resources' (p. 41). This emphasis is perhaps related to the fact, noted above, that the book contains more qualitative observations and suggestions as to how production, etc. may be envisaged than it does specific 'comparative static or dynamic' results (cf. Lutz's complaint that it provides 'no satisfactory explanation of the movement of interest rates over time nor of the structure of the rates at a given moment of time' (p. 310)). It almost certainly explains why Hayek can describe Irving Fisher's *The Theory of Interest* (1930) as 'the most systematic work on the subject which we possess, a formally unimpugnable exposition of the theory of interest' (p. 43) and yet feel that he himself is still called upon to write the very long and complex *Pure Theory of Capital.*[4]

Turning to what is said about rates of profit and interest in the book, we still face the need to make a further preliminary observation, this time about terminology. Throughout the first 350 pages, where money is barely mentioned – and then only to be pushed aside – Hayek consistently refers to the real return on investment as 'the rate of interest' and not as 'the rate of profit'. He does so only reluctantly, however, explaining that while 'It would perhaps be more correct if we referred to this difference between costs and prices as profits rather than interest', it might cause confusion to go against the now 'customary' practice of referring to interest in relation to equilibrium analysis and profit only in connection with dynamic 'abnormalities' (p. 38). Not surprisingly, Hayek reverts to this matter on the opening page of Part IV, 'The Rate of Interest in a Money Economy', repeating that, conventions aside, 'it would probably have been better to refer to this "real" phenomenon either, as the English classical economists did, as the rate of profit, or by some such term as the German *Urzins*' (p. 353). For 'the purposes of this final Part', Hayek uses 'rate of interest' to refer exclusively to money and describes 'the real rate of return as the *rate of profit*' (p. 354). In the rest of *this* section we shall write 'rate of interest [profit]' whenever the former is used to mean the latter! (Was it perhaps rather unfair of Hawtrey, in his review article on *The Pure Theory of Capital*, to complain that the 'price difference' theory confuses interest and profit (1941, p. 285)?)

A 'real' economy

It may be helpful to consider first what Hayek says about the rate of interest [profit] in the first three Parts of *The Pure Theory of Capital* and then to consider separately, in our next subsection, his observations in Part IV. Abstracting from money, Hayek emphasizes that 'the rate of interest [profit] in these conditions is not a price of any particular thing' (p. 38) (cf. the remark of Hicks, 1973b, p. 39, n. 1, that in 'an "Austrian" theory, the rate of interest is not the price of a "factor"'). It is, rather, 'a ratio between the prices of the factors of production and the expected prices of their products, which stands in a certain relationship to the time interval between the purchase of the factors and the sale of the product' (p. 38). Now, in a 'stationary equilibrium in a competitive society with capitalistic production' resources are so allocated 'as to make the relative values of the different types of resources exactly proportional to their relative costs of production, where "cost of production" includes the uniform time-rate of return on resources invested' (p. 264). The reference here to uniformity of the rate is not a casual or careless one. After stressing that a stationary equilibrium is 'extremely unlikely ever to be the case in the real world', Hayek reiterates that 'in so far as we are justified in speaking of a tendency towards an equilibrium ... [the] endeavour to distribute investment in such a way as to bring the highest return will necessarily bring about a uniform rate of return. This will be so quite independently of any possibility of lending money' (pp. 265–6; these points are highlighted in a marginal summary, p. 265). (Much earlier Hayek had referred to 'this result, with which every reader will be familiar', p. 38.)

Stationarity, then, involves a uniform rate of interest [profit] but Hayek, of course, is not much concerned with stationary equilibrium, at least in any positive sense. As noted above, he analyses economic time paths in which, in general, relative quantities and relative values are always changing, particularly perhaps in the early stages. 'But it will still be true that, measured in terms of any one commodity, the rate of increase [in the value of an investment] will have to be the same for all commodities. The actual numerical value of this rate of increase will, however, be different, according as one commodity or another is chosen as the standard of comparison or "numéraire"' (p. 167). Although Hayek writes that, 'It is probably unnecessary to emphasise that there is no way in which this multitude of different "own rates of interest" (as Mr. Keynes has called these rates of increase in terms of particular commodities) can be reduced to one single rate which has a stronger claim than any other to be regarded as *the* rate of productivity of investment' (p. 168), he nevertheless remarks of any attempt to distinguish between value change and real productivity that, 'the search for this philosopher's stone is probably still being pursued by some economists' (p. 169). Alas, no probable searchers are named!

While rates of increase in value between any two given dates must, when appropriately expressed, be equal for all investments, there is no need for the rate of increase between, say, t and $(t + \theta)$ to equal that between, say, $(t + \theta)$ and $(t + 2\theta)$. All that is required with respect to different time periods is that the product of the two rates just referred to be equal to that between t and $(t + 2\theta)$, etc.; see pp. 172–3, 184.

A 'money' economy

How are rates of profit and rates of interest related to one another? 'As has been explained earlier in this volume, its task is to lay the foundations for the treatment of these problems, not to discuss them in any detail' (p. 354). In an equilibrium position, with unchanging money expenditure for any given length of time, 'There would be differences between the rates of profit people expected to earn in their own businesses and the rates of interest at which they would be willing to lend and to borrow, corresponding to the different degrees of risk. But the net rate of interest would tend to be equal to the net rate of profit' (pp. 355–6). On the margin, the rates of return on all assets – allowing for risk, etc. – will tend to be equalized (pp. 358, 385–6) and, with respect to money, at least, liquidity preference will play an important role.[5] Making a distinction between the rate of profit and the marginal rate of profit (e.g., p. 399), Hayek goes on to stress that when account is taken of the different degrees of liquidity of all the various kinds of assets, monetary and non-monetary (pp. 399–400), 'the marginal rate of profit and the rate of interest not only need not be identical but may actually move in opposite directions', when liquidity preference changes (p. 399). Thus 'the connection between the money rate of interest and the profitability of investment becomes even looser than we have so far assumed' (p. 399). It must be recognized, then, that 'for assets possessing different degrees of liquidity, we shall at any moment have not one uniform rate of return but a long series of different rates of return' (p. 401). This fact would have no great significance for the preceding argument if the relative rates of return from different assets were to be constant: 'But this is of course very far from being so' (p. 402). We have by now moved a long way from the single, uniform rate of return result 'with which every reader will be familiar' (p. 38).

Circulating capital, fixed capital and durability

Few readers of *The Pure Theory of Capital* are likely to forget Hayek's striking discussion (pp. 46–9) of the contrasts between what he labels the 'Austrian' and the 'Anglo-American' approaches to capital theory.[6] Although these contrasts are set out 'in a rather trenchant and even exaggerated form [, it] is of course not claimed that the description of either of these approaches in its extreme form does justice to the real position. Indeed one of the tasks of the following pages will be to amalgamate the two lines of thought into a coherent whole' (p. 46). The 'Anglo-American' approach is characterized, in part, as giving exclusive emphasis to fixed capital, to very durable goods which need to be replaced only periodically, and as taking the supply of capital goods to be given for the comparatively short run. The 'Austrian' approach, by contrast, is characterized, in part, as emphasizing circulating capital and non-permanence as the key feature of capital goods, with the result that the stock of those goods is constantly being used up and reproduced (pp. 47–8; we have summarized here the first three of Hayek's ten contrasts). In Chapter VI, it is made clear that, with reference to tools and machinery, the word 'durable' relates not to length of calendar time life, *per se*, but is used rather 'to describe goods that are not destroyed in a moment by a single act of use but can be used repeatedly or continuously over a period of time' (pp. 78–9). Hayek is, of course, well aware of the existence of produced inputs of (effectively) unlimited life; see, for example, his discussion of a 'tunnel' (pp. 88–9) and his explicit reference to the concept of a '*Rentengut*' (p. 329).

What is Hayek's attitude towards this 'Austrian' circulating capital/'Anglo-American' fixed capital contrast? On the one hand, as noted above, he is perfectly conscious that his list of ten contrasts (pp. 47–9) is schematic and exaggerated and, indeed, says that one of the tasks of the book is to amalgamate the two lines of thought (p. 46). Nor does this caution disappear after the early pages of the work, for we are warned much later that any 'simple dichotomy' between fixed and circulating capital 'probably does almost more harm than good, by suggesting what appears to be almost a difference in kind instead of stressing the continuous variation over a wide range of the relevant attributes of the various capital goods' (pp. 323–4). This is soon reiterated: 'any sharp division into two distinct categories of capital goods, such as circulating and fixed capital, is likely to do more harm than good... The division into two separate groups becomes seriously misleading if it treats one part of capital as being permanent, and the other part as involving no waiting whatever: all the problems of capital are then evaded' (pp. 329–30).[7] On the other hand, Hayek's conception of amalgamating the 'Austrian' and the 'Anglo-American' approaches to capital theory certainly does not amount to striking some sort of average, or 50–50 balance, or compromise between the two. As he writes later, immediately after the phrase 'all the problems of capital are then evaded', cited above:

> The fact is rather that even in the shortest of short runs the capital equipment is not given but is eminently variable... It is for this reason that we have persistently argued that circulating capital in this ordinary sense of the term possesses the characteristic attributes of capital in a higher degree than fixed capital, and that in consequence those theories which tend to stress the importance of goods in

process rather than of durable goods have contributed more to the understanding of the important problems in this field'. (p. 330).[8]

Hayek's attitude is, then, not easy to pin down in any sharp characterization, for it would seem to require both that attention should not be directed exclusively to circulating capital and that the latter should receive the greatest emphasis and should, so to speak, set the tone for the whole of capital theory.

However one decides to portray Hayek's overall view of the structure of capital, that view must certainly encompass the presence of fixed capital – durable capital in the 'repeated use' sense of durable. Many pages of *The Pure Theory of Capital* are, after all, devoted to the consideration of fixed capital. Yet it was not silly of Hicks to refer to 'the old Austrian capital theory, a theory which (we can now see) was more competent to deal with circulating capital than with fixed' (1973b, p. 133). Nor was it entirely inappropriate for Smithies – over 30 years earlier – to urge that durable goods are the central problem for Austrian theory (which here means for Hayek in his book): 'No wonder that in the Austrian theory, stress is laid on circulating capital' (1941, p. 771).[9] For Hayek himself is well aware of the complications, to put matters no more strongly, to which fixed capital gives rise. He points out, for example, that 'in the case of durable goods the input function which we have used in connection with goods in process is not directly known... all that is initially given as a technological "datum" is the output function' (p. 127). Eight pages later, Hayek introduces the fact that durable goods are not produced instantaneously but have a gestation period and highlights, in a marginal summary, the 'Difficulties of combining the period of gestation and the period of use in one diagram' (pp. 135–6). And, nothing daunted, he then notes that, 'Compared with the real world, of course, even this case of a durable good which is made without the help of other durable goods... and which then serves consumption directly without further co-operation from other current input, is still very much simplified' (p. 138). In a good (i.e., bad) example of his occasional practice in *The Pure Theory of Capital* of waving his hands in the face of a serious theoretical issue, Hayek then writes: 'But it is not necessary here to follow up these complications in all their details. It is quite sufficient to have elucidated the principle according to which even the most complicated patterns of this sort can be described by one input function' (p. 138). But had Hayek really done what is claimed in this last sentence? His sympathetic critic Lutz, for one, was certainly not persuaded. In his 1943 review article he argues, on both p. 303 and p. 304, that Hayek's input curve cannot be constructed when durable goods are involved, i.e., in practically all cases; on p. 304 he argues also that once the construction period of a durable good is taken into account, Hayek's output curve cannot be constructed either. 'In most practical cases we can therefore draw neither an input nor an output curve' (1943, p. 304). It would seem prudent to take this conclusion of Lutz's to be correct, unless and until it is shown explicitly how the input and/or output curves may be constructed in the relevant cases; Hayek's bland assurance is certainly no adequate substitute for a demonstration. It is for this reason that the present paper does not consider further Hayek's well known – but perhaps not well understood – input functions and output functions, to which so much space is devoted in *The Pure Theory of Capital*.[10]

One formal way of expressing the problem for the input function and the output function is to say that real world production processes involve elements of both joint demand and joint supply. And Hayek himself explicitly introduces these very concepts. In his Chapter VI, already referred to earlier in the present section, Hayek introduces the continuous input–point output and point input–continuous output cases (pp. 66–7) and then remarks that 'we must mention another way of describing [these two cases] which seems to bring out the relevant peculiarities even more clearly ... The first case ... give[s] rise to a *joint demand* for factors ... The second case, where it is a question of the durability of the good, ... gives rise to a *joint supply* of services' (p. 67).[11] The point is repeated later when, against the marginal summary note 'It is not always possible to connect individual units of input with individual units of output', Hayek observes that,

> The popularity which the examples of the growing of trees or the maturing of wine have enjoyed [results from their closeness] to this simplest of cases, the "point input –point output" case. But to assume that all cases of investment can be treated on these lines is to evade the main problems. As we have seen, the relationship between the product and the input used will as a rule be in the nature of a joint demand for resources ... or of a joint supply of products ... or it will be a combination of both ... frequently the only technical link which we shall be able to establish will be the connection between a stream of input stretching over a period of time and a stream of output stretching over another period of time. (pp. 151–2)

Why then did Hicks, after saying that, 'The "Austrians" ... thought (or hoped) that there was some way in which fixed capital could be "reduced" to working capital', continue 'but it has *now* become quite clear that this cannot be done' (1973a, p. 192; emphasis added)? At one level, at least, this seems to have been quite clear to Hayek already in 1941, even if there was also his more optimistic hand-waving (p. 138) referred to above. Hicks perhaps means by 'now' merely 'since the time of the Hayek seminar in 1931–5', for he refers in this context to Sraffa's *Production of Commodities*, to 'the work of the Linear Programmers [and to] the discussions that have been based on von Neumann', while explaining that it is the element of joint supply which makes fixed capital a formidable complication (1973a, p. 192). Yet the reference to Sraffa and von Neumann only raises another obscurity in Hicks's claim that we now know the 'Austrians' to have been wrong in thinking (or hoping) that fixed capital could be reduced to working (circulating) capital, for it is just that very reduction which *is* effected by the von Neumann–Sraffa treatment of fixed capital! That treatment does not reinstate the input function or the output function but it does, in formal terms, render *all* capital goods *circulating* capital goods.[12]

Before concluding this section on the characterization of capital goods, we may note – albeit very briefly – that Hayek, in *The Pure Theory of Capital*, is far from assuming throughout the existence of unlimited possibilities for smooth substitution of one kind or another within production. Thus complementarities and rigidities in proportions are frequently referred to (see, e.g. pp. 25, 62, 153, 187, 203, 328–9). In Chapter XVI, 'The Marginal Value Product of Investment: The Problem of Attribution (Imputation)', pp. 204–7 are devoted entirely to matters connected with rigid input proportions. A later part of the same chapter is given over to another kind of rigidity, in this case concerning produced durable inputs the lives of which cannot be varied (pp. 207–10). (So-called 'partial rigidities' are considered in the remainder of the chapter, pp. 212–5). Hayek is also well aware that there may be an 'input which can be used only in one particular "stage" of production ... Such input we shall call completely *specific* input' (p. 251). While he suggests that 'Specificity in this extreme form will probably be of very rare occurrence' (p. 251), Hayek nevertheless considers the significance of specificity at several points (see, e.g., pp. 280, 307, 314, 328). Finally, we note briefly Hayek's concern with 'Discontinuity of replacement' in the case of 'goods of very great durability and of which comparatively few are in existence (e.g., railway engines or even bridges)' (p. 129). As he points out, 'It is undeniable that for such goods production and replacement will inevitably be discontinuous, and that in consequence the composition of the stock of such goods in existence will undergo periodic changes' (p. 129; in Hawtrey's judgement, 1941, p. 290, Hayek exaggerates the importance of discontinuities).

What, then, is one to say of Hayek's overall vision of the capital structure in *The Pure Theory of Capital*? As noted above, he fully acknowledges the importance of durable capital goods and yet considers that circulating capital goods are, in some important sense, more truly representative of the essential problems of capital theory. Hayek himself makes it quite clear that 'Austrian' theory must be able to take in its stride the continuous input–continuous output case and yet he provides no convincing demonstration that his input functions or output functions can adequately represent this case. Moreover, Hayek's hand-waving reference to production of durable goods by means of other durable goods (p. 138) is far from meeting Shackle's concern that the construction of input and/or output functions 'is made immeasurably more difficult by a fact which Hayek seems quite to ignore', namely the fact of Leontief-like input–output relations (1988, pp. 181–2). Thus while it may be hard to depict accurately Hayek's account of capital structure, it is still harder to accept that account as really convincing.

Relative prices, the value of capital and the amount of waiting

While it may not be easy to discern Hayek's positive theory of capital or to see that it is correct, it is reasonably straightforward to understand his nega-tive, critical view of certain other theories and to appreciate that his criti-cisms thereof are well founded. Both this and the subsequent section will consider some negative, critical aspects of Hayek's book.

Hayek is very conscious that relative commodity prices are unlikely to be the same at different levels of the rate of interest. In Chapter XXI, 'The Effect of the Accumulation of Capital on the Quantities Produced and on Relative Prices of Different Commodities', Hayek considers the effects of 'capital deepening' and takes this to be associated with 'a fall in the rate of interest' (p. 286). He suggests that 'it is almost impossible to explain the changes in the relative values of different types of capital goods without going back to the factors which determine the changes in the relative values of the different kinds of pure input' (pp. 287–8). Disclaiming any ambition to give a full explanation of this latter question, Hayek provides some account of it (pp. 288–92) and then returns to the question, 'How does a change in the rate of interest affect the relative prices of different capital goods ...?' (p. 292). Hayek rejects the idea that 'the relative prices of the intermediate products ... could change permanently only to the relatively small extent to which the direct interest element in their cost changed' (p. 292). This is because the 'much more important' effect of an interest rate change on prices is claimed to be 'through its effect on the demand for the intermediate products and for the factors from which they are produced' (p. 293). What-ever one's assessment of this last claim might be, Hayek is associating a change in the rate of interest with a change in the relative prices of produced commodities.

Hayek's Chapter XXI discussion, just referred to, concludes with a for-ward reference to Chapter XXVII, 'Long-Run Forces Affecting the Rate of Interest'. (Note that the former chapter is in Part III and the latter in Part IV.) Some eight pages of Chapter XXVII deal with the effects on prices of an increase in the rate of profit – such an increase 'cannot be lastingly without effect on the relative prices of the various kinds of input and on the methods of production that will appear profitable' (p. 378). For it involves a general rise in the price of output relative to all kinds of input and it is impossible for such a 'rise in the price of output to leave the relative prices of the different kinds of input unaffected' (p. 381). If relative input prices *were* to remain unchanged then the various time rates of profit earned on different units of input would become unequal; hence a change in the 'uniform time rate' of profit requires changes in relative input prices (pp. 381–2). The adjustment to the change in the rate of profit will involve both changes in production methods and alterations in product prices (pp. 383–6).

Hayek was, then, quite well aware of a link between any uniform rate of interest (profit) and relative values. Whether he managed to take full account of this connection in his own analysis is less clear – certainly Hawtrey and Lutz, for example, were not persuaded that he did. Thus Hawtrey complains that 'Professor Hayek fails to carry through his analysis without assuming over and over again the measurability of capital or of input as aggregates' and insists that 'the mere existence of a "real" rate of interest determined competitively requires' given relative values for both outputs and physical capital inputs (1941, p. 289). Lutz considers that at many points Hayek took *both* the rate of interest and relative output values as given (1943, p. 304). These charges need not be pursued here, however, for Hayek's undoubted awareness of the issue – as opposed to his ability to deal with it – is all that is relevant for his criticism of other theories. For example, given that aware-ness, it would be surprising were Hayek to advocate taking the 'value of aggregate capital' as a datum for economic analysis. No such surprise awaits the reader – to the contrary, Hayek is a fierce critic of any such procedure.

Hayek's warnings against any attempt to treat a 'given value of capital' as a 'capital-supply' datum for economic analysis begin already in his Chapter I, 'The Scope of the Inquiry', (see pp. 5–6, 8–10), resurface immediately in Chapter II, 'Equilibrium Analysis and the Capital Problem' – where p. 16, n. 1 refers to 'the vague concept of a given supply of free capital' – and run throughout Chapter VII, 'Capital and the "Subsistence Fund"'. It would be otiose to cite every statement from the book bearing on this matter and the following will perhaps suffice. In Chapter VII, just referred to, Hayek notes that economists have often spoken of the stock of capital 'as if it could be treated as a homogeneous "fund", an "amount of waiting", or as a given quantity of "capital disposal" or of "pure capital" in the abstract' (p. 93). Whatever limited uses such expressions might have, Hayek continues, 'much more far-reaching assertions have been made about the real existence of such a fund which I cannot but regard as pure mysticism ... I am afraid, with all due respect to Professor Knight, I cannot take this view seriously because I cannot attach any meaning to this mystical "fund"' (pp. 93–4). Later, in Chapter XIX, 'The General Conditions of Equilibrium', and precisely in the context of discussing price relationships and the rate of return, Hayek writes:

> There is no supply of capital in the abstract, no 'fund' of 'waiting' or 'capital disposal' (or whatever else the terms are by which this mystical quantity has been

described), which would form a datum in the determination of those prices. In particular, there is no 'real' magnitude called 'free capital' which exists in any way apart from the concrete capital goods, and which could be regarded as being available for investment in, and in this sense constituting the demand for, the capital goods. (pp. 266–7; see also p. 192)

Hayek is no less forthright in Chapter XXII, 'The Adjustment of the Capital Structure to Foreseen Changes', where he laments that 'the majority of economists have succumbed at one time or another [to] the temptation to regard the stock of "capital" as a quasi-homogeneous, quantitatively determined magnitude which can, like the supply of any other factor of production, be treated as a datum of economic analysis. One of the main conclusions of the whole of the preceding discussion is that the supply of capital can *not* be treated as a single quantity in this sense' (p. 294). Quoting Pigou (1935, p. 239) as claiming that 'capital' is 'an entity capable of maintaining its quantity while altering its form' (p. 294), Hayek insists that the introduction of such a 'fictitious magnitude', such a quantity of 'some common substance which could be preserved irrespective of changes in its composition' (p. 295), would be permissible only in a stationary state. But it would then be of little use! Such a given quantity would be useful only in the analysis of unforeseen changes and it is precisely in this context that such a theoretical construction is impermissible (pp. 295–6). According to Kirzner (1976, p. 134), 'Böhm-Bawerk declared that [J.B.] Clark's concept of capital was mystical' (in *Positive Theory of Capital*, Volume 2) and it will be clear that Hayek in *The Pure Theory of Capital* shares this view very firmly, extending it to Knight, Pigou *e tutti quanti*.

Lest the above should seem to leave too implicit the link between the dependence of relative values on the rate of interest and the non-existence of a given value of capital, we may note Hayek's explicit statement, in Chapter XV, 'Input, Output, and the Stock of Capital in Value Terms', that 'the value of the capital stock [at any moment, under stationary conditions] depends not only on the shape of the input function [i.e., on technical conditions, I.S.] but also on the rate of interest' (p. 199). The value of a given, equilibrium set of capital goods is not independent of distributional considerations.

Hayek is no more sympathetic to the idea of a given 'amount of waiting' than to that of a given value of capital. (Of course, as has already emerged above, the two ideas are often intertwined.) He does, it is true, 'make provisional use of this vague term ["amount of waiting"]' in Chapter VI (p. 73) but the very words 'provisional' and 'vague' already serve notice that the concept is not to be taken too seriously. The same is true of his Chapter VII reference to 'the vague but much used concept of the "amount of waiting" available' (p. 90). In Chapter XI, 'The Productivity of Investment', the concept is firmly set aside in the context of a criticism of the Jevons, Böhm-

Bawerk and Wicksell analysis (p. 140). Hayek rejects the idea that our ability 'to wait for part of the product of the existing resources.... [can be] expressed in terms of a single "amount of waiting"' (p. 141). In part, this is because 'in many cases (in all cases where durable goods are concerned) we cannot say in any general way, and on purely technical grounds, how long the different parts of the total amount of input invested will remain invested' (p. 143). 'But this is not all' (p. 143). Because the value of each specific investment of an input grows at the compound rate of interest, 'the amount of waiting involved in a particular investment is not simply proportional to the length of the investment period and the value of the input invested, but is dependent also on the rate of interest' (p. 144; a note attached to this sentence draws attention to a related observation by Wicksell in *Lectures*, etc., p. 184). Hence 'when we compare two different investment structures, it will not always be possible even to say, on purely technical grounds, which of them involves the greater amount of waiting. At one ... rate of interest, the one structure, and at a ... different rate of interest, the other structure, will represent the greater amount of waiting' (p. 144). There is thus no hope of adequately describing any production method, for the purposes of economic theory, in terms of the 'amount of waiting' which it demands (p. 145) and similar objections arise 'in the concept of a given supply of waiting' (p. 146, marginal summary). Beyond any 'vague' and 'preliminary' uses, the concept of the 'amount of waiting' is firmly expelled from 'Austrian' capital theory in Hayek's book.

It is curious that in the second section of his review article, Smithies should have written that Hayek assumes 'capital to be of a given equilibrium value' (1941, p. 769 n. 10). Smithies notes that Wicksell made such an assumption, even whilst knowing that he should not do so (p. 770), and wishes this same error upon Hayek, despite abundant contrary evidence; Smithies's own footnote (p. 769, n. 10) suggests that he may have felt rather nervous about this attribution. Lutz, in his review article, was far more perceptive in this regard, noting that Hayek is well aware that the subsistence fund cannot be considered as a datum determining equilibrium (1943, p. 306) and that what Hayek does treat as a datum, by contrast, is the (non-equilibrium) initial stock of physically specified capital goods (p. 307). In his later review article (1950), Fabbrini not only specifies correctly all the data of Hayek's analysis (at p. 271 he lists the initial capital stock, technical conditions, agents' preferences and the distribution of resources) but emphasizes throughout Hayek's approach to a Walrasian–Paretian analysis. He writes, for example; 'it seems to me that he has taken the Austrian theory a step forward: a step, however, which leads towards the Walrasian theory, and not beyond it' (p. 278, our translation).

The average period of production

The reader of *The Pure Theory of Capital* need not wait long to learn of Hayek's assessment of this venerable concept, for on the second page of the Preface one is told that the 'average period of production' is an 'almost useless' conceptual tool (p. vi). The matter is taken up already in Part I where, in Chapter VI, Hayek asserts that the 'concept of an average period of production ... is not only unnecessary but is also highly misleading' (p. 76). The explanation comes later, however, in Chapter XI, 'The Productivity of Investment', where Hayek notes that, 'All attempts to reduce the complex structure of waiting periods, which is described by the input functions *and* the output functions, to a single aggregate or average investment period ... are bound to fail because the different waiting periods cannot be reduced to a common denominator in purely technical terms' (pp. 141–2). Such a period 'cannot be regarded as something that is independent of, or as a datum determining, the rate of interest' (p. 143). Nor is it ensured in principle that every 'average' period must be inversely related to the rate of interest, for whatever may be the general tendency, it is 'quite possible that ... a fall in the rate of interest will create ... in the case of some individual factor the effect ... that it will be invested for shorter periods' (p. 292).

Thus far we have – in the interests of clarity, it is hoped – kept separate discussion of the value of capital, the amount of waiting and the average period but they are, of course, closely related (as, indeed, some of the above quotations have already shown). We may therefore conclude this section by noting two passages which bring these concepts together. In Chapter XV, 'Input, Output, and the Stock of Capital in Value Terms', Hayek notes that, 'even given the rate of interest, we could not determine the value of the stock of capital if, instead of having a full description of the range of investment periods ... we knew only the aggregate or average of these periods' (pp. 199–200). At a given rate of interest, the same average period can 'correspond to different quantities of capital' for different technical conditions and, moreover, the *ordering* by value of capital may itself depend on the level of the given rate of interest (p. 200). It would be quite futile, then, to seek for any useful relationship between an average period and the aggregate value of capital. Earlier, in Chapter XI, 'The Productivity of Investment', Hayek brings the various concepts together in a remarkable passage which deserves to be quoted at some length.

> In short, there is no way in which the variety of technical periods during which we have to wait, either for the products of different kinds of input or for particular units of the product, can be combined into an aggregate or average which can be regarded as a technical datum ... But as the size of the product will clearly depend on the technical combination of the different kinds of input, it obviously cannot be represented as a function of any such aggregate or average period of investment ...

We must therefore base the following analysis on the multiplicity of data provided by our description of the investment structure, without trying to combine them into a single productivity function of waiting or of capital. (p. 145)

A quarter of a century later, the famous symposium on so-called 'paradoxes' in capital theory, in the *Quarterly Journal of Economics* for November 1966, added much detail with respect to multiple switching, capital reversing, etc., but the central point about the non-existence of simplified, aggregate representations of production, whether in 'value of capital' terms or 'average period' terms, had already been clearly stated by Hayek in his book. It is unfortunate that (if memory serves), Hayek's book received very little attention during the 'capital theory debates' of the 1960s and 1970s (cf. the remarks of Lachmann, 1975, pp. 1–3).

Traditional relationships
It is not to be inferred from Hayek's clear rejection of any 'aggregate' production function that, in *The Pure Theory of Capital*, he asserts no traditional relationships between economic variables. In the closing chapter of Part II (Chapter XVIII), for example, Hayek refers without any apparent hesitation to 'the fall in the rate of interest accompanying the accumulation of capital' (p. 242). Similarly, the rate of return on investments is said to fall as the amount invested increases (p. 257); 'an increase of capital relatively to the quantity of other factors of production', it is said, 'will lead to ... a fall in the rate of interest [and] the adoption of longer or more roundabout methods of production' (p. 269). On p. 283 one reads that, 'Any additional investment (even while it is only expected) will thus cause a shrinkage in the return on all capital' and soon afterwards that if the rate of interest is lowered a factor 'will evidently have to be redistributed between the different stages [of the production process] so that more will go to the earlier and less to the later stages.... [This only restates] conclusions with which we are already familiar' (pp. 290–1). As a final example, consider Hayek's assertion that 'in so far as labour succeeds ... in raising real wages it will tend to bring about a substitution of capital for labour or a transition to more capitalistic methods of production. The net effect would probably be that fewer workmen would be employed with more capital per head' (p. 347).

It is not entirely transparent what one is to make of such assertions, given Hayek's own clear awareness of the grave difficulties involved in, say, a statement to the effect that roundaboutness has increased. Our uncertainty in this regard is reinforced when, for example, we recall that on p. 292 – *immediately following* the passage just cited, from pp. 290–1, on 'conclusions with which we are already familiar' – Hayek states clearly that 'some individual factor ... may well be ... invested for shorter periods' when the rate of interest falls![13] It would seem that, in his book, Hayek rejects several traditional analytical tools, often retains traditional conclusions (not in itself illogical, of course, since the use of faulty tools could have led to correct conclusions), sometimes expresses those conclusions in ways ruled out by his own rejection of traditional tools, and occasionally even seems to argue against those very conclusions.

Concluding remarks

Hayek's *The Pure Theory of Capital* is, then, a complex work. His 'consistent plans' analysis is not the form of analysis which Hayek would really have liked to use. He provides ways of thinking about capital theory but little in the way of specific, constructive results. Moreover, these 'ways of thinking' tend to be inconclusive in a more general sense, it being unclear precisely how Hayek sees the place of circulating capital and how he could defend consistently some of his more traditional statements – but clear enough that his input functions and output functions are of decidedly limited usefulness. On one thing, however, it is possible to make a quite unambiguous statement; by 1941 Hayek had already provided a convincing dismissal of any attempt to employ the aggregate value of capital, or an aggregate amount of waiting, or an average period of production as a datum in theoretical economic analysis.

Notes

1. It may be helpful to note at this point that 'a mathematical appendix in which I had at one time hoped to restate the central theoretical propositions in algebraic form' (p. viii) had to be omitted from the published version of *The Pure Theory of Capital* and also Hayek's remark, 'But I am not sure that its abandonment is to be regarded as a loss'. We understand that readers will eventually be able to judge this for themselves, since the mathematical appendix is to be included in Volume XIII of Hayek's *Collected Works*.
2. An important consequence of that lack of concern is Hayek's rejection of the use of the distinction between net and gross investment – or, therefore, net and gross income – and of the concept of 'maintaining capital intact'. See, for example, pp. 12–13, 298–9, 335–6 and (1941a).
3. See also Fabbrini (1950), p. 266, where Hayek's Chapter III is seen, in part, as being implicitly a response to Myrdal and, above all, Lindahl. More generally, the whole of Fabbrini's section 3, 'Il metodo d'analisi', pp. 262–7, is very perceptive, as is, indeed, the whole of his long review article.
4. A probable secondary reason is that Hayek, in his book, wishes to emphasize the 'productivity' aspect, rather than the 'time-preference' aspect, and *not* to present as 'even-handed' an account of the two aspects as does Fisher. Time-preference is played down in Hayek's main text and his Appendix I, 'Time Preference and Productivity', is devoted precisely to urging the greater importance of the latter factor. Yet Hayek soon had second thoughts on this matter. Replying to Lutz in November 1943, he recognized that perhaps he had appeared to give too little importance to the 'time preference aspect' and acknowledged that, 'It is in this respect more than in others that I am now most conscious that my exposition requires revision' (1943, p. 311). By February 1945 Hayek had published his 'Time-Preference and Productivity: A Reconsideration', which contains the interesting remark that, 'Though I had thought that I had made every effort to escape the "static"

approach which has had such an unfortunate effect on the theory of capital, in this particular respect I seem still to have been misled by it' (1945, p. 22).

5. At p. 356, n. 2, Hayek – with a hint of irritation – draws attention to the fact that he had already in 1929 published a work in which the rate of interest in the short run was said to be 'determined by considerations of banking liquidity' and that an English translation was published in 1933.

6. Hayek is not entirely happy with the label 'Austrian' (p. 46) and it is amusing to note that when discussing this very contrast Hicks (1973a, p. 192) refers to the other component as simply 'the American version of neo-classical theory', the Angles being exonerated.

7. This statement might well remind one of Sraffian criticism of what Hicks (1973a, p. 192) describes as 'the *Production Function* school' of neoclassical theory. And it may be noted in this context that, in introducing his list of ten contrasts, Hayek mentions explicitly that 'the classical English economists since Ricardo, and particularly J.S. Mill (the latter probably partly under the influence of J. Rae), were in this sense much more "Austrian" than their successors' (p. 47, n. 1).

8. Smithies, whose 'review will be frankly critical [written by] a renegade from the Austrian faith' (1941, p. 767), refers explicitly to this passage and cruelly suggests that it really applies to Hayek's beliefs, rather than to objective relative contributions.

9. To this sentence Smithies appends an interesting footnote (p. 771, n. 14), on what he takes to be the diffidence with which Wicksell approached capital theory and the latter's setting aside of durable goods. Smithies cites p. 186 of Wicksell's *Lectures on Political Economy*, Volume One, in support of his interpretation, which perhaps reflects in part his own short-run emphasis.

10. For helpful remarks on these functions see, for example, Fabbrini (1950), pp. 269–71; Hawtrey (1941), pp. 283–4, 289; Meacci, Chapter 2, this volume; Shackle (1988), pp. 174–9.

11. At p. 67, n. 1, attached to this last sentence, Hayek quotes – slightly inaccurately – Wicksell's reference, in *Lectures*, etc., p. 260, to the annual uses of a capital good as constituting a kind of joint supply.

12. It may not be entirely inappropriate at this point to recall Burmeister's argument of 1974, that Hicks's 'neo-Austrian' theory, of 1973b, has little or nothing to add to the von Neumann analysis.

13. We might note, too, Hayek's claim in Chapter XXVII, 'Long-Run Forces Affecting the Rate of Interest', that 'the rate of interest and profit may be higher in a rich community with much capital and a high rate of saving than in an otherwise similar community with little capital and a low rate of saving' (p. 396).

References

Burmeister, E. (1974), 'Synthesizing the Neo-Austrian and Alternative Approaches to Capital Theory: A Survey', *Journal of Economic Literature*, **XII**, June, 413–56.

Fabbrini, L. (1950), 'La teoria del capitale e dell' interesse di F.A. Hayek', *Rivista internazionale di scienze sociali*, **22**, 250–86.

Hawtrey, R.G. (1941), 'Professor Hayek's Pure Theory of Capital', *Economic Journal*, **LI**, June–September, 281–90.

Hayek, F.A. von (1941), *The Pure Theory of Capital*, London: Routledge & Kegan Paul 1941 and 1950. The 1950 edition was used here.

Hayek, F.A. von (1941a), 'Maintaining Capital Intact: A Reply', *Economica*, new series, **8**, August, 276–80.

Hayek, F.A. von (1943), 'A Comment', *Economica*, new series, **10**, November, 311.

Hayek, F.A. von (1945), 'Time-Preference and Productivity: A Reconsideration', *Economica*, new series, **12**, February, 22–5.

Hicks, J.R. (1973a), 'The Austrian Theory of Capital and its Rebirth in Modern Economics', in J.R. Hicks and W. Weber (eds), *Carl Menger and the Austrian School of Economics*, Oxford: Clarendon Press.

Hicks, J.R. (1973b), *Capital and Time. A Neo-Austrian Theory*, Oxford: Clarendon Press.

Kirzner, I.M. (1976), 'The Theory of Capital', in E.G. Dolan (ed.), *The Foundations of Modern Austrian Economics*, Kansas City: Sheed and Ward.

Lachmann, L.M. (1975), 'Reflections on Hayekian Capital Theory', paper presented at the Allied Social Science Associations Meeting, Dallas.

Lachmann, L.M. (1976), 'On Austrian Capital Theory', in E.G. Dolan (ed.), *The Foundations of Modern Austrian Economics*, Kansas City: Sheed and Ward.

Lutz, F.A. (1943), 'Professor Hayek's Theory of Interest', *Economica*, new series, **10**, November, 302–10.

Machlup, F. (1977), 'Hayek's Contribution to Economics', in F. Machlup (ed.), *Essays on Hayek*, London: Routledge & Kegan Paul; New York: New York University Press, 1976. (Earlier version in *Swedish Journal of Economics*, **76**, December 1974, 498–531.)

Pigou, A.C. (1935), 'Net Income and Capital Depletion', *Economic Journal*, **XLV**, 235–41.

Shackle, G.L.S. (1988), 'Hayek as Economist', ch. 13 of *Business, Time and Thought*, London: Macmillan. (First version in D.P. O'Brien and J.R. Presley (eds), *Pioneers of Modern Economics in Britain*, London: Macmillan, 1981.)

Smithies, A. (1941), 'Professor Hayek on *The Pure Theory of Capital*', *American Economic Review*, **31**, December, 767–79.

Wicksell, K. (1934), *Lectures on Political Economy. Volume One. General Theory*, London: Routledge & Kegan Paul. (Swedish original 1901.)

2 Hayek and the deepening of capital

Ferdinando Meacci

Speaking in 'The Hayek Story' of the 'drama' of economic theory in the 1930s Hicks (1967) says that the only thing that Keynes and Hayek had in common was their intellectual descent from Wicksell, although Wicksell plus Keynes said one thing; Wicksell plus Hayek another. Focusing on the Wicksell–Hayek line, he later concludes that what this line leads to is not where Hayek intended to go, i.e. the theory of the business cycle, but where the economists of one generation later went in droves, i.e. the theory of economic growth.

This conclusion is hard to share for, in addition to obscuring something that Keynes and Hayek had in common, i.e. the idea that money may affect the volume and direction of production, it may also obscure the role that this idea was to play in the history of economic thought ever since.

Hicks's conclusion, however, fits in well with the scope of this paper, whose purpose is to examine an aspect of Hayek's theory which is unrelated to the disequilibrating role of money (and therefore to the business cycle) but which is nonetheless implicit even when it is this role that Hayek is dealing with. This paper, therefore, will not be concerned with the 'disturbing outside forces' (money) which – to use Hansen and Tout's analogy (1933) – make the pendulum swing and which were largely responsible for the Keynes–Hayek drama.[1] Rather, it will be concerned with the 'peculiar internal structure' of the pendulum itself, that is, with the nature and role of time-consuming methods of production in a dynamic economy. In particular, the paper will be focused on an intriguing type of change these methods are subject to. This change was called by Hawtrey (1937) 'deepening the capital structure', or 'capital deepening', or 'deepening' for short.

Hayek's treatment of this phenomenon will be assessed with regard to what he argued both when this expression was not yet in use, as is the case with *Prices and Production* (1931), and when, this expression having become fashionable before the publication of *Profits, Interest and Investment* (1939) and *The Pure Theory of Capital* (1941), the underlying phenomenon was extensively dealt with by Hayek even in the sections of these works where he refrained from using Hawtrey's new expression.

The paper is divided into three sections. They correspond to the three different phases which Hayek's treatment of capital deepening went through. These phases culminated in the three publications mentioned above and can be identified, respectively, by the names given, either by Hayek or by his critics, to the central topics debated in each of them. These topics are the concertina effect; the Ricardo effect; and the input and output functions.

The concertina effect

The expression 'concertina effect' was implied in a note added by Hayek to the first German edition of *Prices and Production* (1931, p. 91) and was later made a catchword by Kaldor (1942) when he set out to criticize the second version of this effect (to be discussed below). The first version (which is the one provided in *Prices and Production* and discussed in this section) is rendered by Hansen and Tout as follows: 'A lengthening of the process of production caused by forced saving (the money supply not having been held neutral) cannot possibly be permanently maintained, but must necessarily be followed by a shortening in the process of production' (1933, p. 134).

While, as will be argued below, something is missing in this otherwise correct exposition of Hayek's reasoning, it is worth noting immediately that the focus of Kaldor's critique is not the Austrian concept of the 'degree of roundaboutness', which instead he defended against Knight's criticisms and even tried to improve by introducing his own concept of the 'degree of capital intensity';[2] nor is it the notion of an increase or of a decrease in this degree. Indeed, the concept of roundaboutness, and the associated notions of lengthening and shortening, can be fruitfully used without resorting to the concept of the 'average period of production' which spelled so much trouble for the Austrian theory of distribution (a topic to be neglected here as much as the Austrian theory of the trade cycle) and which was eventually rejected by Hayek himself (1941) as an unnecessary and misleading tool.

However narrow the focus of inquiry of this paper may be relatively to the scope of Hayek's *Prices and Production*, it is nevertheless broad enough to encompass Hayek's best known assumption as well as the least noticed of his implications. This assumption is that resources are *fully employed* when the cycle begins. The implication is that the output of consumers' goods increases (decreases) only if their period of production is lengthened (shortened). The assumption and the implication are intertwined in Hayek's reasoning in the sense that the existence of unused resources is not 'a *necessary* condition for an increase of output'; and that, starting 'at a condition of equilibrium when no unused resources exist', his purpose is to discuss 'the increase of output made possible by a transition to more capitalistic methods of production' (1931, pp. 34–5). This makes clear what is implied in a number of different passages of *Prices and Production*, namely that there is a necessary relationship between lengthening (shortening) and the subsequent increases (decreases) in the output of consumers' goods.

The idea that a lengthening of the production period is normally required for a given amount of direct labour to be capable of turning out a greater output of consumers' goods belongs to Böhm-Bawerk who designated it as the 'principle of higher productivity of roundabout methods of production'. It should be noted, however, in regard to overall consequences, that a greater output provided by a given amount of direct labour is not the same as a lower amount of direct labour required by a given level of output. As we shall see better below, the difference between these two cases is crucial not only in understanding two different types of lengthening, but also in identifying a usually neglected turning point in the development of the theory of capital in the 1930s.

In his attempt to apply Böhm-Bawerk's principle to his new theory of the trade cycle, Hayek went beyond the static domain in which this principle had been left by Böhm-Bawerk. The outcome of this effort is ambiguous, to begin with, with regard to Hayek's famous triangular figures as they seem to improve, on the one hand, but end up blurring, on the other, Böhm-Bawerk's insight. While the improvement consists in accommodating, within the same geometrical construction, the two points of view from which it is possible to look at a capitalist economy, i.e. its vertical and horizontal integration (a meaningless distinction in an economy without capital), the confusion creeps in when, after recalling the relationship between lengthening and the 'greater quantity of consumers' goods', Hayek proceeds by dealing with changes in 'the proportion' (i.e. in the ratio between the amount of intermediate products which is necessary to secure a given output of consumers' goods and this very output) without noticing that this proportion may increase either because its numerator increases more than its denominator; or because the former increases without any increase (or even with a decrease) in the latter. Furthermore, the proportion between the volume of intermediate products and the volume of consumers' goods (two physical magnitudes) is one thing; the proportion between the value (in terms of money) of the former and the value (in terms of money) of the latter is another. While it is inevitable in *Prices and Production* that this second type of proportion increases (in the context of a constant money supply) as lengthening occurs (for, as Hayek points out, the prices of consumers' goods tend to decrease in these circumstances by more than the income of original means of production), nothing can be said about changes in the first type of proportion (it could indeed rise, fall or remain constant) even if a measurement of the two terms were possible.

Hayek's failure to grasp the different meanings of this proportion seems to be at the root of his explicit identification of 'stages' (downward movement of goods) with 'firms' (upward movement of money). This identification, besides ultimately blurring the distinction between horizontal and vertical integration which was initially brought to the forefront, seems in turn to be responsible for another, more general and dangerous, assumption of *Prices and Production*. Since this assumption is more crucial than is currently believed, it is worth quoting fully the note where it is stipulated (letters in brackets are added to identify sentences):

[a] So long as we confine ourselves to the real aspects of the capital structure the triangular figures may be taken to represent not only the stock of goods in process but also the stock of durable instruments existing at any moment of time. [b] The different instalments of future services which such goods are expected to render will in that case have to be imagined to belong to different 'stages' of production corresponding to the time interval which will elapse before these services mature (...). [c] But as soon as it is tried to use the diagrammatic representations to show the successive transfers of the intermediate products from stage to stage in exchange for money it becomes evidently impossible to treat durable goods in the same way as goods in process since it is impossible to assume that the individual services embodied in any durable goods will regularly change hands as they approach a stage nearer to the moment when they will actually be consumed. [d] For this reason it has been necessary, as has been pointed out in the preface, to abstract from the existence of durable goods so long as the assumption is made that the total stock of intermediate products as it gradually proceeds towards the end of the process of production is exchanged against money at regular intervals. (1931, pp. 40–41, n. 2)

A close examination of [a] and [b] reveals that these two sentences rest on two different notions of time. While under [a] time is regarded as an *ingredient* which is necessary for turning different inputs into the required output, under [b] time is regarded as a *container* in which 'instalments' of the services incorporated in durable goods are periodically released for their use in production. The neglect of this difference seems to be at the root, in [b], of a certain confusion between the concept of *stages* (which relates to the notion of time as an ingredient) and the concept of *periods* (as intervals of time as a container). Now, since the conclusion in [c] is derived from this confusion, [c] is also flawed. Indeed, if it is impossible 'to treat durable goods in the same way as goods in process' it is not because each instalment of their services is released in a different stage or because 'it is impossible to assume' that they change hands on each release, but because durable goods (unlike goods in process) release their services in different periods of the same stage. This confusion eventually leads to Hayek's decision to abstract, in [d], from durable goods and accordingly to base the whole model on what appears to be a strictly *working-capital assumption.*[3]

Hayek's working-capital assumption is not without consequences for the credibility of the principle of roundaboutness on which the logical structure of *Prices and Production* is based. In effect, the credibility of this principle is based on the role played in production by *instrumental* capital as distinct from *working* capital. These two kinds of capital are defined by Hawtrey, in the light of the principle of roundaboutness, as follows:

> Even if we conceive of the use of capital as essentially a device for utilizing the technical advantages of a more prolonged period of production, we still find a place for the conception of capital as an accumulated stock of wealth. At any moment of the productive process those productive operations which are already past will have left their mark in some material objects which embody their contribution to the process as a whole. These material objects fall into two broad classes, instrumental capital and working capital. (1937, p. 9)[4]

Now it should be noted that it is instrumental capital, rather than – as Hayek assumes – working capital, that must increase for the output of consumers' goods to increase in the first place. The former type of capital cannot, however, increase, let alone be created, unless the period of production of consumers' goods is lengthened. Furthermore, the period of production is one thing; that section of it which Hawtrey calls 'period of process' is another:

> One part, which we shall call the *period of process*, is the time occupied by the productive processes applied to the material composing the commodity itself, without regard to the time taken in the construction of the instruments used in those processes. It is the period of production as it would be if every instrument were treated as an original factor of production and if the only capital were working capital. The rest of the period of production is that which is composed of the respective ages and periods of production of the instruments used. (1937, p. 11)

A reformulation of the principle of roundaboutness according to this terminology implies that lengthening the 'period of process' is no condition for increasing the output of consumers' goods unless, given the full-employment assumption, the remaining part of the period of production increases in its turn. If this were not the case, an increase in output would either turn out as an increase in its *weight* (each unit of output being more working-capital intensive – and more expensive – than before), or result from the employment of previously *unused* capacity at every stage of the 'period of process'. But this implies, in the former case, the adoption of those roundabout methods that Böhm-Bawerk (1884–89, vol. III, pp. 1ff) would reject as 'unwisely chosen';[5] in the latter, the existence of those very 'unused resources' which Hayek assumes away in *Prices and Production*. Indeed, it may well be that a lengthening of the 'period of process' is associated with an increase in the output of consumers' goods. But this by no means entails that, however associated with each other, such a lengthening is, under conditions of full employment, the *cause* of this increase. The only thing that can be maintained in this case is that, if the output of consumers' goods increases along with a lengthening of the 'period of process', it is because the period of production, not the 'period of process', has been lengthened in the meantime.

To conclude: while an accumulation of instrumental capital is normally the result of a lengthening of the period of production of consumers' goods, an increase of working capital may or may not be associated with a lengthening of the 'period of process'. If it is associated, the output of consumers' goods increases *because* the period of production has also increased. If it is not, the output of consumers' goods increases *because* some resources, previously unused, have found employment. Unless, therefore, the period of production is confused with the 'period of process' and instrumental capital with working capital (which is what Hayek does according to Hawtrey), the two most crucial assumptions of Hayek's 1931 model, i.e. the working-capital assumption and the full-employment assumption, are untenable and lead the model to self-destruction.

The Ricardo effect

We have seen above that Hayek's model revolves around Böhm-Bawerk's principle of roundaboutness. We have also seen that, however badly Hayek may have applied this principle to the explanation of the trade cycle and however much he may have spoilt it with his confusions or assumptions about working and instrumental capital, firms and stages, stages and periods, his model conforms to the old Austrian tradition of looking at the lengthening of the production period from the point of view of its *output-expanding* effect. Now it is interesting to note that, when Kaldor came to criticize Hayek's *Prices and Production* in 1939, he disregarded this aspect and concentrated instead on something that Hayek had initially ignored, i.e. on the *labour-saving* effect of lengthening. Accordingly, whilst Hayek had adopted, again in Böhm-Bawerk's footsteps, the point of view of the economy as a whole, Kaldor developed his critique by concentrating from the very beginning on the behaviour of individual firms in relation to the choice of the optimal 'degree of capital intensity'.[6] After pointing out that an increase in this degree implies the installation of 'superior equipment, with a greater labour-saving capacity' (in the sense that this equipment, being either more 'automatic' or more 'durable', requires either less 'co-operating labour' or less 'invested labour' per unit of output), and that the excess capacity normally associated with the late phase of the boom is due to the growing underconsumption (resulting from the widening gap between income and demand) and to the emergence of labour scarcity as the boom unfolds, Kaldor argued that a continuous increase in the degree of capital intensity is required to counterbalance these two phenomena in order to postpone the breakdown of the boom. Moreover, he argued that this is impossible – and the breakdown of the boom inevitable – because, as capital intensity increases, the 'marginal productivity of capital intensification' falls below the level of the interest rate.[7]

Kaldor's attempt to provide an alternative explanation of the trade cycle is here taken into consideration only in so far as it contributed to shifting Hayek's focus of analysis away from the (higher and lower) stages of production on to the (profit maximizing) behaviour of firms; and away from the type of lengthening which results in an increase in the volume of output on to a type of lengthening which results, irrespective of changes in the volume of output, in a decrease in the cost per unit of output (or an increase in profit per unit of output). Now it is interesting to note that, when he came to counteract Kaldor's critiques, Hayek took up Kaldor's new approach as if this were the same as the one adopted in his previous trade cycle model, and made use of this approach to demonstrate, against Kaldor's strictures, that his previous conclusions still held true. This is how Hayek's 'Ricardo effect' was born.[8]

Kaldor's treatment of the implications of an increase in the degree of capital intensity was preceded by a momentous distinction put forward by Hawtrey in his book *Capital and Employment* (1937).[9] Here Hawtrey attempted to reformulate in a dynamic context, much as Hayek and Kaldor had done, Böhm-Bawerk's static analysis except that the analytical tools developed in this book are used to criticize both Hayek's and Kaldor's arguments. The most relevant of these tools is the distinction between 'capital widening' and 'capital deepening'. Hawtrey's initial formulation of this distinction runs as follows:

> The process by which the capital equipment of a community is increased may take two forms, a 'widening' and a 'deepening'. The widening of the capital equipment means the extension of productive capacity by the flotation of new enterprises, or the expansion of existing enterprises, without any change in the amount of capital employed for each unit of labour. The deepening means an increase in the amount of capital employed for each unit of labour'. (1937, p. 31)

Following Hawtrey, who pointed out that deepening 'involves an increase in the period of production and a change in the structure of production' (i.e. in the totality of the time-consuming processes existing at a moment of time) while widening 'involves no change in either', Hayek first stressed that investment in labour-saving machinery 'would not aim at producing a larger final output', and second, and in an attempt to trace the Austrian origins of Hawtrey's distinction, likened this distinction to Wicksell's distinction (1934) between 'growth of capital in height' and 'growth of capital in width' (Hayek, 1939, pp. 39–40).[10]

Both Hawtrey's and Wicksell's distinctions were eventually used by Hayek to introduce and support (with particular regard to their 'deepening' and 'height' aspects) his own arguments about what he called the 'Ricardo effect'. This name, as is widely known, was given by him to 'the proposition that a rise in wages will encourage capitalists to substitute machinery for labour and vice versa' (1939, p. 8).[11] The proposition was originally used mostly in its 'vice versa' version, i.e. in the sense that 'a rise in the price of the product (or a fall in real wages) will lead to the use of relatively less machinery and other capital and of relatively more direct labour in the production of any given quantity of output'. Its role, in Hayek's new version of his theory of the trade cycle, was to prove that since output prices increase (real wages fall) when the demand for consumers' goods increases, the concertina effect will now work the other way (in the sense that, as the boom unfolds, 'shallowing' overtakes 'widening' and methods of production become unduly 'direct' rather than unduly 'roundabout'), although Hayek's central thesis that a rise in the demand for consumers' goods will lead to a fall in the demand for capital goods still holds true in the background.[12]

Hayek's new focus on the behaviour of firms (rather than on the multiplication of stages) with regard to the substitution between labour and machinery for a given level of output seems to account for his decision to shed in *Profits, Interest and Investment* the working-capital assumption he had adopted in *Prices and Production*, and to base his new version of the concertina effect on a notion of capital whereby this is considered in its two classical components of *circulating* and *fixed* capital.[13]

This distinction was not ignored (with some contradictions) in Hayek's first version of the concertina effect.[14] He went so far on that occasion as to claim that 'the central idea' of this version was 'by no means new'; that this idea was already in the theories that traced the collapse of the boom to 'the conversion of too much circulating into fixed capital', and that the reason why these theories did not prove more fruitful 'seems to have been that the concepts employed, particularly the concepts of the different kinds of capital, were too uncertain in their meaning to give a clear idea of what was really meant'. It should be objected, however, that Hayek's treatment of this old distinction, far from eliminating, may indeed have added to the 'uncertainty' surrounding it. For, on the one hand, no conversion of circulating into fixed capital can ever take place in a model (as the one put forward in *Prices and Production*) where fixed capital is simply assumed away; on the other, the terms 'working' and 'circulating' are not two different names for the same thing: while the notion of working capital is based on the idea of goods in process, i.e. of goods that sooner or later will be turned into consumers' goods, the notion of circulating capital is based on the idea of a *return* either of consumption goods in the context of the process of (social) *reproduction*, or of money in the context of the process of (interindividual) *circulation* (from the moment it is spent to the moment it is earned). Now it is the latter (not the former, and typically classical) idea that Hayek brings out when, in setting out the mechanism by which a rise in output prices and in profits should lead to a shortening of the period of production, he resorts to the concept of the 'rate of turnover' of the whole or of any part of the capital of an individual firm. Furthermore, given Hayek's claim that 'all these doctrines trace back to Ricardo's doctrine of the conversion of circulating into fixed capital, developed in the chapter 'On Machinery' in the third edition of his *Principles*' (1931, p. 101), it should be noted that Ricardo's problem does not arise from too much capital being invested relative to what is available, but from a given capital suddenly changing its composition from a *right* (circulating) to a *wrong* (fixed) form.[15] In short, it is not because it is impossible to complete the construction of new machines that according to Ricardo a crisis occurs (if it did, it would mean to him something different from what it does to Hayek). Besides, the concern with the 'coordination problem' which plays so large a role in Hayek's thought is basically non-existent in Ricardo in that his 'capitalist' is an omniscient subject who knows exactly what he can do and what the outcome of his choices will be. Indeed, the existence of a coordination problem in Hayek, and its absence in Ricardo, are by themselves sufficient to reveal a fundamental difference in method between these two authors. This difference consists in the fact that Ricardo's approach is basically *static*, Hayek's is essentially *dynamic*.

The question of the static and the dynamic method in Ricardo and Hayek has been recently raised by two authors (Moss and Vaughn, 1986). After noting that Hayek, in dealing with the Ricardo effect, eventually referred his readers both to Ricardo's chapter 'On Value' and to his chapter 'On Machinery', these authors maintain, with regard to Hayek, that the whole of his theory belongs to dynamics; and, with regard to Ricardo, that while the latter's chapter 'On Value' belongs to statics, his chapter 'On Machinery' belongs to dynamics.

As for the statics versus dynamics issue, it should be noted that Ricardo's argument is focused in both chapters on what happens after a change has taken place; and that the study of what happens after a change is not the same as the study of the *process* of adjustment brought about by such a change. Yet, it is this process that Hayek explicitly deals with (see particularly 1942, pp. 231 and 234). Furthermore, while the study of 'what happens after a change' is focused in Ricardo's first chapter on changes in the *values* of commodities (produced with unequal proportions of circulating and fixed capital or with fixed capitals of unequal durability) resulting from an initial change in wages, in his thirty-first chapter the focus is shifted to the change in *wages* resulting from an initial (and sudden) change in the proportion of circulating and fixed capital. The two problems are very different: while the former arises in the context of the classical theory of *value*, the latter arises in the context of the classical theory of *wealth*. If, as in Schumpeter (1954, p. 595), the Ricardo effect is referred to the problem of the first type, it would be better to call it the 'Ricardo value effect'. Since, however, this effect is a problem that arises exclusively in the context of the labour theory of value, it is impossible both to think that this is what was in Hayek's mind (not only because his theory of value was completely different but also because the theory of the business cycle is nothing but a theory of the fluctuations of wealth) and to make use of this type of effect in the current discussion.

As for the second version of the Ricardo effect (i.e. the machinery question), it has already been observed that Ricardo deals with it in two different ways depending on whether a change in wages is the effect or the cause of the introduction of machinery (Zamagni, 1984). It is here worth adding that, however different from one another, these two cases are equally unrelated to the value problem mentioned above (where a change in wages is viewed exclusively as a cause) and are instead two different aspects of the machinery question as dealt with in Ricardo's machinery chapter. Accordingly, both cases will be classified here under the expression 'Ricardo machinery effect' to highlight the difference between the wealth effect due to the introduction of machinery and the value effect due to a change in wages (Ricardo value effect). On the other hand, it should also be added that the difference between the two cases of the machinery effect is not only a question of what is the cause, and what the effect. It is also a question of whether the phenomenon at issue is studied from the point of view of an individual (capitalist or firm) or of the economy as a whole. For, on the one hand, no 'poverty and distress' would follow if the conversion of the circulating into the fixed form of a given capital did not affect the economy as a whole. On the other hand, Ricardo's famous passage 'machinery and labour are in constant competition and the former can frequently not be employed until labour rises' refers, partly in contrast with the general context of the chapter, to the behaviour of individual firms (capitalists) facing a change in factor prices. The substitution of labour by machinery resulting from a rise in wages and the impoverishment of workers resulting from a conversion of circulating into fixed capital are phenomena so different from one another that the former may occur without the latter (as is typically the case when the conversion is financed by new savings). To stress the difference between these two phenomena in the sense that one relates to the behaviour of individual firms, the other to the evolution of the economy as a whole, we shall call the first type of the Ricardo machinery effect 'Ricardo microeffect', and the latter type 'Ricardo macroeffect'.

Given the two types of the Ricardo machinery effect and the static approach needed to grasp both their content and their difference, it becomes possible to understand in what sense Moss and Vaughn, in the article mentioned above, ended up, in their attempt to defend Hayek against Kaldor's critiques, by 'getting hold of the wrong end of the stick'. For, instead of criticizing – as they actually do – Kaldor's comparative static analysis on the grounds that both Hayek's Ricardo effect and Ricardo's machinery effect are framed in the context of dynamic analysis (which seems correct in the former case but incorrect in the latter), they would have rather based their critique on the difference between the behaviour of firms responding to changes in factor prices and the fall in wages brought about in the economy as a whole by a (sudden) conversion of circulating into fixed capital (the central theme of Ricardo's machinery chapter). In fact, this difference was missed by Kaldor and was, albeit unsatisfactorily, used against him by Hayek himself when the latter pointed out that Kaldor's criticisms were based on a misunderstanding of the difference between changes in the structure of production and changes in the productive equipment, as well as in his tacit assumption that the new labour-saving equipment to be bought and installed by individual firms was thought to be 'waiting in the shops' (p. 244 ff): a point of view which is obviously valid for an individual firm but not for the economy as a whole.

Input and output functions

We have seen above that the study of the phenomenon of capital deepening was made impossible, in the first version of the concertina effect, by Hayek's working-capital assumption as well as by the output-expanding effect of lengthening. We have also seen that, in the second version of this effect, the study of this phenomenon was conversely made necessary by Hayek's urge to prove Kaldor wrong on the latter's own ground, i.e. in the discussion of the question of 'the installation of superior equipment with a greater labour-saving capacity'. We have finally noted that, in moving from the first to the second version, Hayek became more and more conscious of the dynamic aspect of his theory and ended up either by contrasting it with the static element in the arguments of his critics (such as Kaldor) or by identifying it with the static aspect of the thought of some of his predecessors (such as Ricardo).

Now the time has come to realize that, as this round of controversies drew to a close, Hayek possibly became aware of a weakness which had not yet been eradicated from his writings and which even Kaldor had failed either to notice or to attack. This weakness consisted in Hayek's total or partial inability to go beyond the continuous input–point output model implied in his initial publications and particularly in *Prices and Production*. Indeed, if Kaldor had failed to explain how the introduction of labour-saving machinery implies an alteration in the continuous input–continuous output relations of a dynamic economy, Hayek himself had done little more, in his reply to Kaldor's criticisms, than criticizing the latter's failure. Hence his new attempt to come to a final reckoning not only with Kaldor (and Keynes) but also with himself. This is how *The Pure Theory of Capital* was born.[16]

We have seen above that Hayek was forced to shed his working-capital assumption when he first came to deal with the phenomenon of capital deepening and that his initial reaction was to move back to the traditional distinction between circulating and fixed capital. This distinction played an increasing role in Hayek's thought and was eventually given a systematic treatment in Chapter XXIV, 'The Mobility of Capital' and in Appendix II, 'The Conversion of "Circulating" Capital into "Fixed" Capital' (1941). An examination of this treatment is here worthwhile for it reveals the specific place occupied by Hayek's theory in the context of the more general theory of capital. This examination will be focused, first, on the relationship between Hayek's Chapter XXIV and Appendix II, and second on the relationship between Hayek's own distinction (plus the related conversion of one type of capital into the other) and the same topic as dealt with by the classical writers who allegedly inspired him.

As for the distinction, Hayek starts in *The Pure Theory of Capital* by claiming that 'the customary definition' identifies fixed capital with *durable goods* and circulating capital (which is to him a synonym for working capital) with *goods in process*.[17] He then proceeds by noting that this definition leads to two different distinctions depending on whether they are based on the length of the period during which a good will 'retain a particular physical shape' or will 'remain within the precincts of a particular enterprise' (1941, p. 324). Possibly mindful of Smith's confusions in this respect, Hayek seizes the opportunity to emphasize that the second criterion 'is highly important from the point of view of the individual entrepreneur' but becomes irrelevant from the point of view of society as a whole. He also points out that, although this distinction was arrived at by the classics from the point of view of the individual entrepreneur, 'what they really had in mind was a distinction from the point of view of society as a whole' (1941, p. 325).

This conclusion is extraordinary not only in its own right but also in view of Hayek's following remark that it is because this was the classics' true point of view that they (Ricardo) came to consider circulating capital as exclusively made up of wage goods and therefore as coinciding with the wages fund.[18] What must be questioned, however, is the inference that Hayek draws from this conclusion. This inference consists in his belief that the classical distinction, if properly understood, can be reformulated on the basis of his new criterion of 'the remoteness from ultimate consumption of a particular capital good'. Hence his very reformulation of what was called above the 'Ricardo macroeffect':

> The proposition that a conversion of circulating capital into fixed capital will bring about a reduction in the rate of output due to that capital is not strictly correct if we define fixed capital as durable goods and circulating capital as goods in process, but becomes true if we define the two kinds of capital ... according to their final distance from consumption. (1941, p. 428)

But it should be objected that 'if we define the two kinds of capital according to their final distance from consumption' the 'reduction in the rate of output' reduces to a truism while Hayek's criticism of Ricardo's alleged 'confusion between the stock of circulating capital and the flow of income derived from it' appears to be misplaced. For this confusion would really be committed only if Ricardo did, or had to, share Hayek's own distinction. But this is obviously not the case, as Hayek himself implies in his own arguments about the point of view of society as a whole praised above. The fact is that Hayek's distinction is different from Ricardo's (and the classics') on at least two different accounts: first, because Hayek, who starts from a notion of capital as the aggregate of all non-permanent resources, regards circulating and fixed capital as the aggregates of, respectively, the most and the least non-permanent resources (rather than as the aggregates of goods with, respectively, the 'right' and 'wrong' form as indicated above); secondly because, as Hayek himself implies again in Chapter XXIV of *The Pure Theory of Capital*, his new distinction is called for by his new method (which, unlike Ricardo's, belongs to dynamics) and by his new purpose (which, unlike Ricardo's again, is to provide an explanation of industrial fluctuations). Accordingly, Hayek's eventual proposition that the Ricardo macroeffect 'is connected with changes in the time dimension of capital in general (or the substitution of a growth of capital in height for a growth in width) irrespective of whether this is in connection with a relative increase of fixed capital or not' (1941, p. 426), though consistent with his own method and purpose and though partly true (in so far as the macroeffect is related to changes in the time dimension of capital), is either untrue or unfaithful in so far as these changes are viewed as disassociated from a relative increase of fixed capital.

Having examined Hayek's distinctions between circulating and fixed capital and between goods in process and durable goods, we are now in a position to examine his related distinction between the *duration* of the process of production and the *durability* of goods. This will bring us closer to the core of *The Pure Theory of Capital* and to its two rather obscure notions: the 'input function' and the 'output function'.

The analysis of the relationship between duration of process and durability of goods emerges in Hayek's theory, first as a result of Hayek's reaction to the fact that in *Prices and Production* (which is focused on changes in the structure of the economy as a whole) he had contemplated a process of some duration but no durable goods, and second as a consequence of his attempt to elaborate upon the Ackerman–Wicksell treatment (which is focused on the forward-looking decisions of entrepreneurs) of the optimal durability of goods in the context of the continuous input–continuous output framework.

Hayek's analysis starts with the 'ideal' cases of continuous input–point output and point input–continuous output: while the first case represents a joint demand for inputs employed through a period of time and leading to an output all of which matures at the end of the period, the second case represents a durable good produced at a given moment which continuously gives rise to a joint supply of its services over a period of time. The continuous input–continuous output case eventually results from a combination of these two cases and actually reflects the more realistic phenomenon of a durable good (continuous flow of output) resulting from a period of production of particular duration (continuous application of inputs). In this context the role of Hayek's input and output functions is to highlight from the point of view of a planning individual (however blurred this point may be by the mismatch between the titles and contents of Part II and Part III of *The Pure Theory of Capital*) the 'two different ways' in which time may enter the 'period of investment', i.e. 'the interval between the application of a unit of input and the maturing of the quantity of output due to that input' (1941, p. 69).[19] While an input function tells us how much and for how long an input should be invested before a durable good is finished, the output function indicates by how much and for how long a finished durable good should be productive of final services.[20] Hence Hayek's belief that his input and output functions are appropriate tools for dealing with the lengthening of the period of investment either on the side of the input function, or on the side of the output function or on the sides of both. From this arises the possibility, which however is never explicitly discussed in *The Pure Theory of Capital*, of representing the phenomenon of capital deepening by a tilt of the balance between the input function and the output function towards the former so that the 'amount of investment of capital', as distinguished by Jevons (1871, ch. VII) from the 'amount of capital invested', is shown to increase.[21]

We have seen above that Hayek tends to identify a process of capital deepening directly with Ricardo's conversion of circulating into fixed capital, and we have just seen that he is led by his notions of these two kinds of capital to represent (without noticing the difference between Ricardo's and the Ackerman–Wicksell approaches) the latter conversion in the same way as the former process, i.e. with a tilt in the balance between the input function and the output function. When, however, he comes to deal explicitly with the process of capital deepening in Chapter XX, 'The Accumulation of Capital', of *The Pure Theory of Capital* (1941), he does it in the only way in which this process can *not* be identified with the Ricardo macroeffect.

This way is paved by Hayek in the Introductory Chapter. Here the conception that additions to the stock of capital 'always means additions of new items similar to those already in existence' is stigmatized as being responsible for the unfortunate idea that capital may be regarded as 'a simple, physically determined quantity' and that the rate of interest may be consequently explained as 'a simple (decreasing) function of this quantity' (1941, p. 10).

So, when this issue is taken up again in Chapters XX–XXIII with the purpose of discussing the adjustments brought about in a dynamic economy by changes (foreseen and unforeseen) in the data (the first of which is a change in the supply of savings), Hayek starts by stressing that 'on our assumptions, and for the economic system as a whole, the growth of capital can take the form of a growth in "height", or of "deepening", *only*' (p. 270, italics added). The assumption that makes this 'only' necessary is again the full employment assumption.[22]

Now, however undeniable it may be that the increase of capital that takes place under these conditions necessarily gives rise to a process of deepening, it should be noted that this very process has little to do with the Ricardo macroeffect if only because this effect is based on the assumption that total capital (circulating plus fixed) does *not* increase. Indeed, whilst Hayek's discussion of the deepening of capital in *The Pure Theory of Capital* is based on the cross assumptions of constant population *and* increasing capital, Ricardo's discussion of the conversion of circulating into fixed capital in his machinery chapter is based on the cross assumptions of constant population (for, if the latter decreased by as much as circulating capital after the conversion, no 'poverty and distress' would result from the introduction of machinery) *and* constant capital. What the two discussions have in common is the analysis of the immediate impact of a change in the ratio of total capital to population in Hayek, and of circulating to fixed capital for a given total capital and population in Ricardo.

Due to the difference between these authors' assumptions, it is no wonder, therefore, that the immediate impact of the introduction of machinery is viewed as different in the two cases. While in Ricardo this is a fall in gross revenue, in Hayek it is a change in technical coefficients of new machines. Thus Hayek presents himself as a follower of that line of thought which regards Ricardo's famous chapter on machinery as an early study of technological unemployment rather than as an 'excellent illustration' (Schumpeter, 1954, p. 680) of the theory of the wages fund. Following Schumpeter's alternative interpretation, it can conversely be argued first, that the Ricardo macroeffect consists in a destruction of circulating capital (wages fund) with changes in the technical coefficients of new machines being an unnecessary effect; and second, that the Ricardo macroeffect can be viewed (along Austrian lines though not in the light of Hayek's input and output functions) as an increase in the 'amount of investment of capital' with the 'amount of capital invested' remaining constant. This implies *inter alia* that the Ricardo macroeffect is a particular type of deepening; and that, therefore, it is nothing but a particular type of a particular type of lengthening.

Notes

1. A detailed story of this drama has recently been written by McCormick (1992).
2. Kaldor's 'degree of capital intensity' is defined as the ratio between 'initial cost' and 'annual cost' involved in the production of a certain stream of output (see Kaldor, 1939, p. 123; see also 1937). Some limits of this notion will be discussed below. For an early critique in the context of trade cycle theory see Hawtrey (1940).
3. This assumption may also be due to Hayek's desire to elaborate upon the notion of 'working capital' (which had just been utilized by Keynes in his *Treatise on Money*, 1930) with the purpose to derive some contrasting conclusions from this very notion. The dangers implicit in this assumption were eventually noticed by Hayek himself who tried to get rid of it in the article 'On the Relationship between Investment and Output' (1934). But, although the justification for the 1931 working-capital assumption is reformulated in the 1934 article in the weak sense that 'considerations of space made it impossible to show how durable goods could be included in the scheme', the latter article seems to add new intricacies, rather than a clear solution, to the problems posed by *Prices and Production*. It is also interesting to note that the role of Hayek's working capital assumption was overlooked by Kaldor who, indeed, referred to Hayek's example of the islanders who have to abandon the construction of an enormous machine because they run out of food before the machine is ready to produce it (Hayek, 1931, p. 94; Kaldor, 1942, p. 152) as if this example faithfully represented Hayek's 1931 model.
4. It should be noted that the circulating–fixed capital distinction to be discussed below, albeit compatible, does not coincide with Hawtrey's distinction between instrumental and working capital (goods).
5. It is interesting to note that this point was later taken up by Hayek himself in *The Pure Theory of Capital* (1941, p. 60 ff) in a further attempt to defend the principle of roundaboutness from its critics.
6. It should be noted that, given the point of view of the individual firm in terms of which Kaldor's 'degree of capital intensity' is formulated, this concept cannot be considered identical (contrary to Kaldor's suggestions) either with the 'degree of roundaboutness of production' or with 'the proportion of embodied labour to current labour per unit of output' with which it is identified by Kaldor himself. Indeed, these two notions relate to the state of the economy as a *fait accompli* rather than to the process of decision making by individual firms.
7. The 'marginal productivity of capital intensification' is, first, defined by Kaldor as 'the ratio between the increase in profit (per annum) and the increase in the amount invested, when the *scale of planned output* is assumed to be given'; and is, second, contrasted with Keynes's marginal efficiency of capital which Kaldor redefines as 'the ratio between the increase in profits (per annum) and the increase in the amount of capital invested, when the *method of production adopted* is assumed to be given' (1939, p. 131, n. 1, Kaldor's italics). Since, however, Kaldor notes that only the *cost* of labour, and not the *produce* of labour, figures in his definition (1942, p. 159), it should be objected that a better name for his new notion should be 'marginal *efficiency* of capital intensification', and that this notion need *not* correspond to Jevons's 'marginal productivity of waiting' (see Kaldor, 1942, pp. 158–9 and Kaldor, 1939, p. 131, n. 1).
8. It must be noted that this accounts for the 'analytical' rather than for the 'dialectical' origins of Hayek's discussion of the Ricardo effect. The latter origins can be detected in Hayek's introduction to his *Profits, Interest and Investment* and seem to reside in his effort to prove himself however right and (Keynes and) Kaldor however wrong.
9. In view of the obscurities contained in this book, it might be interesting to note with Kaldor (1938) that while its theme is the role of fluctuations of short-term and long-term investment in the causation of the trade cycle, its central thesis is that the variations in the amount of stocks held by 'traders' (entrepreneurs) are responsible for the trade cycle itself.
10. It is interesting to note that the relevance of this distinction is due, in Hawtrey's rather than in Wicksell's view, to the fact that 'the motives by which capital outlay is actuated'

are different for the two forms of investment, and that these forms are differently inter-twined in different phases of the trade cycle (see Hawtrey, 1937, chs III–V).

11. It will here be taken for granted, as Kaldor argued in his second attack on Hayek, that 'the proposition of Ricardo and that attributed to him by Professor Hayek are not the same – the assumptions are different, the mode of operation is different, and the conditions of validity are quite different – so that any criticism made against Professor Hayek's 'Ricardo effect' would not necessarily apply to Ricardo' (1942, p. 154). This thesis was later endorsed by Ferguson (1973) and other authors (albeit not by, for instance, O'Driscoll, 1977, p. 121).

12. It is this proposition that Kaldor (1942) aimed to destroy and Hayek (1969) tried later to strengthen again by putting forward three further 'elucidations' of the Ricardo effect.

13. See Hayek (1942, p. 225).

14. See the appendix to Lecture III of *Prices and Production* (1931, pp. 101–4).

15. This distinction is due to Hicks and Hollander (1977). For its usefulness in the interpreta-tion of Ricardo's machinery chapter and for a detailed discussion of other points raised in this article with regard to this chapter see Meacci (1985).

16. In this sense Hayek's article 'On the Relationship between Investment and Output' (1934) looks like an announcement of *The Pure Theory of Capital* after being, as Hayek himself admitted, a reaction to *Prices and Production* (ibid., p. 209, n. 2). While the reaction consisted in moving to the analysis of 'the two different ways in which time may be a condition to the production of the ultimate services to the consumer' (i.e. to the analysis of the role of 'durable goods' as distinct from 'goods in process') the announcement materialized in an early treatment of the continuous input–continuous output framework coupled with a muddling application (not to be discussed in this paper) of the logic of discounting.

17. It is difficult to see in what sense this was a 'customary' definition in Hayek's, let alone in the classics', times. For instance, while Hawtrey regarded circulating capital as 'the sum of a trader's working capital and his net cash resources' (1937, pp. 87 and 107), Keynes regarded working capital as 'the aggregate of goods in course of production, manufacture, transport and retailing' (such as food and textiles but also houses and railways 'the consumption of which must be spread over a period') (1930, pp. 103–4). Furthermore, it is worth noting that the circulating/fixed capital distinction differs from the working/instrumental capital distinction at least in the sense that the former relates to *capital*, the latter to capital *goods*; and that durability is indeed a characteristic, but not the most distinguishing, feature of fixed capital.

18. This is another instance of Hayek's familiarity with the method of vertical integration as well as an interesting proof that this method was by no means unknown to the classics. The relationship between the category of circulating capital, the wages fund and the point of view of society as a whole is discussed in Meacci (1985; 1989).

19. It is here impossible to dwell on the concept of 'period of investment' (which relates to the logic of individual behaviour) as distinct from the 'period of production'. It is worth distinguishing, however, between the 'period of production', the 'average period of pro-duction', and the 'amount of waiting'. While no use has here been made of the last two concepts (and of the rate of interest which enters their definition), the first one has been utilized here on the assumptions that machinery, as Wicksell (1934, p. 134) pointed out, may be regarded as 'indirectly employed' labour rather than as 'saved-up' labour; and that it is possible to speak, as Böhm-Bawerk himself pointed out (1884–89, Vol. III, pp. 1 ff), of lengthenings or shortenings of the period of production without any need to know its *actual* length.

20. It is interesting to note that what is called in *The Pure Theory of Capital* 'input function' was called by Hayek himself on a previous occasion 'investment function' (1934). This earlier expression seems more appropriate than the new one not only because it highlights better the notion of 'sinking' or 'locking' the inputs (which is the process actually implied by the input function and generally highlighted by the term 'investment'), but also be-cause it would fit what appears to be a better expression (never mentioned by Hayek) for the output function itself, i.e. the 'disinvestment function'.

21. See Hayek (1941, pp. 135–6) who, however, confines the difference between his analysis and that of Jevons to the fact that while Jevons's approach is static, the subject of his own investigation is 'the connection between *changes* in the shape of the input function and *changes* in the shape of the output function' (ibid., p. 140, Hayek's italics).

22. It is interesting to note that this assumption is reintroduced in *The Pure Theory of Capital* with the implicit purpose of discrediting Keynes's recent theories. This purpose is particularly visible in the implications of Hayek's statement that 'the analysis still proceeds in real terms'. These implications seem to be that every accumulation of capital necessarily results in a variation in the methods of production; that Keynes's notion of accumulation refers, on the contrary, to the (rare or outdated) widening type; and that the maximum to be expected from a process of widening is that it might take the form of an expansion of capital-intensive industries at the expense of others without any change in their respective techniques ('thickening' of capital). This purpose was eventually admitted by Hayek himself in a letter dated 1970 where he stated that the evolution of his thought had been affected by the fact that 'for Keynes and the Keynesians all investment was supposed to aim at what we then called 'widening' of capital while the 'deepening' of capital was completely neglected' (see Ferguson, 1973, p. 7, n. 22).

References

Böhm-Bawerk, E. von (1884–89), *Kapital und Kapitalzins*; in G.D. Huncke and H.F. Sennholz (eds) (1959), *Capital and Interest*, North Holland: Libertarian Press, 3 vols.

Caravale, G. (ed.) (1985), *The Legacy of Ricardo*, Oxford: Basil Blackwell.

Ferguson, C.E. (1973), 'The Specialization Gap: Barton, Ricardo, and Hollander', *History of Political Economy*, **5**, 1–13.

Hansen, A.H. and H. Tout (1933), 'Annual Survey of Business Cycle Theory: Investment and Saving in Business Cycle Theory', *Econometrica*, **1**, 119–47.

Hawtrey, R.G. (1937), *Capital and Employment*, London: Longmans.

Hawtrey, R.G. (1940), 'The Trade Cycle and Capital Intensity', *Economica*, **7**, 1–15.

Hayek, F.A. von (1931), *Prices and Production*, London: Routledge and Sons. The 1935 revised edition was used here.

Hayek, F.A. von (1934), 'On the Relationship between Investment and Output', *The Economic Journal*, **44**, 207–31.

Hayek, F.A. von (1939), *Profits, Interest and Investment*, London: Routledge and Sons.

Hayek, F.A. von (1941), *The Pure Theory of Capital*, London: Routledge & Kegan Paul, 1941 and 1950.

Hayek, F.A. von (1942), 'The Ricardo Effect', *Economica*, **9**, 127–52. Reprinted in *Individualism and Economic Order*, Chicago: University of Chicago Press, 1948.

Hayek, F.A. von (1969), 'Three Elucidations of the Ricardo Effect', *Journal of Political Economy*, **77**, 274–85.

Hicks, J. (1967), 'The Hayek Story' in J. Hicks (1967), *Critical Essays in Monetary Theory*, Oxford: Clarendon Press.

Hicks, J. and S. Hollander (1977), ' Mr. Ricardo and the Moderns', *Quarterly Journal of Economics*, **91**, 351–69.

Jevons, S. (1871), *The Theory of Political Economy*, London: Macmillan.

Kaldor, N. (1937), 'The Controversy on the Theory of Capital', *Econometrica*, **5**. Reprinted in *Essays on Value and Distribution*, London: Duckworth, 1960.

Kaldor, N. (1938), 'Hawtrey on Short- and Long-Term Investment', *Economica*, **5**, 461–7. Reprinted in *Essays in Economic Stability and Growth*, London: Duckworth, 1960.

Kaldor, N. (1939), 'Capital Intensity and the Trade Cycle', *Economica*, **6**, 40–66. Reprinted in *Essays in Economic Stability and Growth*, London: Duckworth, 1960.

Kaldor, N. (1942), 'Professor Hayek and the Concertina Effect', *Economica*, **9**, 359–82. Reprinted in *Essays in Economic Stability and Growth*, London: Duckworth, 1960.

Keynes, J.M. (1930), *A Treatise on Money*, London: Macmillan.

McCormick, B.J. (1992), *Hayek and the Keynesian Avalanche*, London: Harvester Wheatsheaf.

Meacci, F. (1985), ' Ricardo's Chapter on Machinery and the Theory of Capital', in G. Caravale (ed.) (1985).

Meacci, F. (1989), 'Different Divisions of Capital in Smith, Ricardo and Marx', *Atlantic Economic Journal*, **17**, 13–21.

Moss, L.S. and K.I. Vaughn (1986), 'Hayek's Ricardo effect: a second look', *History of Political Economy*, **18**, 545–65.

O'Driscoll, G.P. (1977), *Economics as a Coordination Problem*, Kansas City: Sheed Andrews.

Ricardo, D. (1821), *On the Principles of Political Economy and Taxation*, Cambridge: Cambridge University Press, 1951.

Schumpeter, J.A. (1954), *History of Economic Analysis*, New York: Oxford University Press.

Wicksell, K. (1934), *Lectures on Political Economy*, 2 vols, London: Routledge and Kegan Paul.

Zamagni, S. (1984), 'Ricardo and Hayek Effects in a Fixwage Model of Traverse', *Oxford Economic Papers*, **36**, *Supplement*, 135–51.

PART II

SOCIALIST CALCULATION

3 Hayek on information and socialism

Erich W. Streissler*

An innovation?

'One of the more immutable of the immutable economic laws is that every sentence in the *Wealth of Nations* will eventually become a book', wrote Gordon Tullock (1969, p. 287) in the Hayek 'Festschrift'.

In the case of Hayek, one extract from Adam Smith apparently even became the nucleus of a Nobel prize-winning idea. It is this:

> the obvious and simple system of natural liberty establishes itself of its own accord. Every man, as long as he does not violate the laws of justice, is left perfectly free to pursue his own interest his own way, and to bring both his industry and capital into competition with those of any other man, or order of men. The sovereign is completely discharged from a duty, in the attempting to perform which he must always be exposed to innumerable delusions, and *for the proper performance of which no human wisdom or knowledge could ever be sufficient*; the duty of superintending the industry of private people, and of directing it towards the employments most suitable to the interest of the society. (Smith, 1776 [1976, IV, ix, p. 687], italics added)

This extract is not merely incidental to Adam Smith's argument: it is much rather the key, in which he presents his ideal system, 'the obvious and simple system of natural liberty', i.e. the free enterprise system. Immediately afterwards, Smith – in a justly famous passage – presents what he thinks the proper agenda of the state, the 'three duties' of 'the sovereign'. Although it is so widely known and quoted, no one before Friedrich August von Hayek had, however, pondered the true significance of the phrase that 'no human wisdom or knowledge could ever be sufficient' to direct private people 'towards the employments most suitable to the interest of the society'. This passage, by the way, tells us immediately what Hayek understood by socialism. Any 'sovereign', i.e. any administration with coercive powers, which tries to direct 'private people' in their 'employments', practices 'socialism' as he understands it. The motive is of no importance: the public authority attempts to do something 'for which no human ... knowledge could ever be sufficient' and is therefore 'socialist' . To attempt to do so is not only sure proof of utter folly, but also shows arrogant presumption, contempt for other people's abilities by those who perpetrate this rash act, as Adam Smith pointed out in

* This essay was first published in *Wirtschaftspolitische Blätter*, **39** (1992), 258–83.

another memorable extract (following the famous 'invisible hand' passage): 'The statesman, who should attempt to direct private people in what manner they ought to employ their capitals, would not only load himself with a most unnecessary attention, but assume an authority which could safely be trusted, not only to no single person, but to no council or senate whatever, and which would nowhere be so dangerous as in the hands of a man who had folly and presumption enough to fancy himself fit to exercise it.' Before that Smith had remarked that 'every individual, it is evident, in his local situation judges much better than any statesman' (Smith, 1976, IV, ii, 10, p. 456). Here we have Hayek in a nutshell: his strictures on the intellectual haughtiness of the 'constructivist' (see, e.g., Hayek, 1952, 1975); his doubts even of the wisdom of assigning too many economic duties, particularly the rights of economic redistribution, to parliaments (e.g. Hayek 1960); and, finally, his best known notion of 'dispersed knowledge'.

But after all, these ideas were just those of Adam Smith, gleaned from two central passages in one of the best known and most widely read books in the history of social thought! Could one of the greatest and most influential social philosophers of the twentieth century have made his reputation and gained a Nobel prize merely by rehashing Adam Smith? That is the first puzzle in the history of thought we have to turn to.

But there is more to puzzle us. Did not Hayek always stress his indebtedness to Carl Menger, the founder of the Austrian (or Vienna, or Menger) School of Economics (to the extent, of course, that Hayek stressed his intellectual indebtedness to any one at all)? His last book, *The Fatal Conceit – The Errors of Socialism* (1988), in a sense the summary of his life's work, after David Hume, Adam Smith and Sir Karl Popper, and excluding self-quotation, most often quotes Carl Menger, together with the great author on liberalism and scientific method, John Stuart Mill. But is it not Menger who is to be credited with initiating the modern vogue of seeing economics as a science centring around information? Menger, who was very close in his ideas on social institutions and social interaction to Adam Smith?[1] Hayek himself regards Menger as the most important author after Adam Smith in creating an evolutionary concept of society – and the use of information in society, of course, lies at the heart of evolution. He says: 'Another great economist, Carl Menger, a little more than a hundred years after Adam Smith, clearly perceived that "this genetic element is inseparable from the conception of theoretical science"' (Hayek, 1988, p. 146; the quotation is from Menger, 1883). May we not truly say: 'The stress on informational content is one of the respects in which Menger was very modern … Hayek, who in the third generation of Austrians is the economist closest to Menger's thought, has turned his attention since 1945 increasingly towards economic problems of information transmission and information content'? (Streissler, 1972). So we have found in Menger a second famous economist from whom Hayek might have borrowed the ideas on the significance of information in economics and society.

What has all this to do with the debate on socialism? Hayek first applied his ideas on the significance of the use of information in society in 1935 – though they were fully developed only by 1945 – in his attack on the feasibility of socialist planning (Hayek, 1935, 1937, 1940, 1945). And that attack was only part of the so-called Mises–Lange controversy on socialism. Ludwig von Mises (1920) ostensibly had made the same points already more than a dozen years earlier. Mises had conceived the notion that socialism could not work because it lacked the information of market prices. It was not only that 'socialism' – a concept to which Mises gave a new meaning, making it synonymous with every kind of economic planning by the government – that 'socialism' thus defined was not quite efficient; it had by necessity to be totally lacking in any economic efficiency because it lacked the very measuring rod of efficiency, those highly, if not to say solely, informative market prices. But Mises himself had borrowed the core of this idea from Friedrich von Wieser (see Streissler, 1986, pp. 101 ff), the successor to Carl Menger and Menger's pupil in the 'habilitation', himself (together with Mises) the most important teacher of Friedrich August von Hayek. Already in 1884, Wieser had written about the need to economize by correctly computing marginal productivities and assigning correct prices to factor uses: 'Even the government of a social state would have to bow to this necessity' (a few pages previously he had spoken explicitly of 'socialism', Wieser, 1884, pp. 178 and 169).

Smith, Menger, Wieser and Mises – that makes four famous economists altogether from whom Hayek could have taken ideas on information: the notion of the significance of the use of knowledge in society, and in particular of the difficulties which certain types of economic organization or certain types of economic policy may encounter if they disregard the problem of the creation, gathering and transmission of economic information, just seems to have too many fathers to credit Hayek with it. His record may seem to suggest a piece of advice most derogatory to economic science and to its scientists: if a young scholar asks you how he should go about gaining a Nobel prize in economics you might answer: 'Take the well-known idea of four of the best known leaders of the profession; repeat this idea often enough; and you are sure to gain the Nobel prize (as proof of this: just look at Hayek)!' For Hayek did get his Nobel prize in large measure for his ideas about information – and, in extension, about socialism.[2] His own Nobel Memorial Lecture (1974) shows that he thought this his main achievement. And today he is certainly best known for his work in this field.

Before we turn to a closer examination of what was, in fact, Hayek's pathbreaking idea on information, let us very briefly survey the possible objections to the workability of socialism. As far as I can see there are four.

1.   There is the incentive argument. If there is no reward for superior economic performance, if there is no reward for risk taking, if all incomes are equal, if the rule 'to each according to his needs' (and not according to his deserts) more or less prevails, then there is no incentive to produce much or to satisfy other persons' needs.
2.   There is the property rights argument. In the narrower sense this does not argue the incentive effects of private property of the means of production. Rather the property rights argument states that there will not be efficient risk taking, and decision taking in general, if decision taking and responsibility are divorced; and in particular if the areas of responsibility are neither clearly defined nor clearly demarcated from each other.
3.   There is Hayek's information argument. A centralized economic decision-taking agency will just not have the information necessary to guide economic activity correctly. Hayek, the purist, used this argument nearly exclusively.
4.   Even if it had sufficient information, a central agency might not have sufficient coercive power to control the subordinate decision-taking units.

Adam Smith on 'Socialism'

The question whether Smith, Menger, Wieser and Mises fully anticipated Hayek on economic information can best be dealt with by inquiring exactly whether they used the same arguments against 'socialism'. As strict classical liberals (apart, perhaps, from the rather devious Wieser) they would have wanted to do so. Did they then use the same intellectual arguments against it that Hayek did? The answer is a clear 'no' in each case, even in the case of Mises. And this shows that Hayek did, indeed, have much deeper arguments of economic information than his precursors.

We take up Smith and Menger on 'socialism' in this and the following section. After a digression on Roscher's ideas on socialism, we shall turn to the differences between Mises (and Wieser) and Hayek next, then consider Hayek's position in greater detail, and finally turn to an evaluation of the question how significant his ideas were as an explanation of the demise of nearly all the 'really existing' socialist systems from 1989 to 1991 and to methodological conclusions.

From the very beginning Hayek had a highly inclusive definition of socialism. In his inaugural lecture as professor in London, published in 1933, he says:

> I have discussed planning here rather than its older brother socialism, not because I think there is any difference between the two (except for the greater consistency

of the latter), but because most of the planners do not yet realise that they are socialists and that, therefore, what the economist has to say with regard to socialism applies also to them. In this sense, there are, of course, very few people left today who are not socialists. (Hayek, 1933, p. 135)

So all 'interventionist' economic policy – to use Mises's term – is Hayek socialism.

What did Adam Smith have to say against this kind of 'socialism', against interventionism? As I quoted him at the very beginning of this paper, it is 'folly and presumption' even to attempt it, because for its 'performance ... no human wisdom or knowledge could ever be sufficient'! And 'in his local situation ... every individual ... judges much better than any statesman'. But if we look closer, we realize that the arguments of Smith come in a particular context: he denies the possibility of what today we would call an industrial policy, the long-run employment-creating policies of the 'mercantile system', the attempts to stimulate exports by artificial means and all attempts to limit competition (expressly named in the first quotation given) between industries, professions and individuals. To put it in Hayek's terms: he doubts that there is sufficient information for a particular kind of socialism.

Further, if we press Adam Smith and ask him with Hayek where the 'impossible' socialism ends and the 'possible' one begins, whether the same argument about the lack of information does not apply everywhere in the field of interventionism, Smith, the pragmatist, eludes us. With him the lack of information of the 'sovereign' or of the 'statesman' is merely a general presumption, subject to numerous exceptions. How many there are has been impressively demonstrated by Lord Robbins, the liberal British economist who brought Hayek to London and was his closest colleague for many years, and by Jacob Viner, for many years the doyen of classically liberal American economists (see Robbins, 1952; Viner, 1958 and Winch, 1969).

One has to read every word in the quotation from Smith at the beginning of this paper: even competition is limited by 'the laws of justice', which apparently the 'sovereign' can fathom! Among many other exceptions Smith enumerates:

Those exertions of the natural liberty of a few individuals, which might endanger the security of the whole society, are, and ought to be, restrained by the laws of all governments; of the most free, as well as of the most despotical. The obligation of building party walls, in order to prevent the communication of fire, is a violation of natural liberty, exactly of the same kind with the regulations of the banking trade which are here proposed. (Smith, 1976, II, ii, p. 324)

The duty to build fire walls may be a legitimate general rule in the sense of Hayek; but bank regulation certainly is not. Adam Smith, in fact, was all for (limited) government action both in the case of positive and of negative external effects. He would not, for example, have opposed an environmental policy on principle. Hayek, on the other hand, always avoided the issue of 'market failure' due to external effects. Adam Smith would have more or less echoed John Stuart Mill: 'It is hardly possible to find any ground of justification common to ... all (the admitted functions of government), except the comprehensive one of general expediency; nor to limit the interference of government by any universal rule, save the simple and vague one, that it should never be admitted but when the case of expediency is strong' (Mill, 1848 [1976; Book V, ch. 1, para 2, p. 800]). But then the Hayek question is, how do we know what 'general expediency' is? What, in fact, is 'expedient'?

Next, for Adam Smith the point about the insufficiency of 'human wisdom or knowledge' is merely subsidiary. As the second quotation at the beginning of this paper shows, his main argument is that government intervention is in general above all 'a most unnecessary attention' (and to Smith it is justified, as we have seen, where it is necessary). It is unnecessary because what is necessary is already achieved due to the self-interested actions of individuals, as long as they are left free to act. Or as Hayek himself put it in 1933: 'From the time of Hume and Adam Smith, the effect of every attempt to understand economic phenomena ... has been to show that, in large part, the coordination of individual efforts in society is not the product of deliberate planning, but has been brought about, and in many cases could only have been brought about, by means which nobody wanted or understood'. To this Hayek adds, and I think here he already exceeds his 'Adam Smith brief': many social institutions 'could not possibly be the result of deliberate regulation because nobody understood them' (Hayek, 1933, p. 129). We have to be very careful in reading and interpreting Smith. Smith's *Wealth of Nations*, which had become a totally uninteresting book by 1926, at the 150th anniversary of its publication, and of which Schumpeter (1954, p. 185) could still say that it 'contained no really novel ideas', was so powerfully revitalized exactly by Hayek that, when we read it today, we have to ask ourselves just where Smith ends and where Hayek begins.

It follows that in judging the 'really existing' socialist systems Smith would much rather have used the (lack of) incentive argument than the (lack of) information argument. At least in the case of the large corporation, which – according to the socialist and Austromarxist Hilferding – is, together with the institutions of financial markets, already 'fraudulent, capitalistically adapted socialism' (Hilferding, 1910), Smith argued in incentive terms:

> The directors of such companies ... being the managers rather of other people's money than of their own, it cannot well be expected, that they should watch over it with the same anxious vigilance with which the partners in a private copartnery

frequently watch over their own ... Negligence and profusion, therefore, must always prevail, more or less, in the management of the affairs of such a company. (Smith, 1976, p. 741)

How much more he would have said that of state owned enterprises!

I conclude: Smith's statement that 'for the proper performance' of interventionist economic policy 'no human wisdom or knowledge could ever be sufficient' is not to be taken literally. He expounded only a subsidiary argument, a partial argument, and one liable to numerous exceptions. With Hayek the argument became central, was generalized, and held without exceptions. In the terminology of Spengler (1968) the shell and the core of the argument changed place, and that is the hallmark of many great scientific innovations. It is surprising how little Hayek used the ancient (lack of) incentive argument in his strictures on socialism. He nearly exclusively used only his own information argument.

Menger on socialism: the Rudolf Lectures
And what about Carl Menger, another central author with a 'stress on informational content' as his key to economic understanding? This interpretation of Menger is my own (Streissler, 1972), and not even that of Hayek. In the introduction to his edition of Menger's works Hayek (1934) merely said, certainly correctly: 'To [Menger] economic activity is essentially planning for the future' (p. 400). But rational planning as such does not imply that some individual or institution or the government are devoid of information others have. Hayek always stressed the subjectivist content in Menger's thinking. Now if the individual alone knows about his subjective evaluations of goods, this might imply that government can never plan for individual wants, because it cannot know them. Actually, as we shall see, Menger did make this point, but not, as far as I can see, in his published works. Once more, however, this is a point subtly different from that made by Hayek: with Hayek it is a lack of information of the central agency about what the individual knows concerning other agents, their actions, concerning circumstances and conditions around him etc., but not a lack of information about individual evaluations. It may be that to Menger his subjectivist position was so important because it did argue against 'socialism'; but this point is not the main point in Hayek.

There are, indeed, many information arguments in Menger's *Principles*. On the very first pages we are told that one of the four 'prerequisites' for 'a thing to become a good', is 'human knowledge of (the) causal connection (between) satisfaction (and) need' (Menger, 1871 [1950; p. 523]). 'Entrepreneurial activity includes: (a) obtaining information about the economic situation; (b) economic calculation – all the various computations that must be made if a production process is to be efficient' (p. 160), a remark which seems to point immediately towards the calculation debate under socialism. And economic progress, too, is defined by Menger in cognitive terms. It is the 'increasing understanding of the causal connections between things and human welfare' (p. 74).

Yet these informational arguments are still unconnected with each other and appear to be important, but not absolutely vital to the general theme developed by Menger. Furthermore, the information concerned seems to be of a rather technical nature in each case. And above all, with Menger we certainly have a diversity of subjective wants, but never explicitly a diversity of information. Both Menger and Hayek criticize Adam Smith for his too exclusive emphasis on such a technical phenomenon as the division of labour. But while Menger merely says 'economic progress' should also be seen as an increase in our understanding (pp. 72 and 74), Hayek had by 1937 come round to confront the division of labour with a 'division of knowledge'. To Hayek, from then on, this was the 'really central problem of economics as a social science' (Hayek, 1937, p. 49).

Thus there is a decided family likeness between the informational arguments of Menger and Hayek. And how could it be otherwise, with Hayek always stressing his allegiance to the Austrian – or, as he often said, the Menger – school? Hayek, of course, was also the rediscoverer of the half-forgotten Carl Menger. And once more we have to ask ourselves whether nowadays all of us do not read Menger mostly with Hayek's eyes . Thus, once more, an argument in Menger's scientific 'shell' or, at best, a semi-core argument of Menger's became a core argument with Hayek.

The proof is again in Menger's arguments on socialism. These are not to be found in Menger's published work. But ample evidence of his position can be gleaned from the lecture notes of Crown Prince Rudolf of Austria, unearthed by Brigitte Hamann.[3] Menger lectured Rudolf in 1876, when the Crown Prince was just turning eighteen, mainly on questions of economic policy. The Crown Prince had to write down what Menger taught him from memory after the end of each lecture. Rudolf echoes Menger after a brief discussion of 'the Communists' views' as follows:

> The so-called Socialists do not go as far as the Communists. They demand neither the complete abolition of private property nor that of the inheritance laws, but rather a limitation of the institutions named above, in particular of landed property.
>
> The proposals listed may not be realizable at all, but they are definitely not to be realized under present conditions. They presuppose a well developed community spirit, a high level of education, less egoism among subjects and great moderation, wisdom and unselfishness among rulers.

Even if these qualities were present, there would still be considerable draw-backs to be dealt with:

1)   Individual responsibility for one's personal welfare, responsibility for the fate of one's children and with it the large supply of individual energy that we find at present, would seriously diminish as they would lack all personal (individual) motivation.

2)   Under Communism and even under Socialism a despotic system would develop which would suppress any kind of self-determination. Nobody could choose his vocation or profession for himself, but would in all matters whatsoever have to comply with government regulations. (Rudolf, 1876, Notebook II)

Three points are noticeable in this passage. First, Rudolf, i.e. Menger, who speaks through him, does not use any informational argument whatsoever. Of course, he still uses the pre-Mises concept of socialism, viz. socialization of the means of production, in other words a change in property relations, and not centralized economic planning as his criterion of socialism. After Hayek, how-ever, even private property of the means of production could be seen mainly in informational terms,[4] e.g. as a means of risk assignment and therefore of error minimization, as I myself – with the express approval of Hayek – have shown (Streissler 1970). Still, Menger evidently thinks that under socialism the agenda of the state increases; and he sees problems here. Much rather than informa-tional arguments Menger uses motivational and moral arguments against so-cialism, arguments which form part of the (lack of) control reasoning against the feasibility of socialism. In the main, his ideas run along the traditional (lack of) incentive thrust against socialism.

Second, Menger actually was just reading – evidently verbatim and with few additions – the standard German economics textbook of his day to the Crown Prince, viz. Wilhelm Roscher (1854), *Grundlagen der Nationalökonomie* with its lengthy discussion of 'communism and socialism'. If we place the texts side by side we are struck by the extent to which the text of the Crown Prince is just an extremely faithful, but abbreviated student version of Roscher's: the Crown Prince follows Roscher in one idea after the other and uses many of his characteristic words, up to the tell-tale word 'despotic'.

Third, while there is no trace of Hayek's argument that socialism will fail because it cannot utilize all the dispersed information, Hayek's analysis of the consequences of socialism and some of the necessary preconditions for its success is all there. In *The Fatal Conceit* Hayek states: 'Cooperation, like solidarity, presupposes a large measure of agreement on ends as well as on methods employed in their pursuit.' He immediately adds: 'It makes sense in a small group whose members share particular habits, knowledge and beliefs about possibilities' (Hayek, 1988, p. 19). Evidently, the Crown Prince had clairvoyantly anticipated these arguments on moral prerequisites. In *The Road to Serfdom* (1944) Hayek says:

> If (planners) want to plan they must control the entry into the different trades and occupations ... If such control were universally practiced and exercised by a single planning authority, one needs little imagination to see what would become of the "free choice of occupation" promised ... Conditions will be without exception what in some measure they inevitably are in a large organization – or rather worse, because there will be no possibility of escape. (Hayek, 1944, pp. 71–2)

Again, the Crown Prince, had he lived to his father's ripe old age, would not have been surprised to read this in 1944; it was only what he had written in his youth. But this was due neither to his brilliance nor that of his teacher Menger: it was simply all there in Roscher, to whose arguments we shall therefore turn in the next section. They are typical of mid-nineteenth century thoughts on socialism, from which Hayek could profit and which he merely had to revive.

In another place of the lectures to the Crown Prince, in the discussion of the functions of government, i.e. in touching upon what Hayek understood by 'socialism' Menger does, in fact, use the information argument. Here he is evidently summarizing Adam Smith, which shows that in the Austrian school Smith had long been understood in the way Hayek later understood him. The Crown Prince writes:

> Innumerable influences, different for everyone, dominate man's activities; only the individual knows the means for gaining his ends; from unhampered individual development there results a wide range of activities which, in their turn, permit an advanced stage of civilization to be reached. The individual citizen knows best what is of use to him, and he will be most industrious when working for his own personal ends. (Rudolf, 1876, Notebook VI)

This latter half-sentence, which cannot be found in Smith in this context, shows that Menger always tended to stress incentives; and in this respect he presented a novel idea of great importance which, as far as I can see, was not taken up by Hayek. The Crown Prince writes:

> If, however, government were to take the erroneous course of paternalism and of controlling the citizen's most private affairs with the intent of helping, though actually harming, him, then the bureaucracy as the agent of government would have to take charge of economic endeavours and interfere with individual activities ... Freedom and self-reliance in the economic efforts of citizens are the foundation of the overall development of a state; therefore the state has to realize and defend these fundamental principles. By its opposite, by paternalism, it spoils and hinders its own progress and infringes upon the natural rights of its citizens. (Rudolf, 1876, Notebook VI)

This is a highly interesting and important notion: on the cost side of all government activity, even if as such beneficial, we have to add its disincentive effects: citizens unlearn private initiative.

Menger has a further original idea, this time on information, but quite different from Hayek. The Crown Prince writes:

> The variety of work performed follows from the variety of individuals and by its very manifoldness promotes progress in every way; it would be altogether lost with comprehensive bureaucratic controls. Even the most devoted civil servant ... (cannot) cope ... with the diversity of practical life. And therefore one may consider it impossible that all economic activities be treated in a stereotyped (!) way, following one and the same rule. (Rudolf, 1876, Notebook VI)

In other words: government can at best provide a standardized product, e.g. in the social security system. But when, with increasing wealth, demand turns increasingly to more varied and higher qualities of commodities, 'socialism' becomes more and more inept.[5]

Roscher on socialism

Roscher's *Grundlagen der Nationalökonomie* treats the problem of socialism very extensively. In a dense text of altogether close to 600 pages some 25 pages, i.e. Chapter 5 of the first book, deal with 'Community property and private property' of which about a dozen pages pertain particularly to socialism (Roscher, 1854, pp. 139–63). For Roscher (1817–94), professor in Leipzig, wanted to educate German youth not only intellectually, but also morally. Roscher's *Grundlagen* was not merely just another text; it was, so to speak, the 'Samuelson' of German language economics in the third quarter of the nineteenth century and beyond, only more so. It boasted 26 editions from 1854 to 1926. It had noticeable links with the Austrian School of Economics: Menger had dedicated his *Principles* to Roscher and was extremely proud that he (and not e.g. Gustav von Schmoller in Berlin) had succeeded Roscher in the Académie des sciences morales et politiques (Institut de France) in Paris, and both Böhm-Bawerk and Wieser had studied with Roscher. So, Hayek must have learned of the basic ideas of Roscher from his own teachers.

Roscher opens his treatment of socialism with an invocation of the property rights argument: 'As human labour can achieve its fullest economic significance only under the condition of personal freedom, so capital with its productive powers only under conditions of free private property. Who would want to save, i.e. forego present satisfaction, if he were not sure of future satisfaction?' (Roscher, 1854, p. 139, my translation). The last clause, somewhat difficult to translate, runs in German: 'wenn er des zukünftigen Genusses nicht sicher wäre'. Roscher then turns to the causes of a movement towards socialism and, as a historicist, shows that they are recurrent in history. It is 'a malady, which recurs nearly regularly among highly civilized peoples at certain periods of their existence' (Roscher, 1854, p. 147, my translation).

Communists are careless of the form of governments as long as they serve their economic ends, but usually prefer 'despotism'.

Roscher then turns to the problems of the community of property. This could succeed among 'animals and angels' (for which Plato is adduced as crown witness); among human beings it could succeed because of 'true love', within an 'ideal family'. 'Within larger societies this kind of love, however, is to be found only in the highest state of religious enthusiasm, which seldom lasts long' – the Acts of the Apostles being quoted in corroboration (Roscher, 1854, p. 148, my translation). In other words, Roscher foreshadows Hayek's (1988) argument on the extended order! 'Otherwise, as a rule, every participant in the community of property would want to work as little as possible and enjoy as much as possible' (Roscher, 1854, p. 148, my translation), the now so fashionable 'tragedy of the commons' argument. Roscher proceeds to state the free-rider argument explicitly and to quantify it in an example. If all the duties and enjoyments were to be made equal in society, the advantages of the division of labour would be lost, the number of consumers would increase (no restraint on procreation!), all the 'higher goods of life' would disappear and the same basic education for all would mean that nobody would attain 'higher scientific education' (a terrible thought for Roscher, the very highly remunerated professor at an élite institution of learning – see Roscher, 1854, pp. 148–9). Thus Roscher refers to the incentive argument, exclusively and in many variations, in order to show the economic disadvantages of the socialization of the means of production.

From these passages very close to Hayek's *Fatal Conceit*, Roscher next turns to 'the idea of an organization of work..., i.e. a central direction of all consumption and production either through the existing, or a newly constituted coercive government' (Roscher, 1854, para. 82, p. 151, my translation. Roscher uses the German 'Staatsgewalt'). Roscher points out that such a coercive power in the field of economics is deemed necessary for counteracting the disincentive effects. The ground for the transposition by Mises and Hayek of the term 'socialism' from the socialization of the means of production to central planning is thus fully prepared by Roscher. And with this he now turns to give a preview of Hayek's *The Road to Serfdom*. Such a central direction would be 'such despotism as the world had hardly ever known before: a Caesaropapism [note the religious connotation] which would at the same time usurp the power of the housefather' (Roscher, 1854, p. 151, my translation). But the disincentive effects would not be eradicated: 'Even tutelage would be lax because it would not arise out of any personal interest (which would still be the best possible outcome). It is well-known and easily explainable that in the long run state enterprises can never be managed with the same zeal and success as private enterprises' (Roscher, 1854, p. 151 ff, my translation). Roscher thus invokes the lack of control argument against socialism.

And what would one have gained? Many people would regard the distribution of goods as unjust, as the lazy and inept would now get the same as the diligent and efficient. On the other hand, because of the diversity of human talents, the distribution of assets undoubtedly would soon become unequal again. Thus, a once-and-for-all-redistribution is not enough. One has to repeat it again and again (Roscher, 1854, p. 152).

To these discussions, Roscher adds two very interesting new ideas in the following paragraphs. On the one hand, historical investigation shows that community of property is everywhere typical of underdeveloped societies and is discarded in the course of development. On the other hand, there is a countervailing effect: 'Everywhere with the rise in civilization the agenda of government increases' (Roscher, 1854, p. 155, my translation. The German reads 'Überall erweitert sich beim Fortschreiten der Kultur das Gebiet der Staatszwecke'). 'Where is the point at which growing communization ceases to be a gain? This is as easy to determine in general terms as it is difficult in a particular case ... The progress in communal property is welfare-increasing as long as it corresponds to a progress in solidarity' (Roscher, 1854, p. 156, my translation). It would be good if all of us were to become true Christians!

It is astonishing and highly prescient that all this was originally written in 1854! I have thus shown that Roscher uses the incentive argument against socialism copiously and also employs the property rights and the (lack of) control arguments. But against this very background, Hayek's innovation becomes apparent: Roscher never uses the information argument which Menger, closer to Adam Smith, took from the latter. Roscher comes closest to Hayek when he argues not from the point of a difference in knowledge but a difference in morals. On the other hand, many of the main arguments of both *The Road to Serfdom* and *The Fatal Conceit* are seen to be mere nineteenth-century text book stuff. Hayek revived these arguments, elaborated them and garnished them with new supportive examples in contrast to those which Roscher had taken largely from classical and biblical antiquity. But in this case he did no more.

Mises and the beginning of the calculation debate

We have thus seen that as far as the German language literature on socialism is concerned, Karen Vaughn (1980, in an otherwise excellent and highly recommendable article on the so-called 'calculation debate') is wrong in stating 'The literature on the economics of socialism before 1920 is sparse' (p. 538). Rather, before 1920 it had been restricted to questions of the incentive compatibility of socialism. Incentives, however, were closely linked to the values men would want to pursue and, in fact, with their morality. But it was a central tenet of socialist thought that man was only warped in his moral nature by the evil influences of capitalism, and that, freed from the shackles of his serfdom, he would cease to be an egoist and become brim-full of solidarity. The (lack of) incentive arguments were therefore laughed off, if not denigrated as mere signs of the moral depravity of their authors. Marx himself had honoured Roscher with the epithet: a 'puny German plagiarist' (it sounds much harsher and snappier in German: 'ein schmaler deutscher Nachkläffer') and had chided him with 'childish notions' (Marx, 1867 [1967], pp. 157, 251). It was difficult to persist in the incentive argument before any 'really existing' socialist system had provided sufficient experience of how social systems based on socialism actually worked. And even after 1917 it was difficult because of the evident fervour of many socialists (a 'fervour' enhanced by the ability of the system to eliminate forcefully those lacking in fervour!). Had men become 'angels' in the sense of Roscher under socialism? But the sceptical liberal at least knows with Bagehot (1867, p. 86) that 'the human heart is strong and the human reason weak' (he would add, the human heart is strong particularly in hankering after the unattainable). The argument was therefore bound to shift to the 'human reason' side of socialism, to the information problem. Did not socialist authors assume that under socialism men would not only be angels but also omniscient? This shift was achieved by Ludwig von Mises in 1920, reiterated in book form in 1922, defended in 1924 and in 1928 and perfected in the second edition of his book *Die Gemeinwirtschaft* in 1932. In his argument Mises built, as I have already pointed out, on the notion of Friedrich von Wieser that even a socialist community would have to calculate in economic terms if it wanted to be efficient.

The debate is best summarized by quoting Vaughn:

> Mises wrote an article claiming that rational economic calculation was impossible under socialism. This prompted those who favoured socialism to try to refute him and thus forced them to construct a model of [a] rationally administered centrally directed economy. Meanwhile, Hayek wrote two sophisticated and penetrating critiques of the socialist schemes which were in the main ignored. Mises seemed easy to refute, and so, for twenty years, socialists continued to refute the same arguments, thereby avoiding consideration of the more difficult issues raised by Hayek. (1980, p. 537)

Mises had found an important problem and the line of solution, but, as so often with him, could not prove his solution. In fact, with the later Austrians' contempt for general equilibrium analysis, he did not understand this important tool of thought and committed a serious error, if not several such, which marred his argument. At the same time the above quotation from one of the neo-Austrians in the USA shows clearly that the arguments of Mises and Hayek in the calculation debate were quite different.

Mises gave five arguments against the economic workability of socialism. The first was the most apodictic one, the one which simply showed a lack of understanding of economic theory and thus was so easy to refute. Hayek recognized that and therefore did not use this argument. Mises's first argument ran: the theory of economic calculation shows that no economic calculation is possible under socialism. For without prices there is no economic calculation. Prices are only formed in markets, which a socialist society (in the sense of a centrally planned economic system) does not have. Thus socialism is completely impracticable: it lacks the very measuring rod of efficiency, viz. prices, and is therefore completely devoid of any efficiency whatsoever (Mises, 1981. The text reads: 'Die Theorie der Wirtschaftsrechnung zeigt, dass im sozialistischen Gemeinwesen Wirtschaftsrechnung nicht möglich ist ... Wo der Marktverkehr fehlt, gibt es keine Preisbildung; ohne Preisbildung gibt es keine Wirtschaftsrechnung ... Das Problem der Wirtschaftsrechnung ist ... Beweis dafür, dass der Sozialismus undurchführbar ist'). It is irrational, completely unscientific – a charge which infuriated socialists to the utmost.

Now every modern student of economics knows that in a static framework and as a proposition of theoretical impossibility this argument is nonsense. From input–output analysis, or its generalization, activity analysis, and from the theory of duality we know that efficient production can be achieved by planning in quantity terms alone; that, in fact, under the condition of constant returns to scale (which would also be necessary for a competitive market solution) the price solution to the efficiency problem is merely the dual to the quantity solution; that the two solutions thus yield identical results; that production maximization, given factor quantities, yields the same solution as cost minimization given factor prices, which latter case is the Mises framework of thought. Of course, for the quantity solution we have to know all preferences, all production technologies and all initial endowments. It is, apparently, much easier to find out about these data via the competitive market process, than, e.g., via the statistical apparatus of a centrally planned socialist system; but that is the problem of the viability of socialism, not its theoretical possibility: it is cheaper to find out the relevant facts via markets. (In fact, if we add the incentive aspects, it is to all intents and purposes 'impossible' to find out the data through statistical offices, necessarily limited in time and personnel, because the local people, who have to report the data, will have a strong incentive to lie.) Hayek rightly turned attention to this aspect of practicality. Mises, on the other hand, who had hoisted his flag to theoretical impossibility (in the sense of impossibility in terms of models in pure logic), was rightly crucified by the socialist critics.

Efficient 'socialist' systems do exist, and do abound. Every large, integrated enterprise has to calculate internal prices from quantitative data for purposes of internal efficiency. And Walter Eucken (1940), certainly a fervent defender of the free enterprise system, chose the medieval monastery of Bobbio as the very epitome of a centrally administered (i.e. 'socialist' in

Mises's sense) economy. Mises (1932, p. 116) replied that large enterprises could only calculate efficiently because they were working in a still larger framework of market prices; and that the same was true of the Soviet Union. But that is beside the point. The problem of calculation thereby becomes smaller in terms of the equations to be solved (or of its cost), but that cannot change the nature of the possibility or impossibility. The theoretical possibility of efficient economic calculation under socialism had already been shown by Pareto (1897) and, in particular, by Barone (1908). Mises (1932) argued that these authors 'had not penetrated to the core of the problem' ('Pareto ... und Barone... sind nicht bis zum Kern des Problems gelangt'), a remark which shows that he had not understood it.

Mises's second proposition is that, in particular, socialist economies are unable to compute appropriate terms of exchange for material factors of production because these must not be privately owned and therefore cannot be privately exchanged (Mises, 1932, pp. 112–14). In one sense this argument is no better than the first; for a quantity optimizing system would optimize the use of factors of production just the same as that of commodities for final consumption; or, in other words, would compute competitive shadow factor prices for factors as well. In another sense, however, the argument is better: a socialist government could lease its material factors of production at competitive auction prices, as is done, e.g., in free enterprise economies by governments with mining or exploitation rights and as was done in effect by the English great landed estates to their tenant farmers. As sole owner – though not at all sole user – of these material factors of production the government would still remain socialist in the old sense, but not in Mises's new sense, which includes centralized government planning added to that of social ownership of the factors of production (the old definition of socialism). But exactly because 'really existing' socialist systems did have a desire to do at least some central planning (as, among non-socialist authors, Mises was the first to realize), this option of competitive leasing was never taken. Some later socialist systems did make attempts to price consumer goods competitively, but never producer goods. Mises's second argument is thus logically no better than his first. But he had hit upon an aspect of the value system of all socialist systems which precludes them from seeking economic efficiency in the field of factor pricing, be it capital pricing or labour pricing. And the reason was that all 'really existing' socialist systems actually were feudal systems, run in the interest of the central bureaucracy, in the interest of the 'new class' as Milovan Djilas (1957) said; and bureaucracy has no power left if it auctions it off. Had Mises said that a feudal system that does not care about factor use efficiency has to fail, he would have made an extraordinarily prescient forecast. But he merely said that a system with no private property of factors of production can never be efficient, which is wrong in the static case.

In the static case! Efficiency could also be achieved for known once-and-for-all changes in techniques and preferences, i.e. in a comparative statics framework (though Mises once more denied this). But now Mises came round to his third, basically correct, and also very deep argument. Unfortunately this tell-tale final information argument of his against socialism was separated from the first two, which were basically right in thrust but wrong in reasoning, by many pages, in the case of the second edition of *Die Gemeinwirtschaft* (1932) by about 65 pages; and by that time he had already lost his infuriated socialist readers so that none of them realized that he made this point at all: his third argument was that the economy is in constant flux and the economic data necessary for efficient planning are not available (1932, pp. 182–4).

Mises argues that every real economy is in constant motion. Therefore every economic decision has to be geared towards uncertain future events. One does not know what the future will bring forth. All economic action is risk taking, is speculation. To this Mises adds an incentive argument: only in a free enterprise system will the speculator be concerned with the accuracy of his speculative forecast, because only in such a system will a successful speculation be mainly to his own advantage.

Mises's perceptive remarks on this third point are very brief and sketchy, just a few sentences; and it is this point, above all, which was taken up by Hayek and elaborated into a real theory. With this argument Mises leaves the by now well-trodden path of the establishment of general competitive equilibria. There is only one catch: so far no economist has been able to show how a free enterprise system solves this problem of decision taking under uncertainty about the future. What Mises postulates is a case of incomplete futures markets, as we would say today. Here we can prove 'market failure' for a competitive economic system. What Mises says is that in the face of an uncertain future a socialist system will fail much worse than markets would fail. This is a sociological argument or a historical argument, but not one of economic theory. Today, most economists would agree with him, exactly because of our recent historical experience. But they would think themselves on treacherous ground: how does one compare two inefficient systems? One cannot 'prove' Mises's point logically. Nearly all economists would, however, agree that without private rewards there will be little risk taking.

To these three information arguments Mises added two further points, rather as asides. Argument four runs that there will be no economic improvement and no reforms if all enterprises are socialized. This is a pure incentive argument, and stated as such by Mises. Obviously, at least to us today, this point is quite valid. Finally, as point five, Mises remarks that it is impossible to demarcate the spheres of economic influence and decision taking of one individual from that of others in a socialist system. Mises gives no reason why, though we know from historical experience that the point is again a good one: responsibilities get hopelessly tangled and obscured in 'really existing' socialist systems, and, in fact, in all cases of state action. This final argument is a property-rights argument (Mises, 1932, p. 186). Arguments four and five, however, did not become basic for Hayek. I conclude: Mises did introduce the information argument against socialism prior to Hayek; but he got much of it wrong.

Before we leave Mises and finally turn to Hayek, a brief sketch is needed of how the argument of his socialist critics ran. As Karen Vaughn (1980) rightly points out, the main rebuttal of Mises was a debate among English language economists, mainly debating among themselves, in the 1930s, i.e. after Mises had ceased publishing on this point (pp. 535, 537). In contrast to his continental sparring partners, who hardly knew any economics, were completely blinded by Marxism, and had the naivest ideas, his English critics were mainly fully trained academic economists who could spot his errors. The socialist 'solution' to points one and two of Mises was given by the eminent economist Oskar Lange (1936, 1937), improving on ideas voiced by Dickinson (1933) and himself elaborated upon by Abba Lerner (1937, 1977). Both Lange and Lerner were immediate colleagues of Hayek at the London School of Economics. The Lange–Lerner argument runs as follows.

In order to achieve economic efficiency the socialist central authority just has to give each manager of a socialist enterprise two directives. Directive one is to minimize costs in your plant in the production of the commodities you produce. Directive two is to price your commodities at marginal cost and produce and sell as much as is demanded. If all managers were to follow this rule, the competitive market mechanism would be mimicked and efficiency would be achieved. The central office would merely have to see to it that its commands are obeyed. It becomes a board of control.

Note three things in this solution. First, on theoretical grounds, the Lange–Lerner solution is wrong from the point of view of our present knowledge of general equilibrium analysis. Even granting all the necessary assumptions as to demand and cost functions, the Lange–Lerner procedure is still a so-called 'tâtonnement' process, or in everyday words one of trial and error. While the hypothetical supercomputer of the socialist central office, knowing all the data, would have immediately calculated the equilibrium allocations, Lange tries to approach this equilibrium step by step through the decisions of the managers. No proof exists that this procedure is likely to converge to economic equilibrium in general. In fact, Lange had confused (in technical terms) the existence of an equilibrium, which is relatively easy to prove, with its stability, as a student of mine has pointed out in his thesis (Hutschenreiter, 1984). Existence of equilibrium implies that if you have got there, you stay there; while stability implies the much trickier problem whether, if you are not in equilibrium initially, you will ever reach it. In this confusion he is, of course, in good company, including, as is well known, the Nobel Laureate Milton Friedman (1968) who wrote about the 'natural rate of unemployment ... that would be ground out by the Walrasian system of general equilibrium equations'. Second, it is immediately obvious that Mises's third problem cannot be 'solved' by the Lange procedure: how does one design new plants or find new commodities? The procedure of Lange and Lerner is most evidently static. And third, on incentive grounds the argument is naive in the extreme. Why should any manager ever obey the 'two commands' of the central office? If he does not drive his workers hard and if he fires nobody, i.e. if he does not minimize costs, he will be on much better terms with his workers. Furthermore, he can take it easy himself. And if he prices above marginal cost, he will have a surplus, to be used as he likes. A 'central office' simply cannot exercise genuine control.

Hayek's specific contribution

Friedrich August von Hayek developed his ideas on information in the course of the debate on the feasibility of socialism, mainly during the period 1935 to 1945 (see Hayek, 1935, 1937, 1940, 1945), but with important additions up to his last book, published in 1988, which once more dealt explicitly with the problems of socialism. As Hayek's contributions on these topics are so numerous, comprising literally thousands of pages, and were in flux over a considerable period, no attempt will be made to quote him verbatim, with a very few exceptions; and no attempt will be made to trace the development of his ideas historically. This was only necessary for the authors preceding him, in order to gauge his own contribution correctly.

First, Hayek presented his own ideas on the theoretical impossibility of efficient economic calculation under socialism. He made it quite clear that 'impossibility' is not meant to imply that in the static framework of general equilibrium analysis one could not find the efficient solution without using prices, adding that Mises had never meant to imply that. As to the latter point – which has frequently been reiterated by neo-Austrians – I take the opposite line: Mises did, indeed, show no appreciation whatsoever of the general equilibrium argument and thus lent himself to misconstruction. But this can certainly not be said of Hayek. He presented three arguments of his own on 'impossibility'.

The first runs that in the real world goods are not easily specified. This is the quality problem of heterogenous commodities, which has plagued economists now for more than half a century and defies easy solution. If we cannot specify commodities fully, we can, of course, not even write down their supply equations, much less solve the demand and supply equation system even in theory. Furthermore, the central planning office cannot control the managers fully, because, as it cannot fully specify the commodities, it cannot check whether its commands have been obeyed. The point was a very 'modern' one in 1935, when Hayek made it. Nineteenth-century economists had always thought in terms of homogenous, i.e. fully standardized commodities, because their basic market framework was the mechanism of the commodity exchanges. But standardized commodities auctioned on exchanges are only a very small fraction of all commodities. Hayek may have realized this in the course of the imperfect competition revolution (see Sraffa, 1930; Chamberlin, 1933; Robinson, 1933) of price theory, which had just then started. Furthermore the point was of great relevance for really existing socialist systems. We now know that the quality of the commodities constantly declined over time, at least relative to the free enterprise economies, exactly because the planning authorities could not fully control quality. Hayek was extremely prescient in starting to realize that, even if only vaguely, as early as 1935.

Second, Hayek argued that costs were not objectively given, but were mere subjective estimates (Hayek, 1935, 1940). They implied judgements about future values. Theoretically this would mean that even for the determination of present costs we would have to have many futures markets, which do not exist. So we have to make subjective guesses about what future prices would be like. Objectively costs are determinable only *ex-post*, not *ex-ante*. We can use them in order to show to what degree economic agents have made mistakes in the past, but not in order to guide their future actions. Vaughn (1980, p. 550) thinks that Hayek should have made more of this thoroughly neo-Austrian point, a point always latent in the Austrian school with its stress on subjective values; still, Hayek did at least make it. He might also have argued (but did not) that the value of factors is agent specific: one entrepreneur knows better than others how to use factors economically, which plays havoc with aggregate capital valuation (Gorman, 1968). A socialist economy could have found out agent-specific production information only by auctioning off its material factors to managers; but even under this institutional arrangement it could have found out only if managers actually were aware of their superior factor use knowledge in advance of actual use.

Hayek's third 'impossibility' theorem is the deepest and the most fundamental of all and was only made by him in 1945 in his famous article 'The Use of Knowledge in Society': knowledge is uncentralizable (see also Hayek, 1940, p. 144, 1945, p. 524) because we do not even know what knowledge we use (1945, p. 527 ff) and therefore cannot communicate it fully to others. Knowledge is thus non-collectible by statistical means (p. 524). It is also contradictory. Only the price mechanism can collect and aggregate such knowledge. The economy consists of 'dispersed bits of incomplete and frequently contradictory knowledge which all the separate individuals possess ... knowledge of people, of local conditions, of special circumstances' (pp. 519, 522) which latter knowledge is much more important than purely technical knowledge. Hayek was the first to spot a deficiency which became of eminent practical relevance: socialist systems were constantly overstressing the economic importance of technical production proficiency and efficiency and constantly underestimating, even dismissing, design, commerce and marketing (1945, p. 521 ff; 1988, p. 89 ff), which in a fully developed market economy actually contribute much more to 'surplus value' than mere production.

As Vaughn summarizes it, Hayek argued that the price system in markets is a 'highly successful means of encouraging the production, transmission and use of information because it takes advantages of decentralization of knowledge and of decision making' (Vaughn, 1980, p. 545). It encourages the production of information because in a free enterprise system agents profit from it. At this point Hayek mixes an incentive argument into his information line of thought. Furthermore, if knowledge is not produced, a central planning authority obviously cannot use it. As we would say today, prices are signals, they are informative in a novel way. Hayek was the first to argue, and to argue at length as early as 1945, that prices economize on the necessary information (1945, p. 525). We do not have to know about the myriad relevant changes the world over; it is enough to look at the highly condensed and one-dimensional information provided by prices. It is because of this very basic argument that 'The Use of Knowledge in Society' has been so much quoted, particularly in the last two decades. As Hayek said in his last book: prices in markets are a way of 'Ordering ... the Unknown' (1988, p. 83).

This brings us round to Hayek's three arguments why a socialist system, even if it were 'possible' in the sense of being at all economically efficient, would be extremely impracticable, i.e. much too costly. The first argument is that the price system in competitive markets collects information extremely cheaply. This is so because any one who buys and sells automatically introduces all the relevant information he has into the pricing process, with the prices changing accordingly. The participant in exchange collects his information voluntarily and often without cost for agents, and always without cost for others if he is a consumer. It has been pointed out that the price system need not reflect quality information correctly (Green, 1977); but, external effects and monopoly aside, changes in prices always signal changes in scarcity correctly. A socialist system, on the other hand, has to have a vast statistical staff to collect its information: bureaucratic staffs, both at the centre and also, interestingly, at the firm level, actually proved to be two or three times as large as in mainly free enterprise economies. This costliness of information collection and processing has been one of the main reasons why 'really existing' socialist systems foundered. Hayek's point (1935, p. 156) went to the very core of the real problem. He made it long before the use of computers became common. The capacity of modern computers slowly reaches the point where the general equilibrium equations of a socialist economy might actually be solved – if, indeed, we could set them up. But it is a rule of thumb that it takes about a thousand times longer than the time of computation to feed the data into the computer; and again a thousand times longer to collect the data. The real problem thus is not the solvability of the equations but the collection of the data and the cost of this collection!

Hayek's second point on the impracticability of socialism is that of the time lag in the adjustment of prices. If any manager who perceives a market disequilibrium has first to consult the central office before he is allowed to change a price, prices are much longer out of equilibrium than in a competitive market system (Hayek, 1940, p. 135 ff). This argument is not valid against the Lange–Lerner model, where managers would be directed to act on their own. But it was very relevant to really existing socialist systems. Firms, e.g., were told never to sell below cost, so that there were no bargain sales. The bad effect of being trained in this rule shows up at the time of writing (1992) in Moscow, where markets have become completely free. When Moscow shops cannot sell their goods at the cost price of the supplier, they send them back to the supplier, and, with perishable commodities, usually after they are spoiled! Hayek added the further point that for practical reasons prices can only be set for whole categories of commodities, so that prices of individual commodities remain uncontrolled (p. 92).

Hayek's third point on the impracticability of socialism had already been briefly touched upon by Mises and is, rather exceptionally for Hayek, an incentive argument. Managers would not take risks in socialism, as they can only lose, if things go wrong and they are blamed, while they would not profit from successful risk taking. In fact, Hayek was the first to remark that managers would therefore only try to please the planning bureaucracy, and, in particular, would always try to follow rules very strictly (Hayek, 1935, p. 174 ff; 1940, p. 141 ff), so as not to be blamed. Such behaviour would prove to be economically dysfunctional. Practice in socialist economies proved Hayek right.

Hayek's arguments on the impractability of socialism thus do not aver that a socialist economy would lack any measuring rod of efficiency. But he points out that such a system will only achieve a much lower degree of efficiency at much higher cost than a free enterprise system. Even his 'impossibility' arguments were taken by sympathetic observers to imply only that: higher costs and lower efficiency (see Barry, 1979). And in a sense, of course, they do only that. By the 1930s, and, in particular, in 1945, after a successfully fought war, socialism in a sense was evidently 'possible'. On the other hand, Hayek would never have written, as Schumpeter still did in 1942: 'Can

Socialism work? Of course it can' (opening words of the third part of his book). His achievement shines all the brighter compared to an outstanding non-socialist economist, like Schumpeter, who was bred in the Austrian subjective value tradition and used subjective information arguments copiously in his own theory of the creative entrepreneur. Yet the example of Schumpeter shows what illusions the blinding light of Walrasian general equilibrium theory could cause in the 1930s and 1940s (though not after the 1960s). In comparison to Schumpeter, Hayek's economic information theory also shows up in sharper relief: while Schumpeter had argued that there would be a few individuals who would be 'pioneers' and great innovators, Hayek thought that all economic decision taking would always be innovation to a greater or lesser degree. Therefore he never explicitly invoked innovation or technical progress in the narrower sense: 'Economic problems arise always and only in consequence of change' (Hayek, 1945, p. 523).

In his later years Hayek developed this concept into an evolutionary idea about social systems and society. A free enterprise system is uniquely qualified to cope with economic change and thus has a decided evolutionary advantage over other social systems. We know so little about the complex social interactions in an extended society: they are too complex for our understanding (Hayek, 1964). We therefore have to face up to it: 'What Cannot be Known Cannot be Planned' (Hayek, 1988, p. 85). It is a fatal conceit to try to do otherwise: both hybris in its perpetrators and the creation of serious scarcities up to the point of death. Hayek's last book, *The Fatal Conceit*, suggests that it is therefore also immoral to 'commit' socialism: in the chase after a mere will-o'-the wisp, personal freedom is sacrificed to repression.

Historical and methodological assessment
In contrast to Hayek, I would regard the chase after socialism not as a mere delusion. It may have been madness, but there was method in it – or, at least, a definable purpose. The really existing socialist societies were wasteful systems of exploitation for and by the nomenclatura. They served the evident interest of a social 'class'. In Marxist terms they did not progress beyond capitalism; they regressed towards feudalism!

The likely extent of their wastefulness, however, was first demonstrated by Hayek – and that in the teeth of rationalist opposition and at the height of rationalist fantasies. How well then does his new information-theoretic line of argument explain the great events of 1989 to 1991, the demise of socialist systems in Europe?

This particular historical event is more convincingly explained by the older lines of argument about the difficulties of socialism, viz. the incentive and the property rights arguments. Hayek's information arguments, on the other hand, are to show the difficulties of all interventionist economic planning: governments can never know enough. They always have too little local information. Hayek is much more damning about 'socialism' (in his sense) in the so-called 'market' economies, all of which are mixed economies. His paradigm is thus much more a paradigm for the future than one to explain the 'really existing' socialist experiments of the past. Hayek's information approach is also vital to explain the lower efficiency level of the 'really existing' socialist systems relative to free enterprise systems, and in particular their evident lack of efficiency in using capital, i.e. producer goods.

But on Hayek's terms the great puzzle remains: how, in the face of this handicap, could the Soviet type economies achieve such astonishing rates of development in the 1950s and up to, perhaps, 1965? Average living standards did improve in them somewhat over a lengthy period. To my mind the answer has to be: up to around 1965 their alternative incentive structure, the religious fervour of the few and the brutal repression of the many, worked, while this incentive system broke down in the last quarter century. The very idea of socialism with a smile on its face is thus necessarily a chimera! But it was Roscher, not Hayek, who pointed out that you cannot run a system for long on religious fervour alone. He might have added: neither can you do it for long by brutal repression of large groups of the population.

Specifically, the really existing socialist systems broke down because they could not adapt to the changed economic conditions after the two oil crises. This would appear to lead to pure Hayek conclusions. Did he not write in 1945: 'Economic problems arise always and only in consequence of change?' But the problem with his explanation here is that the socialist economies knew perfectly well that the oil price – and in consequence all other energy prices – had changed. These were world market prices! They also knew perfectly well that they were ruining their environment. For there the quantity signals were unmistakable. They just ignored the obvious signals. And that is a case of lack of incentives to act – in part. In part it was also due to different value systems. Hayek, evidently, thinks Adam Smith's maxim, 'Consumption is the sole end and purpose of all production', is (as Smith himself thought) 'self-evident', and all economists are brought up on this maxim. Smith (1776) wrote: 'The maxim is so perfectly self-evident, that it would be absurd to attempt to prove it'. But in social decision taking in general it is not self-evident at all. 'Really existing' socialist ideology came close to postulating that production is the sole end and purpose of production. These systems thus deteriorated more and more, as Leontief is said to have remarked, into input–input–systems. But that was a question of priorities, not information about means.

Hayek was much closer to the mark when he pointed out that the quality of products cannot be controlled in a socialist economy. Quality deterioration is cumulative, and it certainly contributed decisively to the systemic breakdown leading up to the demise of socialist states from 1989 to 1991. And as to the choice of the merely production-oriented value system, Hayek in his later years would have pointed out that an economy with such values cannot successfully compete with a free enterprise system, if consumer preferences count at all – and be it only the preferences of generals as consumers of military hardware. In this he would certainly have been right.

Thus Hayek's information-theoretic approach is better in condemning planning in 'market' economies and in explaining the low level of productivity in socialist systems (in the narrower sense) than in explaining their deterioration in the last two decades. His arguments on the evolutionary advantages of free enterprise economies and of competition, on the other hand, explain very well how it was possible for the United States to conquer the Soviet Union in an unbloody war in the 1980s: President Reagan merely had to turn on the competition of a rearmament race and the Soviet Union, forced to compete, must break down. Recently, an important Austrian social democratic politician, who, as a social democrat, does not value competition highly but security very much so, argued with me that President Carter was very wise in trying to forestall competition between the USA and the Soviet Union by mutual confidential talks and mutually agreed respect of spheres of interest. He thought that Reagan's policy of confrontation amounted to wilful taking of high risks and therefore was to be condemned on moral grounds. I answered that on Hayek's theory Reagan actually had faced no risk whatsoever; breakdown of the Soviet Union was so absolutely assured that there was no danger of its starting a nuclear war. As Paul Kennedy (1989) has pointed out, all great power wars have always been won by the economically stronger power; and, I add, since the War of the Great Alliance (1689–97) that was always the power or the powers in whose economy the element of free enterprise was more pronounced – with two exceptions, which clouded our judgement for a while: World War II and the Vietnam War. In both cases a socialist economy did very well. If the Soviet Union was so long overestimated this was due to the CIA and other information services, which most decidedly were not competitive free enterprise information systems!

But here we run up against a definite snag. If we look at information agencies which sell their products on the market and which can inform us about aggregative future developments, e.g. economic developments in whole countries, long-term forecasts of economic trends or even the stock market movements, their performance is very disappointing, not much better than that of the CIA. Furthermore, competing firms, like banks, frequently seem to have blundered in their forecasts of general trends in asset prices. And if some individuals make great fortunes in speculative ventures, this proves above all that the average market performance is poor. There are numerous goods not adequately supplied by the market, in particular most public goods. And frequently market calculation is wrong because of external effects, which by definition do not enter market-relevant calculations. Hayek always avoided an extensive discussion of the problem of external effects in economics, at best mentioning them briefly, e.g. in *The Road to Serfdom*, where he introduces a mere paragraph on them by saying: 'There are, finally, undoubted fields where no legal arrangements can create the main condition on which the usefulness of the system of competition and private property depends' (1944, p. 28 ff). Many of his statements about the informative nature of prices and about 'competition as a discovery procedure' (1978) have therefore to be taken with quite a pinch of salt, because the qualifying clauses are not stated. Might we not therefore even argue, as so much is unknowable and as so much is outside the proper purlieus of a well-functioning free enterprise system, that an individual free enterprise economy, though a member of a class of societies in general superior, might be plagued by so many external effects that it does not perform better than an individual socialist society, which functions particularly well because of a high degree of religious fervour, in spite of the fact that it belongs to a class of societies in general inferior? Information simply is not everything. Hayek is palpably wrong, when he states: 'The empirical element in economic theory ... consists of propositions about the acquisition of knowledge' (1937, p. 33). At least there are also initial endowments, constraints, and even preferences, e.g. about risk taking, which are empirically verifiable.

Hayek was extremely successful with his approach to 'The Use of Knowledge in Society'; and, unusually, the more so as time progressed. In the last twenty years (1972–92), the International Citation Index of the Social Sciences gives 2145 citations of Hayek, with 137 for the article named.[7] And here we have a fascinating aspect in the theory of science. I started out by showing that in a sense many of Hayek's basic tenets were not absolutely new; and we now see that they are not absolutely logically correct, either. Still, a great scientific reputation justly rests upon them. This only shows that Hayek's theory of knowledge is also very well applicable to the learning process of the scientific community. We do not 'know' an idea if it is encapsuled in a few sentences or a mere half sentence, even if it can be found in a well known text. Only one man sees their full significance at first; and he elaborates on it. We only learn a point by elaboration and constant repetition. And overstated propositions, which are 'wrong' in the logical sense, help – rather than mar – the process of reception: lesser men can easily supply the qualifying clauses. By his arguments no less than by the example of his scientific success Hayek proves that the development of knowledge is not a fully rational process.

The qualifying clauses in Hayek's statements can easily be supplied by lesser men. But these qualifying clauses evidently have to run in the direction that market failures do exist, that not all economic policies are therefore *a priori* reprehensible. As Hayek himself put it in *The Road to Serfdom*:

> It is of the utmost importance to the argument of this book for the reader to keep in mind that the planning against which all our criticism is directed is solely the planning against competition – the planning which is to be substituted for competition. This is the more important as we cannot, within the scope of this book, enter into a discussion of the very necessary planning which is required to make competition as effective and beneficial as possible. (Hayek, 1944, p. 31)

But quite apart from the fact that in practice it proves impossible to distinguish clearly between planning for and planning against competition, e.g. in environmental matters, Hayek has also taught us that there is an 'unavoidable imperfection of man's knowledge' (1945, p. 31), and that knowledge is not centralizable. Obviously, Hayek's statement, 'What Cannot be Known Cannot Be Planned', cannot be qualified. How can any government then have the knowledge necessary for the 'planning which is required to make competition as effective and beneficial as possible'? Problems of external effects certainly require very detailed knowledge, and knowledge very difficult to come by. We are faced with what might be termed the 'fatal dilemma' of Hayek. Ultimately, he leaves us in an unavoidable impasse: economic policy is both impossible – and necessary!

Notes

1. This has become clear from the recently discovered notes of Crown Prince Rudolf on the lectures Menger gave him. See Streissler (1990).
2. The Nobel Memorial Prize citation of the Royal Swedish Academy for Hayek said: 'The Academy is of the opinion that von Hayek's analysis of the functional efficiency of different economic systems is one of the most significant contributions to economic research in the broader sense ... He presented new ideas with regard to the basic difficulties of "socialist planning" ... His guiding principle ... was to study how efficient knowledge and information dispersed among individuals and enterprises is utilized'. See Machlup (1976).
3. I have edited these notes which are published under the title: *Carl Menger's Lectures to Crown Prince Rudolf of Austria* (Edward Elgar, 1994). An English translation has been provided by Monika Streissler and David Good.
4. Hayek (1988) says: 'decentralized control over resources, control through several property, leads to the generation and use of more information than is possible under central direction' (p. 86).
5. I rediscovered that argument in an earlier issue of this journal; see Streissler (1971), p. 425.
6. Para. 77 is entitled 'Sozialismus und Communismus'.
7. I owe this quantification to Karl Milford.

References

Bagehot, W. (1867), *The English Constitution*, London and Glasgow: Fontana Classics, 1963 and 1968.
Barone, E. (1908), 'Il Ministro della Produzione nello Stato Collettivista', *Giornale degli Economisti*, **XXXVII**, 409.

Barry, N.P. (1979), *Hayek's Social and Economic Philosophy*, Basingstoke and London: Macmillan.

Buchanan, J. (1969), *Costs and Choice*, Chicago: Markham.

Chamberlin, E.J. (1933), *The Theory of Monopolistic Competition*, Cambridge, Mass.: Harvard University Press.

Dickinson, H.D. (1933), 'Price Formation in a Socialist Community', *Economic Journal*, **XLIII**, 237.

Djilas, M. (1957), *The New Class*, New York: Praeger.

Eucken, W. (1965), *Die Grundlagen der Nationalökonomie*, Jena: Gustav Fischer, 1940, 8th ed. Berlin, Heidelberg, New York: Springer, 1965.

Friedman, M. (1968), 'The Role of Monetary Policy', *American Economic Review*, **LVIII**, 1.

Gorman, W.M. (1968), 'Measuring the Quantity of Fixed Factors', in J.N. Wolfe (ed.), *Value, Capital, and Growth, Papers in Honour of Sir John Hicks*, Edinburgh: Edinburgh University Press.

Green, J. (1977), 'The Non-Existence of Informational Equilibria', *Review of Economic Studies*, **44**, 451.

Hayek, F.A. von (1933), 'The Trend of Economic Thinking', *Economica*, **40**, 121 (inaugural lecture as Tooke Professor, London).

Hayek, F.A. von (1934), 'Carl Menger', *Economica*, new series, **I**, 393.

Hayek, F.A. von (1935), *Collectivist Economic Planning*, London: Routledge.

Hayek, F.A. von (1937), 'Economics and Knowledge', *Economica*, new series, **IV**, 33.

Hayek, F.A. von (1940), 'Socialist calculation: the competitive solution', *Economica*, new series, **VII**, 125.

Hayek, F.A. von (1944), *The Road to Serfdom*, London: Routledge; paperback ed. 1962.

Hayek, F.A. von (1945), 'The Use of Knowledge in Society', *American Economic Review*, **XXXV**, 519.

Hayek, F.A. von (1952), *The Counterrevolution of Science*, Glencoe, Ill.: The Free Press.

Hayek, F.A. von (1960), *The Constitution of Liberty*, London and Chicago: Routledge.

Hayek, F.A. von (1964), 'The Theory of Complex Phenomena', in M. Bunge (ed.), *The Critical Approach to Science and Philosophy. In Honour of Karl R. Popper*, Glencoe, Ill.: The Free Press.

Hayek, F.A. von (1975), *Die Irrtümer des Konstruktivismus und die Grundlagen legitimer Kritik gesellschaftlicher Gebilde*, Tübingen: Mohr, Walter Eucken Institut, vol. 51.

Hayek, F.A. von (1978), 'Competition as a Discovery Procedure', in *New Studies in Philosophy, Politics, Economics and the History of Ideas*, London: Routledge.

Hayek, F.A. von (1988), *The Fatal Conceit – The Errors of Socialism*, vol. 1 of W.W. Bartley III (ed.), *The Collected Works of Friedrich August Hayek*, London, New York: Routledge.

Hayek, F.A. von (1989), 'The Pretence of Knowledge', Nobel Memorial Lecture, 11 December 1974, *American Economic Review*, **79**, Survey of Members, 3.

Hilferding, R. (1910), *Das Finanzkapital. Eine Studie über die jüngste Entwicklung des Kapitalismus*, Berlin, Frankfurt, Vienna: Europa Verlag, 1968.

Hutschenreiter, G. (1984), *Gleichgewicht und Anpassung in abstrakten ökonomischen Systemen*, Diplomarbeit, (mimeo), University of Vienna.

Kennedy, P. (1989), *The Rise and Fall of the Great Powers*, New York: Vintage Books.

Lange, O. (1936), 'On the Economic Theory of Socialism, Part I', *Review of Economic Studies*, **4**, 53; (1937), 'Part II', *Review of Economic Studies*, **5**, 123.

Lerner, A.P. (1937), 'Statics and Dynamics in Socialist Economics', *Economic Journal*, **XLVII**, 253.

Machlup, F. (1976), *Essays on Hayek*, New York: New York University Press.

Marx, K. (1967), *Capital. A Critique of Political Economy*, vol. 1, New York: International Publishers (originally published in German, 1867).

Menger, C. (1871), *Grundsätze der Volkswirtschaftslehre*, Vienna: Braumüller; English translation by J. Dingwall and B.F. Hoselitz, *Principles of Economics*, Glencoe, Ill.: The Free Press, 1976.

Menger, C. (1883), *Untersuchungen über die Methode der Socialwissenschaften und der Politischen Oekonomie insbesondere*, Leipzig: Duncker & Humblot.

Mill, J.S. (1848), *Principles of Political Economy With Some of Their Applications to Social Philosophy*, London: Parker; 1976 ed. by Sir W. Ashley, Fairfield: Aug. Kelley.

Mises, L. von (1920), 'Die Wirtschaftsrechnung im sozialistischen Gemeinwesen', *Archiv für Sozialwissenschaften und Sozialpolitik*, **XLVII** (April), 119.

Mises, L. von (1922), *Die Gemeinwirtschaft – Untersuchungen über den Sozialismus*, Jena: Gustav Fischer, 2nd ed. 1932; reprint Munich: Philosophia, 1981.

Mises, L. von (1924), 'Neue Beiträge zum Problem der sozialistischen Wirtschaftsrechnung', *Archiv für Sozialwissenschaften und Sozialpolitik*, **LI**.

Mises, L. von (1928), 'Neue Schriften zum Problem der sozialistischen Wirtschaftsrechnung', *Archiv für Sozialwissenschaften und Sozialpolitik*, **LVI**.

Pareto, V. (1897), *Cours d'Economie Politique*, vol. II, Lausanne.

Robbins, L. (1952), *The Theory of Economic Policy in English Classical Political Economy*, London: Macmillan; 2nd ed. 1978.

Robinson, J.V. (1933), *The Economics of Imperfect Competition*, London: Macmillan.

Roscher, W. (1854), *Die Grundlagen der Nationalökonomie. Ein Hand- und Lesebuch für Geschäftsmänner und Studierende*, Stuttgart: Cotta; 26th ed. 1926; quotations from 5th ed. 1864.

Rudolf, Crown Prince of Austria (1876), *Politische Ökonomie, Hefte*, January – August, mostly written in his own hand (but corrected by Menger), Österreichisches Staatsarchiv (Haus-, Hof- und Staatsarchiv), Vienna.

Schumpeter, J.A. (1942), *Capitalism, Socialism and Democracy*, New York: Harper.

Schumpeter, J.A. (1954), *History of Economic Analysis*, London: Allen and Unwin.

Smith, A. (1776), *An Inquiry into the Nature and Causes of the Wealth of Nations*, London: Straham and Cadall. Glasgow edition by R.H. Campbell and A.S. Skinner, Oxford: Oxford University Press 1976.

Spengler, J.J. (1968), 'Exogenous and Endogenous Influences in the Formation of Post-1870 Economic Thought: A Sociology of Knowledge Approach', in R.V. Eagly (ed.), *Events, Ideology, and Economic Theory*, Detroit.

Sraffa, P. (1930), 'Increasing Returns and the Representative Firm: A Criticism', *Economic Journal*, **40**, 89.

Streissler, E.W. (1970), 'Privates Produktiveigentum – Stand und Entwicklungstrends der Auffassungen in kapitalistischen Ländern', in *Eigentum – Wirtschaft – Fortschritt, Veröffentlichungen der Walter-Raymond-Stiftung*, vol. 12, Cologne: Hegner.

Streissler, E.W. (1971), 'Liberale Wirtschaftsordnung – aktueller denn je – Versuch einer materialistischen Geschichtsinterpretation', *Wirtschaftspolitische Blätter*, **18**, (5–6), 419.

Streissler, E.W. (1972), 'To What Extent Was the Austrian School Marginalist?', *History of Political Economy*, **4**, 426.

Streissler, E.W. (1986), 'Friedrich von Wieser, the Bard as Economist', in N. Leser (ed.), *Die Wiener Schule der Nationalökonomie*, Vienna: Böhlau.

Streissler, E.W. (1990), 'Carl Menger on economic policy; the lectures to Crown Prince Rudolf', *History of Political Economy*, **22**, suppl., 107.

Streissler, E.W. (1994), *Carl Menger's Lectures to Crown Prince Rudolf of Austria*, Aldershot: Edward Elgar.

Tullock, G. (1969), 'The New Theory of Corporations', in E.W. Streissler et al. (eds), *Roads to Freedom – Essays in Honour of Friedrich A. von Hayek*, London: Routledge.

Vaughn, K.J. (1980), 'Economic Calculation Under Socialism: The Austrian Contribution', *Economic Enquiry*, **XVIII**, 535.

Viner, J. (1958), 'Adam Smith and Laissez Faire', in *The Long View and the Short*, Glencoe, Ill.: The Free Press.

Wieser, F. von (1884), *Über den Ursprung und die Hauptgesetze des wirtschaftlichen Wertes*, Vienna: Hölder.

Winch, D. (1969), *Economics and Policy – A Historical Study*, London: Hodder and Stoughton.

4   Hayek and market socialism

Bruno Jossa

The main purpose of this paper is to discuss whether the arguments against, and criticisms of, socialism that Hayek set forth in his complex theoretical system are merely directed against a strictly centralized economic system or also against market socialism in all its possible forms.

Given the variety of market socialism models and the perhaps scant awareness of this form of social organization even among professional economists, a convenient procedure will be to refer constantly to a well defined model. Accordingly the following section of this paper will expound in detail the ideas of Oscar Lange concerning market socialism; thereafter three sections will be concerned with analysing Hayek's ideas on market economy, with a view to verifying whether they can also be applied to the market socialism theorized by Lange in the writings of his mature years; then two sections will discuss the ideas of Hayek concerning the distribution of income, always in connection with market socialism.

The conclusion reached in this study is that there is hardly anything, in Hayek's theoretical system, that might be of use for a critique of those models of market socialism that we feel are the most interesting ones.[1] At first sight such a conclusion is likely to seem surprising, for Hayek was unmistakably an avowed enemy of any model with even the vaguest socialist connotations. Yet Hayek himself stated that one of his most valuable contributions was 'the demonstration that the difference between socialists and non-socialists ultimately rests on purely intellectual issues capable of a scientific resolution and not on different judgments of value' (Hayek, 1973a, p. 6). 'Socialism', he also wrote, 'is not based merely on a different system of ultimate value from that of liberalism, which one would have to respect even if one disagreed; it is based on intellectual error which makes its adherents blind to its consequences' (Hayek, 1976a, p. 136; also see Hayek, 1976b, pp. 295–6 and 304–5).[2] If there is some truth in these contentions, then the fact that the several proposals of market socialism stem from value judgments thoroughly different from Hayek's must be deemed irrelevant in judging Hayek's thought concerning this issue, given the absence, in his writings, of any logical or theoretical arguments against those proposals.[3]

As is well known, the core idea of Hayek's theoretical construction is the notion of a spontaneous or self-generating order, a concept which Austrian economists consider a sort of 'first principle of economics' (see O'Driscoll,

1977, p. 116); accordingly a large part of the Austrian economists' research was concerned with exploring and discussing the implications of the notion of market economy as a spontaneous order first set forth by Mandeville and Hume.[4] Yet it will be convenient to point out right from the start that this idea was shared and extensively dealt with even by Lange, so that it is hardly conceivable that any of the arguments in Hayek's theoretical system based on the idea that the market order arises independently of human will and awareness should prove effectual in confuting a Langean model of market socialism.

The Langean model of market socialism

According to Lange, 'the evolution of the capitalist mode of production itself prepared conditions in which the new socialist system of relations of production becomes both possible and necessary' (see Lange, 1958, p. 87). Unlike other socialist authors, however, Lange contended that when firms are taken up by the state, economic laws continue to act themselves out fully as objective laws operating 'regardless of whether people are conscious of them or not, and regardless of whether or not they conform to human intentions' (see Lange, 1958, p. 54). In Lange's view 'the historical process develops like a process of natural history, even though it is the result of conscious and purposive human actions' (p. 79);[5] and this applies both to capitalism and to socialism. In socialism, Lange wrote, 'the technical and balance laws of human behaviour and the laws of interplay of human actions continue to operate objectively, independently of human will and consciousness', because they are phenomena that neither the socialist nor other production modes can rule out (p. 82). 'Yet the social ownership of the means of production enables these laws to give results intended by man' (p. 82). Thanks to the social ownership of all firms, Engels wrote, 'the laws of his own social action, hitherto standing face to face with man as laws of nature foreign to, and dominating him, will then be used with full understanding, and so mastered by him' (see Engels, 1878, p. 392); and in commenting on this passage, Lange stated that 'it is necessary to bear in mind the difference between the spontaneity of operation and the objective character of economic laws' and made it clear that the social ownership of all firms, far from suspending the working of economic laws or their mechanical and objective nature, creates 'conditions in which these economic laws operate in such a way that their effects coincide with the aims of man' (see Lange, 1958, p. 83).

Lange also clarified that 'the basis of the management of the national economy should be the autonomous socialist enterprises. Such enterprises should function as teams of people implementing common social tasks, personally interested in the favourable outcome of these tasks' (Lange, 1956, p. 43); and in the 1942 lectures he stated:

the socialist idea is that, though socialism advocates public enterprise, it does not advocate government enterprise and activity in the sense indicated, but rather wants to see the public institutions which are charged with the operation of our productive system to be autonomous institutions, independent from the political state. (Lange, 1942, p. 4).

In Lange's view public corporations must be run according to criteria of strict efficiency. His argument is that the main purpose in nationalizing firms is to keep in check the all-powerful economic sway of bourgeois society, e.g. private capital, and not to replace one kind of management with another. In other words, the nationalization of firms is intended to bring about really effective economic policies not impaired by private interest; it strives to make possible a purposive use of the *levers* at the disposal of the public hand and not to put 'administrative methods' in place of the market.

In short, according to Lange, as soon as the main production means have been nationalized, the management of the economy will have to be hinged on public corporations and these will have to be run efficiently, in keeping with the economic principle of minimum cost, by granting both managers and workers a share of the net income produced by them. This, as is well known, results in saying that socialist firms should be managed in the same way as capitalist ones, with a view to maximizing profits.[6]

As mentioned above, Lange's idea is that the transition to socialism puts man in a position to use economic laws purposely while continuing to respect them; and the objective nature of economic laws, their independence of human intentions and consciousness, determines that the only way in which they can be used is to create 'conditions in which these economic laws operate in such a way that their effect coincide with the aims of man'. This means that in a Langean socialist market economy the state must first of all create the 'legal framework' within which economic activity is to develop and then constantly prefer state intervention of an *indirect* kind, i.e. of a kind not involving the power of its organs to act at discretion in order to achieve concrete purposes. It goes without saying that according to Lange the ultimate end of the state in framing effective economic policies is the attainment of the multifarious purposes usually assigned to it; however, far from putting direct state action in place of market mechanisms, the economic policy advocated by Lange uses the levers of public intervention to channel the spontaneous market forces in a direction suited to bring about the intended results.

Hayek and market economy
Most of Hayek's criticisms of socialism are found to lose their grip when set against a modern interpretation of socialism as an authentic market economy. The greatest fault that Hayek imputed to socialism, the one which led him to talk of a 'fatal conceit', is the underlying idea that planning should take the

place of the market, that the state, instead of creating an abstract framework within which citizens can freely move, should vest in its organs power to take any actions they may deem expedient in view of the attainment of concrete purposes.[7]

But Hayek is known to have strenuously opposed any state intervention whatsoever in the economy, even action of an 'indirect' kind grounded on market mechanisms. And he went so far as to maintain that to control a spontaneous order was 'a contradiction in terms' (see Hayek, 1988, p.84).

So what are we to think of this last proposition? In this author's opinion it is evident that the spontaneous nature of the market order and its lack of any rational foundation can by no means prevent man from striving continuously to improve it. Hayek contended that man 'will therefore have to use what knowledge he can achieve, not to shape the results as the craftsman shapes his handiwork, but rather to cultivate a growth by providing the appropriate environment in the manner in which the gardener does this for his plants' (Hayek, 1975, p. 34). But a gardener takes action in a myriad of different manners, by watering and manuring the ground and by pruning, grafting and propping plants, by moving them from one place to another, by creating shelters, etc. Why then should man, who expends all such effort in correcting the working of natural phenomena, be prevented from modifying and improving the order of the market, which is not even a natural one?

Hayek wrote that 'it is possible that an order which would still have to be described as spontaneous rests on rules which are entirely the result of deliberate design' (Hayek, 1973a, p. 46);[8] and he observed that, as a rule, the economic system is undeniably the result of an evolutionary process, but of a process 'in the course of which spontaneous growth of customs and deliberate improvements of the particulars of an existing system have constantly interacted' (Hayek, 1973a, p. 100). Consequently, Hayek seems to have admitted that in a market economy man is always taking purposive action in order to regulate and direct the spontaneous forces of the market and that this does not nullify the spontaneous self-regulating essence of this order. Why then did he contend that to control a spontaneous order is a 'contradiction in terms'?

A distinction in keeping with the most rigorous liberal thought is that between actions on institutions, which are always allowed, and actions on rules of conduct, which conversely must not be acted upon consciously.[9] It is worth emphasizing that this distinction has nothing to do with the distinction between organization and spontaneous order, for many institutions arise by spontaneous evolution (see Hayek, 1960, pp. 58–9 and Bobbio, 1970, p. 127) and many rules of organization can likewise arise spontaneously (see Galeotti, 1987, p. 290).[10] Neither does it fall in with the distinction between 'government through rules', which Hayek approves of, and 'government through commands', which he rejects, for even rules of organization, like rules of conduct, are mostly abstract (see Bobbio, 1970, pp. 126–7). In the last period of his life, however, Hayek seems to have opposed even actions on institutions intended for a purpose other than restoring the pure order of the market (see, e.g., Arnold, 1980, pp. 231–2).

According to a widely shared interpretation, this aversion of Hayek's to actions on institutions is due to his confidence that social evolution will guarantee the survival of efficient institutions (see, e.g., Houle, 1989, pp. 201–2); but other well known advocates of economic liberalism, among them Viner and Buchanan, have severely criticized Hayek's opposition to institutional reforms by emphasizing that the institutions that are found to survive, and even to thrive, are not necessarily those apt to maximize human capabilities (see Viner, 1961, pp. 116–17; Buchanan, 1975, pp. 130–31 and Buchanan, 1976, pp. 13–24). In other words, according to Viner and Buchanan, cultural evolution does not guarantee the survival of the best institutions.[11] Viner wrote:

> I do not see how this doctrine can be distinguished from 'social Darwinism' or from that 'historicism', which Hayek has elsewhere so persuasively warned us against. I miss a discussion of the rate of speed at which institutions of the past, like serfdom, slavery, caste, trial by torture, latifundia, religious persecution, head-hunting, and so on, which at least today many regard as *never* having been 'useful', got displaced, through spontaneous forces, by 'useful' institutions. (Viner, 1961, pp. 116–7)[12]

Hayek's contention, however, is not that existing institutions do not admit any improvement, but that man is unable to purposely improve the results of cultural evolution. Many institutions, among them private property, do originate from cultural evolution; and in such a case they are part of the spontaneous market order. Consequently it is institutions originating from conscious efforts on the part of man that, in Hayek's view, are unable to improve the spontaneous order of the market.[13] The point to be made in this respect, therefore, is that the order man's purposive action is unable to improve is exactly the one typical of the economic liberalism advocated by Hayek, viz. that of a perfectly competitive market where the functions of the state are strictly delimited. Otherwise Viner's objection (the permanence of institutions that social conscience condemns) would in itself be enough to confute Hayek's propositions (see Gray, 1980, pp. 164–7; in this regard, also see Diamond, 1980, pp. 247–8 and Petroni and Monti Bragadin, 1986, pp. XIV–XVI).

Law and legislation

But what is the rationale underlying Hayek's contention that institutions (apart from those intended to establish a perfectly competitive order) must never be brought into being through purposive human action?

To clarify this problem Hayek himself deemed it necessary 'to consider more fully the precise relation between the various kinds of rules which people in fact obey and the resulting order of actions' and, in particular, to examine the rules of law (Hayek, 1973a, p. 45).

As is well known, according to Hayek a really liberal constitutional order is one in which Parliament is empowered to pass, not just any kind of laws, but only general rules of proper conduct arising through spontaneous evolution. In Hayek's opinion, the strict enforcement of the principle of the separation of powers requires indeed that the notion of law be conceived of, in a narrow sense, as a general rule of just conduct applicable to all citizens (see, e.g., Hayek, 1973a, chs 5 and 6 and Hayek, 1973d, pp. 9–16). In order to further clarify this point, Hayek drew his well known distinction (reflected even in the title of his *magnum opus*; see Hayek, 1973a, 1976a and 1979) between law and legislation; and he made it clear that in a really liberal constitutional order the legislative body is merely called upon to pass statutes fitting in the category of law proper, while government bodies are expected to provide only sundry services not involving any recourse to coercion and to restrict their use of coercive action merely to obliging people to pay their taxes or to observe the general rules of just conduct passed by Parliament (see Hayek, 1973a, pp. 72–4 and 124–44; Hayek, 1979, pp. 105–27; also Hayek, 1973b, pp. 142–5).[14]

At this point it would be useless to discuss whether a provision of law by which Parliament enforces the wage structure (viz. a kind of action which, as will be shown below, is a distinctive feature of the form of market socialism we are addressing in this paper) is a *kind* of law Hayek would have approved of. In all likelihood it is not. Hayek would have termed it, not a law in the narrow sense of the word, a rule of just conduct, but an act of legislation and, moreover, a legislative provision by which the state sets out to attain an end Hayek strenuously opposed.[15]

But the problem we are setting out to solve here is obviously not whether Hayek (a lifelong opposer of any form whatsoever of socialism) did or did not approve of market socialism. Our purpose is to verify whether Hayek's works contain any *logical* arguments that may induce us to extend the definition of 'fatal conceit' also to the form of socialism here under review. And the first and most general reflection we are led to set forth, in this respect, is that Hayek, who clearly approved of a government levying taxes and duties and fixing the salaries of its own officers, could by no means devise any logical arguments in support of the contention that a Parliament should abstain from enforcing a wage structure that the representatives of the majority of the citizens were to deem, by a decision freely made, to be better than the one arising spontaneously in the market.

In Barry's view Hayek's distinction between law and command 'is not a logical one, because he says that both laws and commands are in the same logical category in contrast with facts, and that *laws gradually shade into commands the less general they become'* (see Barry, 1979, p. 83; italics added); and the same is true of the distinction between law and legislation, since rules of organization are usually also both general and abstract and the only difference, in this respect, between law and legislation lies in the greater or lesser degree of such general nature (see Leoni, 1961, pp. 68–70; Hamowy, 1978, p. 103–5 and Hamowy, 1982, p. 382 et seq.].[16] And this entails that there can hardly be any logical arguments effectual in criticizing a decision only because it was enforced by means of an act of legislation.

While contending that 'law serves, or is the necessary condition for, the formation of a spontaneous order of actions' (Hayek, 1973a, p. 112), Hayek also wrote that the spontaneous evolutionary processes of law 'may lead into an impasse from which it cannot extricate itself by its own forces' and that 'the fact that law that has evolved in this way has certain desirable properties does not prove that it will always be good law or even that some of its rules may not be very bad' [Hayek 1973a, p. 88); and this shows that one cannot altogether dispense with legislation.

In Hayek's own words, rules of law are 'those rules which, because we can deliberately alter them, become the chief instruments whereby we can affect the resulting order' (Hayek, 1973a, p. 45); and he admitted not only that 'a spontaneous order may rest in part on regularities which are not spontaneous but imposed' (see Hayek, 1968, p. 74), but also that 'although undoubtedly an order originally formed itself spontaneously because the individuals followed rules which had not been deliberately made but had arisen spontaneously, people gradually learned to improve those rules' (Hayek, 1973a, p. 45), which amounts to acknowledging that conscious action can and must change a spontaneous order.[17]

Spontaneous order and liberalism
In Gray's view, a spontaneous order is a value-free notion devoid of any normative content. Spontaneous evolution may lead to a social system founded on freedom or, conversely, to tyranny: and, indeed, 'the road to serfdom' as theorized by Hayek is a process by which society slowly and unconsciously heads toward an illiberal statist system.

As was made clear by Buchanan and Tullock, in the absence of appropriate safeguards put in place by constitutional rules, competition for the vote generates a context of overall legal warfare and leads, by its very nature, to policies envisaging more and more intervention. Against the will of the majority of the people, society thus begins to head toward a totalitarian state. And such a process toward totalitarianism can correctly be termed as spontaneous, since competition for the vote, which is typical of unlimited democracy, by generating the warfare of every man against every man, results in behaviours which, though resorted to with intent to pursue the interest of the moment and in the absence of a design to increase state intervention in the economy, end up by favouring a statist system. Consequently, 'if spontaneous order is to be understood in this value-free way, it will have no necessary connection with individual liberty' (Gray, 1984, pp. 121–2). On the other hand, if Hayek insists on negating the existence of laws governing evolution, then it seems clear that in his view spontaneous evolution can generate both freedom and its reverse, tyranny (also see Barry, 1979, pp. 142–3 and Lagueux, 1989, pp. 94 et seq.).

If this is how things stand, it is not clear how it is possible to contend that socialists are the enemies of freedom because they want to substitute a conscious design for spontaneous evolution. If, indeed, spontaneous evolution can easily lead to totalitarianism, how can Hayek maintain that totalitarianism is the outcome of a purposive human design?

There is general consensus of opinion that the definition of freedom as *negative* freedom and the consequential distinction between liberty and liberties are crucial notions of Hayek's thought. In Hayek's own words, 'the difference between liberty and liberties is that which exists between a condition in which all is permitted that is not prohibited by general rules and one in which all is prohibited that is not explicitly permitted' (Hayek, 1960, p. 19). And there is likewise consensus about the fact that it is in consequence of this particular view of liberty as negative freedom ('all is permitted that is not prohibited') that, in Hayek's opinion, all those who want to impose a purposive design upon society are turned into its enemies (see Tomlinson, 1990, pp. 20–21).

On the contrary, it has been shown above that general and abstract laws may well result in imposing a purposive design upon society and that consequently a society can undoubtedly be organized (within given limits, obviously) according to a deliberate design and nevertheless continue to be free, e.g. continue to be a society in which, in Hayek's words, 'all is permitted that is not prohibited'. Consequently, there seems to be no link between the notion of liberty as negative freedom and the critique of purposive intervention into the social order by reason of its alleged paving the way for totalitarianism.

One of the arguments on which Hayek bases his opposition to conscious control of the social order is that reason is not a faculty enabling man to explain and judge society from a position outside and above it, but the product of human evolution and civilization (see Hayek, 1960, p. 24; Hayek, 1978, p. 20 and Kukathas, 1989, pp. 61–2 and 103–5). Quoting Hayek, Kukathas writes: 'because he sees reason as unable to "rise above" the civilization that produces it, or identify an Archimedean point from which to view the world, he argues that "the social process from which reason emerges must remain free from its control"' (see Hayek, 1960, p. 38 and Kukathas 1989, p. 61). Yet, even granting Hayek's thesis of the limits of human reason, it seems evident that the short-comings of cognition are in themselves not enough to justify the contention that man must *never* control social evolution (for a different critique of Hayek's stance on this point, see Kukathas, 1989, pp. 79–83).

In an early article discussing the Hayekian distinction between true and false individualism, Harrod observed that the main aspect of individualism Hayek set out to vindicate was the respect of spontaneous order and that he contrasted 'this doctrine with the rationalist approach which assumes that Reason can provide blue-prints which solve all human problems' (Harrod, 1946, p. 438). In Harrod's view, however, the conflict to which Hayek drew attention was not between liberalism and socialism, but between conserva-tism and radicalism.

In other words, in Harrod's view the association of individualism, liberal-ism and defence of tradition on the one hand and rationalism and socialism on the other is 'a confusion between two separate issues' (see Harrod, 1946, p. 439) and – what is of greater concern to us here – the juxtaposition of tradition and reason as two irreconcilable opposites is a polemic distortion denoting 'a certain tendency to dogmatism and exclusiveness which cannot validly be maintained in the field of political studies' (Harrod, 1946, p. 435).[18] Indeed there is no doubt that spontaneity and control can be reconciled and that it is necessary to search for the best combination of them.

In the light of the above it is possible to conclude, on this point, that whereas Hayek disapproved of actions on institutions intended to improve the spontaneous order of the market, he seems not to have devised any logical arguments that could be effectively used to disclaim a political system envisaging state intervention based on 'government through rules' and, con-sequently, also a model of market socialism *à la* Lange.[19] The idea of 'gov-ernment through rules' is central to his thought (see Dietze, 1977 and Barry, 1979, ch. 5), so that no solid arguments can be found, in his writings, to confute a model of market socialism founded on an abstract legal framework within which citizens are allowed to move freely.[20] Hayek's methodological proposal is that 'in the case of complex spontaneous orders we will never be able to determine more than the general principles on which they operate' [Hayek, 1973a, pp. 62–3]; and he is convinced that 'an ideal picture of a society which may be wholly achievable, or a guiding conception of the overall orders to be aimed at, is ... the chief contribution that science can make to the solution of the problems of practical policy' (Hayek, 1973a, p. 65). But Lange's market socialism is exactly the enunciation of the general principles of a prospective ideal society which merely enunciates the rules of the game without claiming in the least to purposely alter the rules of conduct of individuals.

Hayek and the distribution of income

Hayek's works contain a wealth of arguments in support of the thesis that in a market economy the distribution of income cannot, and must not, be altered by purposive human action. What is called a 'fair wage structure', he contended, is incompatible with the order of a competitive economy, so much so that the criteria of justice we are wont to term 'social' would be better described as 'anti-social'. If they were realized, levels of income would decrease and mankind would gradually revert to more primitive levels of civilization. Merit, he maintained, is determined by the results obtained, not by motives. And any criticism of the distribution of income determined by the market is borne of a feeling of envy which, though comprehensible, is to be censured because it contradicts the general interest (see Hayek, 1988, pp. 71–4 and 117–9). In Hayek's opinion 'the most destructive of constructivistic morals is egalitarianism' (see Hayek, 1979, p. 170).

But, in my opinion, Hayek's argument that equality is in contrast with the morals of a competitive society is of little use in disclaiming market socialism. Far from maintaining that everybody is to earn the same income, market socialists only vindicate equal starting opportunities, an idea traditionally subscribed to even by the best liberal tradition (see, for instance, Einaudi, 1964, part III), though not by Hayek (see Hayek, 1946, p. 31 and Hayek, 1976a, pp. 9–10 and 82–4). And again the best way to counter this argument seems to be the observation that Hayek's theoretical system, while containing forceful arguments against the Soviet model, is ineffectual in criticizing market socialism. Whoever sets out to attain equality through the system of recruitment by competitive examination does not run counter to the morals of a competitive society; in a system providing for recruitment by competitive examination merit is assessed based on achievement, in line with Hayek's recommendations, wherefore it does in no way conflict with the need to strive for excellence: on the contrary, in that system there is more emphasis on the recognition of merit than in a system exclusively based on the market.

But the most forceful objection to Hayek's stance concerning this point will come from those who share Okun's well known views: if justice and efficiency are in conflict, as is currently maintained, then the problem is to find the best *trade-off* between the two, not to abstain from intervention altogether (Okun, 1975). Consequently, as Hayek was determined to rule out any action intended to establish a distribution other than that spontaneously generated by the market, the only way open to him was to maintain that there was *no* conflict between justice and efficiency.

In denying the conflict between justice and efficiency, Hayek maintained that the distribution determined by the market is neither just nor unjust. In his opinion spontaneous order and social evolution, though arising from the observance of moral rules, do not generate results that can be described as 'just' or morally acceptable: for, if the activities of single individuals are coordinated in the market thanks to a spontaneous process which puts order into a quantity of facts well beyond the power of perception or control of a single human mind, it would be contrary to reason or, better, impossible to describe this process as just (Hayek, 1988, p. 73). In a market economy it is only success that matters and distribution does not reflect any rules of social justice. 'Evolution cannot be just' (p. 74).

Neither – and this is Hayek's main proposition – can the order of the market be described as unjust. Only results purposely contrived by man can be termed unjust. In particular, to describe the distribution of income arising in the market as unjust is like speaking of injustice in connection with an earthquake or a flood (see Hayek, 1960, p. 137 and, e.g., Plant, 1989, pp. 53–6). 'Justice has meaning only as a rule of human conduct' (Hayek, 1976c, p. 58); what is not the product of the conscious will of man can be considered a misfortune, a natural calamity, but never injustice.[21]

Hayek endorsed the thesis of Pantaleoni, according to whom 'merit is a word void of meaning' (see Pantaleoni, 1925, p. 101 and Hayek, 1976b, p. 179, n. 21);[22] and his essential argument in discussing problems of distribution was consequently that 'the phrase "social justice" is completely devoid of meaning or content' (see Hayek, 1976a, p. 96; also see Hayek, 1973c, p. 13 and Hayek, 1976b).

Granted that the order of the market is neither just nor unjust, human action seeking to alter it can nevertheless be guided by reason and can, and must, tend to bring about a society that social conscience will consider a better one. According to the liberal theorist Nozick, 'no doubt people will not long accept a distribution they believe unjust' (Nozick, 1974, p. 158). Apart from this, however, the fact that the order of the market is not, in itself, either just or unjust does not justify the contention that it cannot be altered so as to bring about a distribution of income deemed by social conscience (as it surfaces in decisions democratically made in Parliament) to be better than the distribution arising spontaneously. Such distribution as arises spontaneously in the market can perhaps be compared to an earthquake or a flood;[23] but, given that man takes action to remedy the damage caused by an earthquake or a flood, why ought he to be prevented from correcting the distribution of income determined by the market?[24]

Egalitarianism, Hayek also said, is a threat to freedom. The idea of a society in which remuneration would be determined by criteria of 'social justice' is illusory, in his opinion, for it is unattainable if only because there is no agreement as to what is meant by optimal distribution of income; yet it is an illusoriness fraught with danger, because it would result in a disastrous loss of freedom (Hayek, 1973b, p. 140). In Hayek's opinion, the free choice of an occupation we are accustomed to is possible 'only if the remuneration one will expect to receive for a job reflects the value the relevant products will carry for those people for whom they are actually being produced' (Hayek, 1976c, p. 430).

Recruitment by competitive examination

The lack of agreement concerning optimal distribution, however, is not an argument against state action intended to establish a more egalitarian distribution. Decisions concerning social justice are political decisions to be passed, as a rule, in Parliament by a majority vote. It follows, therefore, that they are not a threat to freedom. Hayek's contention that freedom is possible 'only if the remuneration one will expect to receive for a job reflects the value that the relevant products carry for those people for whom they are actually being produced', is a statement void of any sense whatsoever, for no economist of any standing would ever maintain in earnest, for example, that the tax levied on the income of an individual is a threat to freedom in that it reduces his net proceeds to an amount short of the marginal product of his work. What Hayek probably wanted to say is that remuneration ought to be commensurate with the objective results of economic activity, and not with the individual merits of the person acting (see Hayek, 1946, p. 21). If this is the case, then his contention sounds something of an overstatement: on closer analysis, it seems to purport that the distributive rule according to which the earnings of a 'factor' must equate its marginal productivity is the only objective rule compatible with freedom.

In other words, whilst rejecting J.B. Clark's old and untenable proposition that the marginalist rules of distribution are the only distributive rules in keeping with justice, Hayek formulated a new but equally untenable proposition, i.e. the one according to which marginalist rules of distribution are the only distributive rules compatible with freedom.[25]

In our opinion, therefore, Hayek's arguments against distributive justice are weak and objectionable and he was forced to admit that according to many the distribution determined by the market did not reflect any ideals of justice. But, given the existence of criteria for establishing whether one kind of distribution is more or less just than another, why should man refrain from attempting to attain a fairer kind of distribution? Merit, Hayek says, is determined by results, not by intentions: but this is a proposition that, though not entirely ungrounded, is in conflict with the whole tradition of Christian thought. In the opinion of Popper, 'We need an ethics which defies success and reward. And such an ethics need not be invented. It is not new. It has been taught by Christianity, at least in its beginnings' (see Popper, 1966, vol. II, p. 277). But even accepting the rationale that merit is to be judged on the basis of the results achieved, who could deny that a system of competitive examination, well devised and strictly enforced, would place even greater emphasis on merit than the market system itself?

A society in which the wage structure results from decisions passed by majority votes and where a well-devised system of competitive examinations is used extensively to balance out demand and supply in the different labour markets is a society where distribution is determined, not by the market, but by purposive choices of man. Nevertheless such a society would still be free, because (apart from the imposition of the wage structure) the conditions of the market would still be determined, as usual, by its own spontaneous rules.

Hayek wrote:

> The complete emptiness of the phrase 'social justice' shows itself in the fact that no agreement exists about what social justice requires in particular instances; also that there is no known test by which to decide who is right if people differ, and that no preconceived scheme of distribution could be effectively devised in a society whose individuals are free, in the sense of being allowed to use their own knowledge for their own purposes. Indeed, individual moral responsibility for one's actions is incompatible with the realization of any such desired overall patterns of distribution. (Hayek, 1976c, p. 58)

But the system of recruitment by competitive examination is exactly 'a scheme of distribution' devised for a society in which men are perfectly free and for a well organized state; consequently it is in no way incompatible with individual moral responsibility.

Conclusions

We have tried to clarify, in this paper, that the core issue in a comparative analysis of capitalism and market socialism is not the spontaneous nature of the market order, but the kind of rules to be enforced. Thus one will have to decide, for instance, whether purposely contrived rules should, or should not, impose restrictions on the accumulation of personal wealth; whether they are, or are not, to guarantee equal starting opportunities for everybody; whether they are to encourage competition in the market or in examinations for competitive recruitment to the public service, etc. Faced with these options, Hayek declared himself clearly in favour of rules which did not enforce any restrictions on the accumulation of personal wealth or guarantee equal starting opportunities, and he definitely opposed recruitment by competitive examination, even within a well designed scheme; but as there are no logical arguments anywhere in his works in support of his stance on these points, a necessary conclusion is that his choices were entirely based on *a priori* value judgements. It has been pointed out that

> many of Hayek's arguments are, like Hume's, largely negative. They do not so much establish a case for accepting particular liberal principles as show what

problems face the critics of liberal individualism who wish to restructure society to ensure the distribution of benefits and burdens in accordance with, for example, preferred conceptions of desert or need or merit. (Kukathas, 1989, p. 84)

But as for possible objections that could be raised against a proposal of market socialism with fully autonomous firms, for instance objections concerning incentive systems, risks of authoritarianism possibly entailed in the monopoly of production means, drawbacks inherent in a systematic separation of ownership and control,[26] etc., it will be worth emphasizing again that they have never been specifically dealt with in any of Hayek's works.[27]

As mentioned above, whatever his strictures against socialism, Hayek constantly opposed centrally planned economies and not market socialism with autonomous firms. But 'to attack an extreme position when it is not clear that a more moderate position is open to the same *kind* of objections', Viner wrote, 'may be, depending on the historical context, to attack a straw man' (Viner, 1961, p. 109).[28] Consequently it is not surprising that hardly anything is to be found, in Hayek's writings, for an effective critique of market socialism with autonomous firms.

Notes

1. As has rightly been observed, the only alternative to the free play of market forces that Hayek conceives of is an institution in which it is the government that makes all the decisions (see Dasgupta, 1982, p. 214 and Tomlinson, 1990, pp. 23–4).
2. In the wake of Mises, Hayek too was an advocate of a value-free economic science. Viewed against the background of the arguments quoted above, however, this is not in contrast with his impassioned vindication of economic liberalism (on this paradox of Austrian economic thought, see Kirzner (1976), who tries to solve the apparent contradiction, and Sowell (1987), who conversely sees Hayek as one of the greatest exponents of one of two conflicting 'visions' differing in aspects of a non-scientific nature).
3. In this connection, Barry wrote that 'part of the task of unravelling Hayek's complex system of ideas involves separating normative statements from scientific' (see Barry, 1979, p. 5).
4. For an enunciation of the neo-Austrian research programme, see Rizzo (1982) and Langlois (1982). An exposition of Hayek's thought concerning the nature of market economy is found, e.g., in Barry (1979), ch. 3, Gray (1984), part II, and Jossa (1992a).
5. In this connection Lange quoted Engels (1886), p. 354 and reported the very words of Marx (1867), p. 92: 'my standpoint is one from which the development of the economic formation is viewed as a process of natural history'.
6. The propositions of Lange discussed here are consequently not those expounded in the celebrated 1936–37 article (Lange, 1936–37), but those he set forth in later years. For a more detailed analysis of Lange's thought concerning market socialism, see Jossa (1991 and 1992b). It is worth mentioning, however, that even today theorists analysing Lange's thought on market socialism usually fail to mention that, as early as 1942 and later on in even greater detail in his 1958 treatise, Lange spoke of market socialism with autonomous firms (see, e.g., Lavoie, 1986, pp. 215–21).
7. An author who has still recently contended that 'Hayek, after all, has expended a good part of his critical talents criticizing the theory of market socialism as both impracticable and ethically indefensible' (see Di Quattro, 1986, p. 308) continues to refer to Hayek's early writings of the 1930s and, above all, fails to point out that Hayek's strictures were never directed against market socialism *with autonomous firms*. In connection with Lange's

model with autonomous firms, consequently, one will hardly subscribe to Lavoie's contention that the core issues underlying economic calculations in socialist economies have in no way been affected by the substitution of market socialism for central planning, because market socialism models are still based on the 'abstract formulation of optima at the expense of any consideration of the mechanism by which this aim might be realised' (Lavoie, 1985, p. 123).

8. The above contention has been quoted by several authors and has come in for varying comments; and there are some who contend that it betrays an element of confusion in Hayek's thought (see Houle, 1989, p. 202, n. 1).

9. Among those who contend that Hayek accepts conscious human action on institutions, see, e.g., Kukathas (1989), pp. 86–105.

10. Therefore it is improper to say, as Hayek seems to do, that 'the spontaneous rules are rules of conduct in opposition to the artificially created ones, which are rules of organization' (see Galeotti, 1987, p. 289).

11. Some, however, have gone so far as to take it for granted (and not entirely without reason) that if lashing workers were an efficient system, it would certainly be envisaged in the employment contracts of free workers (see de Meza, 1992, p. 168).

12. For a view in support of Hayek's stance on this point, see, on the contrary, Lagueux (1989).

13. Cagliozzi has rightly argued that the distinction between planned and non-planned institutions is quite a vague one (see Cagliozzi, 1990, pp. 89 et seq.; also see, in this respect, Arnold, 1980, pp. 229–30).

14. For further details and a comment on Hayek's thought on this subject, see Dietze (1977) and Barry (1979), ch. 5.

15. In extolling the universal and abstract character of law Hayek also adds that it must not tend to attain any specific or concrete ends (see Hayek, 1979, p. 109). This claim of Hayek's, however, has rightly been termed unsustainable, since 'all statute law is enacted to achieve certain concrete purposes, whether it be as broad as prohibiting theft or as narrow as proscribing entry into a specific defense installation without authorization' (see Hamowy, 1982, p. 382).

16. Also the distinction between order and organization is consequently a vague one (see Kukathas, 1989, pp. 103–4 and Houle, 1989, pp. 201–2).

17. Among those who want to emphasize that in Hayek's view legislation must often correct law are Dietze (1977), p. 133 et seq. and Shearmur (1986), pp. 212–16.
    For stances recalling Hayek's, see, e.g. Brough and Naka (1989).

18. Views recalling Harrod's are found both in Robbins (1961), pp. 123 et seq., and in Gray (1980), whilst Gray (1984), pp. 129–30, sets forth arguments apt to defend Hayek against criticisms of this kind.

19. As has been written, 'to assert freedom in the political arena is on a lower or less good level than market freedom requires more than an economic analysis' (see Sufrin, 1961, p. 141).

20. According to Hayek, 'nothing distinguishes more clearly conditions in a free country from those in a country under arbitrary government than the observance in the former of the great principles known as the Rule of the Law' (see Hayek, 1944, p. 54).

21. According to Dasgupta, these statements of Hayek's 'are so astonishing that it is hard to believe that he takes them seriously' (see Dasgupta, 1982, p. 216).

22. Since Hayek seems to have approved of some kinds of state action rewarding merit in matters other than economic, some have pointed to the contradiction inherent in his negation of the importance of merit in economic matters (see Wilhelm, 1972, p. 172).

23. According to Dasgupta, any comparison with the blind forces of nature is out of place, for 'to leave society to the mercies of the free-play of market forces is itself a social decision' (see Dasgupta, 1982, p. 216).

24. The problem discussed here is to a large extent a mere issue of terminology and 'if, in a political discussion, a Hayekian were to say to one who describes the market as unjust (or just) that he is guilty of a philosophical 'category mistake', in Hayek's word, the latter is

more likely to regard it as academic pedantry rather than constructive criticism' (see Gordon, 1981, p. 480).

25.   In this connection it will be interesting to note that according to Friedman 'payment in accordance with product has been, and, in large measure, still is one of [the] accepted value judgements or institutions' (see Friedman, 1962, p. 167).

26.   As for the separation of ownership and control in Austrian theory, see, e.g., Reekie (1984), ch. 6.

27.   Perhaps it is useful explicitly to remark that the arguments against market socialism which are set forth in Hayek's well known writings on economic calculation in socialism (Hayek, 1935 and 1940 and Vaughn, 1980) are not relevant for a market socialism with autonomous firms (in which managers and/or workers are rewarded with a share of the profits).

28.   On the extent to which a historical perspective is lacking in Hayek's works, see, e.g., Schumpeter (1946), p. 647 and Wilhelm (1972), pp. 171–2.

References

Arnold, R.A. (1980), 'Hayek and Institutional Reform', reprinted in Wood and Woods (1991).

Barry, N.P. (1979), *Hayek's Social and Economic Philosophy*, London: Macmillan.

Bobbio, N. (1970), 'Dell'uso delle grandi dicotomie nella teoria del diritto', in Bobbio (1977).

Bobbio, N. (1977), *Dalla struttura alla funzione; nuovi studi di teoria del diritto*, Edizioni di Comunità.

Brough, W.T. and S. Naka (1989), 'Man, the Market and the Transfer State', in Leube and Zlabinger (1989).

Buchanan, J.M. (1975), *The Limits of Liberty Between Anarchy and Leviathan*, Chicago; partial Italian translation *I limiti della libertà*, Quaderni di 'Biblioteca della libertà', no. 16, 1978.

Buchanan, J.M. (1976), *Law and the Invisible Hand*, reprinted in *Freedom in Constitutional Contract* (1979), College Station, Texas.

Cagliozzi, R. (1990), *Oggettività e intenzione nell'analisi economica*, Napoli: Liguori.

Chilosi, A. (ed.) (1992), *L'economia del periodo di transizione*, Bologna: Il Mulino.

Dasgupta, P. (1982), 'Utilitarianism, Information and Rights', in Sen and Williams (1982).

De Meza, D. (1992), 'Critical review of T. Eggertsson, *Economic Behaviour and Institutions'*, *Economic Journal*, January 1992.

Diamond, A.M. Jr. (1980), 'F.A. Hayek on Constructivism and Ethics', reprinted in Wood and Woods (1991), vol. 3.

Dietze, G. (1977), 'Hayek on the Rule of Law', in Machlup (1977).

Di Quattro, A. (1986), 'Rawls versus Hayek', in *Political Theory*, **14**, May.

Dolan, E.G. (ed) (1976), *The Foundations of Modern Austrian Economics*, Kansas City: Sheed and Ward.

Dostaler, M. and D. Ethier (eds) (1989), *Friedrich Hayek. Philosophie, économie et politique*, Paris: Economica.

Eatwell, J., M. Milgate and P. Newman (eds) (1989), *The New Palgrave, the Invisible Hand*, London: Macmillan.

Einaudi, L. (1964), *Lezioni di politica sociale*, Torino: Einaudi.

Engels, F. (1878), *Antidühring*, English translation London: Lawrence and Wishart, 1955.

Engels, F. (1886), *Ludwig Feuerbach and the End of Classical German Philosophy*, in Marx and Engels (1958), vol. II.

Friedman, M. (1962), *Capitalism and Freedom*, Chicago: University of Chicago Press.

Galeotti, A.E. (1987), 'Individualism, Social Rules, Tradition: the Case of Friedrich A. Hayek', reprinted in Wood and Woods (1991).

Gordon, S. (1981), 'The Political Economy of F.A. Hayek', in *Canadian Journal of Economics*, **14**, August, 470–87.

Grassl, W. and B. Smith (eds) (1986), *Austrian Economics*, Sidney: Croom Helm,

Gray, J.N. (1980), 'F.A. Hayek on Liberty and Tradition', reprinted in Wood and Woods (1991), vol. 3.

Gray, J.N. (1984), *Hayek on Liberty*, Oxford: Basil Blackwell.

Hamowy, R. (1978), 'Law and the Liberal Society: F.A. Hayek's Constitution of Liberty', reprinted in Wood and Woods (1991).
Hamowy, R. (1982), 'The Hayekian Model of Government in an Open Society', reprinted in Wood and Woods (1991).
Harrod, R.F. (1946), 'Professor Hayek on Individualism', in *Economic Journal,* 56, (223), 435–42.
Hayek, F.A. von (1935), 'The Nature and History of the Problem', reprinted in Hayek (1948).
Hayek, F.A. von (1940), 'Socialist Calculation: the Competitive "Solution"', reprinted in Hayek (1948).
Hayek, F.A. von (1944), *The Road to Serfdom,* London: Routledge & Sons.
Hayek, F.A. von (1946), 'Individualism: True and False', reprinted in Hayek (1948).
Hayek, F.A. von (1948), *Individualism and Economic Order,* Chicago: The University of Chicago Press.
Hayek, F.A. von (1960), *The Constitution of Liberty,* London: Routledge & Kegan Paul.
Hayek, F.A. von (1968), 'The Confusion of Language in Political Thought', in Hayek (1978).
Hayek, F.A. von (1973a), *Law, Legislation and Liberty,* vol. I, *Rules and Order*, Chicago: The University of Chicago Press.
Hayek, F.A. von (1973b), 'Liberalism', in Hayek (1978).
Hayek, F.A. von (1973c), 'The Place of Menger's *Grundsätze* in the History of Economic Thought', in Hayek (1978).
Hayek, F.A. von (1973d), *Economic Freedom and Representative Government*, London: Institute of Economic Affairs.
Hayek, F.A. von (1975), 'The Pretence of Knowledge', in Hayek (1978).
Hayek, F.A. von (1976a), *Law, Legislation and Liberty,* vol. II, *The Mirage of Social Justice,* Chicago: University of Chicago Press.
Hayek, F.A. von (1976b), 'Socialism and Science', in Hayek (1978).
Hayek, F.A. von (1976c), 'The Atavism of Social Justice', in Hayek (1978).
Hayek, F.A. von (1978), *New Studies in Philosophy, Politics and the History of Ideas*, London: Routledge & Kegan Paul.
Hayek, F.A. von (1979), *Law, Legislation and Liberty,* vol. III, *The Political Order of a Free People*, Chicago: University of Chicago Press.
Hayek, F.A. von (1982), *Legge, legislazione e libertà,* Italian translation, Milan: Il Saggiatore (1986).
Hayek, F.A. von (1988), *The Fatal Conceit; the Errors of Socialism*, London: Routledge & Kegan Paul.
Houle, F. (1989), 'Hayek et la justice redistributive', in Dostaler and Ethier (1989).
Jossa, B. (1991), 'Keynes and Lange on the public enterprise', in *Contributions to Political Economy,* vol. X.
Jossa, B. (1992a), *Il liberalismo di Hayek,* Naples: Quaderni del Dipartimento di Scienze economiche e sociali, no. 1.
Jossa, B. (1992b), 'Socialismo di mercato e distribuzione del reddito', in Chilosi (1992).
Kirzner, I.M. (1976), 'Philosophical and Ethical Implications of Austrian Economics', in Dolan (1976).
Kirzner, I.M. (ed.) (1982), *Method, Process and Austrian Economics; Essays in Honor of Ludwig von Mises,* Lexington: Lexington Books.
Kukathas, C. (1989), *Hayek and Modern Liberalism,* Oxford: Clarendon Press.
Lagueux, M. (1989), 'Ordre spontané et darwinisme méthodologique chez Hayek', in Dostaler and Ethier (1989).
Lange, O. (1936–37), 'On the Economic Theory of Socialism', *The Review of Economic Studies,* IV (1 and 2), reprinted in Lange and Taylor (1938).
Lange, O. (1942), 'The Economic Operation of a Socialist Society', first published in *Contributions to Political Economy,* 6, March 1987.
Lange, O. (1956), 'How I See the Polish Economic Model', in Lange (1970).
Lange, O. (1958), *Political Economy,* Vol. I, English translation, Oxford: Pergamon Press, 1970.

Lange, O. (1970), *Papers in Economics and Sociology*, English translation, Oxford: Pergamon Press, 1970.

Lange, O. and F.M. Taylor (1938), *On the Economic Theory of Socialism*, ed. by B.E. Lippincott, London: McGraw Hill Book Company.

Langlois, R.N. (1982), 'Austrian Economics as Affirmative Science: Comment on Rizzo', in Kirzner (1982).

Lavoie, D. (1985), *Rivalry and Central Planning: the Socialist Calculation Debate Reconsidered*, Cambridge: Cambridge University Press.

Lavoie, D. (1986), 'The Market as a Procedure for Discovery and Conveyance of Inarticulate Knowledge', reprinted in Wood and Woods (1991).

Le Grand J. and S. Estrin (eds) (1969), *Market Socialism*, Oxford: Clarendon Press.

Leoni, B. (1961), *Freedom and the Law*, Princeton, N.J.: Van Nostrand.

Leube, K.R. and A.H. Zlabinger (eds) (1989), *The Political Economy of Freedom; Essays In Honor of F.A. Hayek*, Munich: Philosophia Verlag.

Machlup, F. (ed) (1977), *Essays on Hayek*, London: Routledge & Kegan Paul.

Marx, K. (1867), *Capital*, vol. I, English translation, Harmondsworth: Penguin Books.

Marx, K. and F. Engels (1958), *Selected Works*, London: Lawrence and Wishart.

Nozick, R. (1974), *Anarchy, State and Utopia*, Oxford: Basil Blackwell.

O'Driscoll, G.P., (1977), 'Spontaneous Order and the Coordination of Economic Activities', in Spadaro (1978).

Okun, A. (1975), *Equality and Efficiency: the Big Trade-off*, Washington.

Pantaleoni, M. (1925), *Erotemi di economia*, Bari: Laterza.

Petroni, A. and S. Monti Bragadin (1986), 'Introduzione' to Hayek (1982).

Plant, R. (1989), 'Socialism, Markets and End States', in Le Grand and Estrin (1989).

Popper, K. (1966), *The Open Society and its Enemies*, Princeton, N.J.: Princeton University Press.

Reekie, W.D. (1984), *Markets, Entrepreneurs and Liberty; an Austrian View of Capitalism*, Brighton: Wheatsheaf Books.

Rizzo, M.J. (1982), 'Mises and Lakatos: a Reformulation of Austrian Methodology', in Kirzner (1982).

Robbins, L. (1961), 'Hayek on Liberty', reprinted in Wood and Woods (1991), vol. II.

Schumpeter, J.A. (1946), 'Review of *The Road to Serfdom*', reprinted in Wood and Woods (1991), vol. II.

Sen, A. and B. Williams (eds) (1982), *Utilitarianism and Beyond*, Cambridge: Cambridge University Press.

Shearmur, J. (1986), 'The Austrian Convention: Hayek's Liberalism and the Thought of Carl Menger', in Grassl and Smith (1986).

Sowell, T. (1987), *A Conflict of Visions: Ideological Origins of Political Struggles*, New York: Quied William Morrow.

Spadaro, L.M. (ed.) (1978), *New Directions in Austrian Economics*, Kansas City: Sheed Andrews and McMeel.

Sufrin, S.C. (1961), 'Some Reflections on Hayek's *The Constitution of Liberty*', reprinted in Wood and Woods (1991), vol. II.

Tomlinson, J. (1990), *Hayek and the Market*, London: Pluto Press.

Vaughn, K.I. (1980), 'Economic Calculation Under Socialism: the Austrian Contribution', *Economic Inquiry*, **XVIII**, October.

Vaughn, K.I. (1987), 'Invisible Hand' in Eatwell, Milgate and Newman (1987).

Viner, J. (1961), 'Hayek on Freedom and Coercion', reprinted in Wood and Woods (1991), vol. II.

Wilhelm, M.M. (1972), 'The Political Thought of Friedrich A. Hayek', reprinted in Wood and Woods (1991), vol. II.

Wood, J.C. and R.N. Woods (eds) (1991), *Friedrich A. Hayek: Critical Assessments*, vols I–IV, London: Routledge & Kegan Paul.

5 Hayek and the several faces of socialism

Laurence S. Moss

The title of this paper is somewhat misleading. I only discuss 'two faces', and it is not socialism per se that really interests me here. Instead, I am interested in the impact that Hayek's forays with certain variants of socialist thought had on the evolution of his scientific work. Hayek's publications spanned seven decades – nearly the entire twentieth century – and it seems to have become commonplace in the secondary literature to remark that sometime during the 1950s Hayek gave up formal theoretical economics for politics, philosophy and history (Caldwell, 1988; Colonna, 1990; Lawson, Chapter 7, this volume). I believe this verdict is somewhat harsh despite the fact that Hayek at one time seemed to agree with it (Caldwell, 1988, p. 513; Hayek, 1967, pp. vii). What I detect in Hayek's economics is something of a fundamental shift in understanding about the nature of the economic system itself. This altered understanding certainly does owe something to Hayek's disputes with the socialist writers as I shall explain below (see Caldwell, Chapter 6, this volume).

The economy can be thought of as a deliberate arrangement or organization such as a huge household that needs to be managed. In this case, various resources are assigned tasks all under the control of a patriarchal leader. The leader strives to maximize some measure of performance, such as household income, family net worth, or household welfare. Hayek's achievement (one that is still not appreciated in our time) was to break with this household management view and maintain that the economic system is an 'ordered structure' consisting of reliable institutions (mostly abstract rules as embodied in customs and business procedures). The abstract rules (rules about property, contracts, commercial ethics and etiquette) are generated spontaneously and assist private households in coordinating their plans and therefore increase the chances that their otherwise separate plans will be fulfilled. For Hayek, the economy is emphatically not a single household. It is a 'catallaxy,' Hayek explained, thereby rehabilitating a much older term in the history of economics.[1]

Although much has been made by modern Austrians of Hayek's supposed abandonment of Walrasian equilibrium models encouraged by the positions he took during the economic calculation debates of the 1920s and 1930s, I do not find this an accurate statement of what actually occurred. As I argue in the next section, Hayek remained keenly interested in the coordinative features of the pricing system. In so far as I believe this is the *essential* problem that is addressed by Walrasian models, I find it difficult to apply the 'anti-Walrasian' label to Hayek, for reasons explained in a later section.

After that I offer some interpretive evidence that refers to the principal argument of Hayek's most ambitious work, *The Pure Theory of Capital* (1941). I show that Hayek remained keenly interested in general equilibrium reasoning despite its limitations and despite its tendency to mask certain problems that interested him in that work. If a 'Hayekian moment' must be found when some critically decisive analytic *volte face* occurred in Hayek's thought, it came when he published his most celebrated and widely read attack against socialism in 1944 under the title *The Road to Serfdom*. That book was written to confront the authoritarian, indeed, violent side of socialism that Hayek found implicit in the programmes of 'socialists of all parties' (1944, p. ii). The argument of this avowedly 'political' tract throws light on the evolution of Hayek's thoughts about the economic system as a catallaxy and not a household. For this reason, I devote a whole section of this paper to that work.

Thereafter I point to the seminal importance of Hayek's Freiburg lecture delivered at the Walter Eucken Institute and published the next year, 'The Confusion of Language in Political Thought,' to identify a heroic shift in Hayek's understanding of the market that gave a specific shape to his writings over the last several decades of his life. The second volume of *Law, Legislation, and Liberty* and, later, his *Fatal Conceit* offer additional clear statements of his views about the economy as a catallaxy (Hayek, 1976a; Hayek, 1988).

Hayek's appreciation of the market order required breaking with the household economics metaphor and appreciating that markets are amazing networks of abstract rules that help coordinate the otherwise separate and diverse plans of individual agents. In the final section, I show that this break with household economics did not require any abandonment by Hayek of his interest in general equilibrium economics.

Lessons from the economic calculation debate

Ludwig von Mises challenged the socialists to explain how they would assign prices and make economic calculations once the buying and selling of the means of production (i.e., capital equipment) were abolished as part of the nationalization of industry (Mises, 1920; 1949). Mises was convinced that no satisfactory solution would be forthcoming and that attempts to instruct government administrators to 'play capitalist manager' would produce only disappointing results.[2] Without stock markets or their equivalent, economic calculation under socialism was logically impossible and reports of famine in the land would soon swamp the office of the socialist minister of production. It was this sweeping epistemological claim coupled with a dismal forecast that infuriated Mises's socialist critics (Mises, 1920, pp. 107–14).

Hayek took up his mentor's fight against the socialists but dropped the categorical assertiveness that coloured Mises's writings. Hayek pointed out certain practical but enormously important difficulties duplicating the market process once nationalization had been completed. According to Caldwell, 'most of what Hayek wrote [during the economic calculation debate] ... could easily be mistaken for the work of standard neoclassical economists' (Caldwell, 1988, p. 534). Vaughn correctly pointed out that many of Hayek's practical problems during the 1920s and 1930s have become the great theoretical issues of the 1970s (Vaughn, 1980, pp. 551–2). Vaughn was referring to the problems of incentives, disaggregated information and information-processing limitations that face all decision makers, especially those who would attempt to fulfil the primary duty of the central planning authority (the allocation of scarce resources so as to make the community more prosperous) (Vaughn, 1980, pp. 551–2; cf. Hurwicz, 1973, and Rothschild, 1973). To Vaughn's list, Streissler added Hayek's emphasis on the heterogeneity of commodities, especially capital goods (see Streissler, Chapter 3, this volume). Vaughn and Streissler also pointed to the Austrian insight that the costs that inform rational choice are forgone opportunities not easily measured by the accounting prices that the socialists were prepared to assign (Vaughn, 1980, p. 550). Apparently the commentators agree that it was 'in response to the arguments of the market socialists that ... Hayek began to develop [his] own insights concerning information and discovery' (Caldwell, 1988, p. 534; Butos, 1985; Caldwell, Chapter 6, this volume).

In 1937, Lange published the second part of his spirited defence of how a socialist economy can operate efficiently while still achieving important socialist goals and objectives such as the elimination of monopoly, cyclical unemployment, distributional inequality and lack-lustre economic growth (1937). Lange offered an elaboration of the 'trial and error' method that was first proposed by Taylor in 1928. The two essays are often read together and are known for offering the 'trial and error' solution to the economic problem of calculation under socialism (Lange and Taylor, 1956).

According to Lange and Taylor, a central planning board would establish all commodity and factor prices as accounting prices initially on a trial basis, with periodic adjustments thereafter. The socialist managers in charge of each establishment (firm) would pledge themselves to follow certain general and abstract rules. The rules included always running production up to the level at which marginal cost of production equals the state-administered selling price; and choosing the cheapest technique of production to produce supply (Lange and Taylor, 1956, p. 73). The central planning board would sequentially revise the accounting prices upwards or downwards to eliminate shortages and surpluses as they might emerge in particular markets. Lange and Taylor claimed that the unintended but not unexpected consequence of this system of 'liberal socialism' is that a set of prices would emerge for all traders that would promote an efficient allocation of resources. They believed that the managerial rules would replicate that pattern of prices suggested by the Walrasian general equilibrium model without the nagging problems of unemployed resources and monopoly.

In a remarkable paper written in 1940, Hayek set out to show that the 'competitive solution' to the economic calculation problem established by Lange and Taylor was not really a solution at all (Hayek, 1940). Hayek carefully examined the managerial rules that were to be established by the central planning board. He stated that they were unworkable because the relevant costs are those related to a 'consideration of the returns expected' from a piece of capital equipment, which cannot be known 'unless there is competition' (Hayek, 1949, p. 229). By competition Hayek meant a process of genuine discovery that arises whenever entrepreneurs compete to reshuffle resources (Hayek, 1969; cf. Kirzner, 1985 and Böhm, Chapter 8, this volume). Hayek (following Mises) insisted that without a genuine market for the means of production such a real competition was impossible under market socialism.

Hayek's several papers on economic calculation under socialism were regarded favourably (Hurwicz, 1973, p. 28). Indeed, his name was immortalized in the burgeoning postwar textbook literature as a prescient critic of liberal socialism. For example, in Halm's text Hayek is presented as being sceptical about the prospect of socialist managers becoming entrepreneurs (Halm, 1962, pp. 208–9). During the 1960s, when the managerial reforms in the old Soviet Union and other parts of Eastern Europe became publicized in the West, Hayek's prescient criticisms of socialist planning were noted (Bergson, 1967, p. 662). In an influential article published in 1967, Harvard economist Bergson reviewed the economic calculation controversy and specifically agreed with Hayek about the practical impossibility of setting prices for 'an entire economy' (p. 662). Unlike his teacher Mises, Hayek had admitted that economic calculation under socialism was logically possible. He maintained, however, that the required calculations would be impossible to administer (Hayek, 1940, pp. 182–3).

In 1980, twelve years after Bergson, Vaughn revisited the older economic calculation controversy and provided a stimulating reassessment of Hayek's position. Vaughn concluded that the economic calculation debate made Hayek critical of Walrasian modelling in economics. In her words, 'Walrasian models [leave] out important features of real markets that generate efficient outcomes,' and economists who try to simulate the results of Walras's simultaneous equations (as Lange and Taylor apparently wanted to do) may end up with a blemished and highly inefficient economy (Vaughn, 1980, p. 535).

For example, Walrasian models consider production a matter of simply combining well defined inputs in accordance with known recipes. In fact, production involves organizational structures and incentive systems that encourage loyalty and hard work. How will a socialist central planning board provide adequate incentives and conduct a responsible monitoring of the managers? Socialist-appointed managers may prove to be disloyal and capable of shirking responsibility and avoiding risky decisions. Hayek maintained that without the threat of job loss and reorganization such as provided by the 'takeover' mechanisms in the market for corporate control, it is unclear how socialist planners can avoid stagnating economies (Hayek, 1940, pp. 200–201).

Second, real-world exchange often involves using equipment that is both special and unique. Well defined markets do not exist for this equipment and the board may not know what to call a particular machine or how to create a market for it. The market system encourages those with specialized information to come forward and take positions by either purchasing special task equipment or investing in organizations that are themselves set up to seize such opportunities.

Hayek insisted that the special task of the price system is to provide incentives that encourage individuals who may possess circumstantially relevant business information to utilize that information. The price system functions to provide for a more effective and efficient allocation of knowledge in society under circumstances where the knowledge is not in any one place (Hayek, 1949, pp. 83–4). In 1976, Hayek described the market order in game-theoretic terms but at the same time harking back to his familiar theme that the price system helps communicate information. Hayek wrote:

> ...the market system. ... is a wealth-creating game ... one that leads to an increase of the stream of goods and of the prospects of all participants to satisfy their needs. ... The chief cause of the wealth-creating character of the game is that the returns of the efforts of each player act as the signs which enable him to contribute to the satisfaction of needs of which he does not know, and to do so by taking advantage of conditions of which he also learns only indirectly through their being reflected in the prices of the factors of production which they use. It is thus a wealth-producing game because it supplies to each player information which enables him to provide for needs of which he has no direct knowledge and by the use of means of the existence of which without it he would have no cognizance, thus bringing about the satisfaction of a greater range of needs than would otherwise be possible. (Hayek, 1976a, p. 115)

The mechanisms of adjustment are impersonal and while the market order can be appreciated, even understood, it cannot be charted, measured and recorded in all its multifarious details. The output of a household can be measured but not that of a complex densely populated market order (Hayek, 1988, pp. 109–15).

Walrasian models not only ignored circumstantially relevant information but assumed that the knowledge that was needed to produce general equilibrium was mostly technological and readily available to all agents without cost or expense (Hayek, 1949, p. 90n). This ruled out any effort to understand another important function provided by the price system, namely, that it facilitates information retrieval and utilization. It does this without the need for first translating that information into a format suitable for central agency data collection. During the 1970s, important efforts were made to reconcile general equilibrium models with complex informational conditions, especially those associated with disequilibrium (Shubik, 1975).

To sum up: Vaughn–Caldwell–Streissler contend that the economic calculation debate informed Hayek as to just how weak the socialists' understanding of the economy really was. Hayek's insights about the market process, especially as a device to encourage the utilization of information, made him impatient with socialists like Lange and Taylor and with other proponents of planning such as Leontief (Hayek, 1976b).

Hayek and general equilibrium

I do not believe that Hayek became disenchanted with general equilibrium tools of analysis as a result of the economic calculation controversy and (thus) retreated after 1940 from economics into politics, philosophy and history. In my opinion, no such disillusionment took place as a result of that controversy, nor of any other controversy, despite Hayek's consistent warning that the equilibrium concepts could mislead.[3] It had been a catechism to Hayek and other Austrians that models, whether they be 'Walrasian' or not, are simply fictions that can be more or less useful in helping us understand an actual market process in time (Hayek, 1941, p. 21). The fictions had to be handled properly because they can easily mislead, as often happened when policy makers drew plans of action from simple equilibrium settings.

Caldwell set the matter right when he wrote, 'it is ... clear that Hayek believe[d] that any legitimate economic explanation must employ *some* notion of equilibrium' (1988, p. 524, original emphasis). Caldwell reminded us that, in 1937, Hayek pioneered an improved notion of equilibrium that addressed the compatibility of agents' plans (Caldwell, 1988; Böhm, 1986). Agents' respective plans will be compatible 'only as long as [their] expectations ... correspond to the external data'. How agents acquire perceptions that come into agreement with one another and with the external data involves considerations about the market process in which information is acquired (Lachmann, 1976, p. 60). Hayek identified the central question of all social science as follows:

> How can the combination of fragments of knowledge existing in different minds bring about results which, if they were to be brought about deliberately, would require a knowledge on the part of the directing mind which no single person can possess? (Hayek, 1949, p. 54)

Apparently, Hayek was bothered about the particular models of his day. They assumed that 'knowledge of the external facts [was] given to every agent' and in this way did not assist in the appreciation of markets and competition as institutional devices that lead to the search, discovery and utilization of those external facts. Hayek advanced a different conception of equilibrium that emphasized the importance of plan coordination over merely reactive mechanical behaviour (Hayek, 1949; cf. Arena, Chapter 10, Volume I of this series).

Hayek also warned that sometimes the almost exclusive focus on final equilibrium conditions, such as the details of the stationary state construction, disguised the importance of the study of market adjustments. He considered it particularly important to understand how the capital stock adjusts to changes in overall market conditions, and he made this the subject of perhaps the greatest and most challenging of his economic works (Hayek, 1941).

Walrasian models in *The Pure Theory of Capital*
The use of the term 'Walrasian' to dismiss certain theoretical models as 'non-Austrian' became commonplace in the writings of various Austrian writers, especially during the Austrian revival of the 1970s.[4] Whereas Kirzner and Lachmann used the term with some deference to scholarly protocol, the Walrasian label became a term of ridicule and derision among the younger members of the reconstituted Austrian school. Indeed, it was used to describe an approach that supposedly stripped economics of much of what modern Austrian writers found important and useful. Thus, one writer complained that Walras's approach 'supplanted classical sequential analysis' and 'contained inner contradictions that had to be resolved before a satisfactory theoretical edifice could be constructed' (O'Driscoll, 1977, p. 150). Another commentator argued that Hayek retreated from equilibrium analysis after recognizing its limitations (Butos, 1985, p. 341). More cautiously, Vaughn suggested that it was the unrealism of the Walrasian approach that bothered Hayek when Lange and Taylor recommended the trial and error procedure for obtaining 'the' Walrasian results (Vaughn, 1980).

During the 1970s, I was not persuaded that Hayek's opposition to Walrasian economics was as total and uncompromising as the modern Austrian writers maintained. I am still not convinced that the textual evidence points to any retreat into the quicksand of radical subjectivism as some writers insist (Butos, 1985). In support of my thesis that Walrasian general equilibrium notions were important to Hayek throughout his career, let me first try to summarize what it was about Walrasian economics that interested Hayek and then demonstrate how he used equilibrium analysis in perhaps his most ambitious theoretical work – *The Pure Theory of Capital* – published *after* the economic calculation debate. There is in that book positive evidence that the Walrasian modelling approach was retained and employed in interesting ways. I shall also point to what is indeed anomalous about the argument of the book (Parts II and III, respectively) that may have started Hayek thinking about how economic activity in the sense of household management by a patriarch produces results that are entirely different from the results produced by a market order.

I shall use the expression 'Walrasian models' to refer to any economic model that emphasizes the interrelationships of known existing markets when they are competitive and individuals have well defined tastes (or plans) that they pursue within a given 'state of the art' and with some knowledge about the resources available to them.[5] Walrasian model builders often delight in showing that (as a matter of logic) an internally consistent set of prices exists such that all markets clear (no shortages or surpluses) and each agent finds that his plans coordinate with the plans of other agents (cf. Butos, 1985, p. 333). In other words, Walrasian models specify the formal relationships that must prevail in any economic system, regardless of its characteristic institutions, where scarce resources are utilized to satisfy wants (Bator, 1957). A stimulating discussion of what is contained in the 'core' of every Walrasian model is in Weintraub (1985, pp. 108–22).

Generations of Walrasian modellers, such as Hahn (1973), Patinkin (1965), and Arrow (1971) have used the Walrasian model to assess the impact different institutions (such as money, bonds or insurance contracts) have on the general equilibrium 'solution'. Comparative static results are then used for a variety of scientific purposes, as a logical aid in deriving hypotheses that are then subjected to empirical testing, or sometimes as a thought experiment that helps us appreciate the significance of the institutions by explaining how they function in a world where the 'interdependence of markets' is all pervasive (Weintraub, 1985, pp. 123–35).

In my opinion, there is nothing 'un-Austrian' about this practice. In this sense, the Walrasian model serves the same purpose for Hahn, Patinkin and Arrow as similar constructs such as the 'evenly rotating economy' did for Austrian writers like Mises (1949, pp. 244–50).

Hayek tried to improve on the general equilibrium approach of his day by emphasizing that the knowledge required to harness the resources of society towards the satisfaction of dispersed and privately held wants was not readily available in one place. Instead of a general equilibrium where all markets simultaneously clear and the passing of time has no significance whatsoever,

Hayek suggested that equilibrium exists only when individuals (who may not know each other) make decisions that produce precisely those results that make the simultaneous completion of their plans possible. In 1941, in the opening chapters of *The Pure Theory of Capital*, Hayek repeated this exact idea:

> The problems of capital or of investment, as here defined, are problems connected with the activity of making provision in the present for the more or less distant future... [An agent's] plans at any moment will be based on the expectations of a certain future state of the market which will allow him to dispose of his product at a certain price. ... But the ... 'state of the market' on which he counts is largely the result of the present decisions of other people. ... This means that although every individual will be guided only by (more or less well-founded) expectations of particular prices, he will actually be performing part of a larger process of the rest of which he knows little; and his success or failure will depend on whether what he does fits in with the other parts of that larger process which are undertaken or contemplated at the same time by other people. (Hayek, 1941, pp. 24–5)

Hayek reflected on his method of analysis as follows:

> The use of the equilibrium method here then means constructing an imaginary state in which the plans of the different people (entrepreneurs and consumers generally) are so adjusted to one another that each individual will be able to sell or buy exactly those quantities of commodities which he has been planning to sell or buy (Hayek, 1941, p. 26)

Hayek explained that his 'fictitious state of equilibrium,' in which the plans of one agent are coordinated with the plans of others, is 'indispensable' in understanding 'phenomena that are *ex definitione* absent in a stationary state' (Hayek, 1941, pp. 19, 27–8). The phenomena that interested Hayek included the processes of production utilized by an advanced industrial economy and how the value of a given stock of capital equipment and the income derived from it was affected by selected changes in economic conditions.

Hayek's *Pure Theory of Capital* was not a mere afterthought or a collection of notebook entries published just before he abandoned economics for politics, philosophy and history. The work is quite fundamental to his economics. Although, as Steedman pointed out, the book is complex and full of enigmas, I am inclined to support Fritz Machlup's verdict that the book is filled with 'some of the most penetrating thoughts on the subject that have ever been published' (Steedman, Chapter 1, this volume; Machlup, 1974).

In my opinion, *The Pure Theory of Capital* is a great theoretical work. It is filled with stimulating statements, clever asides, and lengthy methodological discussions of economic tools and their relationship to the study of capital goods (Hayek, 1941, ch. 2). Hayek presented his ideas nearly always within reach of the familiar Austrian idea that vertically integrated stages of production exist in which semifinished goods produced in the higher orders of production are passed down and sold to consumers in the lowest orders (Colonna, 1990, pp. 60–62). All resources and capital equipment draw their respective value from the expected output they help produce. Since a resource employed today will only 'pay its way' when the goods-in-process are finally sold at a later date, its value today is discounted (that is, each factor of production earns only a discounted marginal product). Hayek explained how the prices prevailing at each sequential state of production must be in a certain definite relationship to each other because markets 'remember' that today's resource is indeed productive only after the lapse of a period of time (Hayek, 1931, pp. 69–100; Hayek, 1941, pp. 285–93; Rothbard, 1962, pp. 502–59).

I shall begin with Part III of *The Pure Theory of Capital* and then discuss Part II. In Part III, Hayek offered a theoretical account of what must happen when there is a sudden shift in a community's willingness to consume. Two theoretical cases are distinguished: one is the fantasy case, in which everyone learns that life on earth is about to end and frantically begins to consume their capital; in the second case, a small part of the population simply decides to increase its saving (Hayek, 1941, p. 254). Hayek analyses the consequences of these (sudden) changes by looking ahead to see what price relationships must be fulfilled in a state of hypothetical general equilibrium. The sequential processes outlined in this part are imagined to occur in order to get us to general equilibrium. Hayek admitted that this analysis had not produced an explanation of the 'actual causal process' involved but was preliminary and necessary to such an investigation (Hayek, 1941, p. 248). In Hayek's words, his results are 'like the tâtonnements in Walras's analysis or Edgeworth's construction of recontracting, as successive attempts of the individuals to find out what the equilibrium position is' (1941, p. 248). Clearly, Walrasian models were important to Hayek's theoretical work and the economic calculation debate did not weaken his interest in this subject or Hayek's resolve to employ this modelling technique.

In Part II of his book, Hayek followed a technique of analysis that he learned from his teacher von Wieser (Hayek, 1941, p. 27n). This technique is of some interest because within just a few years' time Hayek would find the approach misleading and obscuring a proper appreciation of the market process and its operation. To see what is involved here, think of the economy as if it were a huge household. This is the method of analysis in which 'the actions of the different individuals are directed by somebody in accordance with a single plan' – the plan of the dictator or patriarch (Hayek, 1941, pp. 26–7, 99). Wieser's technique was to conceive of the economy as if it were one large household. The two advantages of the household model are that it impounds the diversity of tastes by reducing preferences to a single mind making fundamental decisions, and that the entire economy is managed as if it were a huge single authority and thus there is no need for a price system. In *The Pure Theory of Capital* Hayek termed this 'the case of the centrally directed communist society,' and in an earlier work he spoke of a dictator

> who himself ranges in order the different needs of the members of the society according to his views about their merits [and] has saved himself the trouble of finding out what people really prefer and [therefore] avoided the impossible task of combining the individual scales into an agreed common scale which expresses the general idea of justice. (Hayek, 1935, pp. 216–17; Hayek, 1941, pp. 26–7, 217)

Hayek admitted that the household model must be 'later ... abandoned in favour of the assumption of separate but perfectly matched plans of the different individuals' (Hayek, 1941, p. 27 and 247; cf. Steedman, Chapter 1, this volume). Hayek used this technique to show how the capital equipment must be reorganized by the dictator so as to permanently maintain a larger flow of real income.

In the subsequent Part III, Hayek outlined (as I have already mentioned) the set of price relationships that must be re-established and the sorts of reallocation of equipment that must occur if real income is to be permanently raised as a result of saving. In Part III the rearrangements are brought about not by a central authority but through the price system, which is assumed to be characterized by market structures that are perfectly competitive and agents who have enough timely information such that market prices quickly adjust to provide correct incentives and choke off errors that could result in massive failed investments.

What is the exact relationship that Hayek thought existed between the arguments presented in Part II involving the household management model and the rearrangements necessitated by a small group of net savers interacting in a market setting as discussed in Part III? The connection between Parts II and III is not explained. I guess that Hayek's main point was to show how the impersonal mechanisms of the market will simulate what a rational patriarch would do if he could manage the entire economy as he might manage a household. Consider Hayek's own remarks about his method:

> Until in Part III we explicitly introduce the market, it will be assumed that we have to deal with a closed economic system in which all economic activity is directed by a single will and according to a coherent plan. We shall deal...either with the economy of an isolated individual, or with that of a communist society where all economic activity is directed by a dictator. (Hayek, 1941, p. 99)

Hayek promised to make the transition from a single agent world to the multi-agent world:

> The transition from the study of equilibrium in a 'simple' economy to the study of equilibrium in a competitive economy ... means passing from the analysis of the plans of an individual to the analysis of the compatibility of the independent plans of a number of individuals. (Hayek 1941, p. 247)

According to Hayek, the act of saving requires a shifting around of the ownership and control of the means of production. In a market system, Hayek explained:

> [the resources] are divided between a number of persons. ... [and therefore] it will be necessary to exchange not only different final products but also intermediate products and the services of resources of all kinds. (Hayek, 1941, p. 249)

The ones who save for the future face a reduction in present consumption unless they planned ahead of time and increased their command over present consumers' goods with the idea of trading these goods off for claims to future goods. Hayek wrote:

> if they [the savers] want to maintain their available income at an even level they will have to increase the share of the consumers' goods in their possession which they cede to other members of the community. (Hayek, 1941, p. 257)

But the similarities and differences between the principles that regulate the reallocation of resources in a multi-agent market setting to the principles that regulate the reallocation in a single agent setting were not explored. Whatever Hayek set out to prove, it is clear that the market oriented readjustments explained in Part III produce results that are dramatically different from what the dictator accomplished in Part II. While a certain similarity is apparent, the magnitudes involved raise the spectre of too little private saving in the presence of externalities.[6] If Hayek were aware of the issues presented when attempting to reconcile the household management model of the economy with the market system model, he did not disclose this in the text itself. The issue of differences between the household management model and market order would surface however in a different context. That context was Hayek's blistering attack on authoritarian socialism and its roots in economic planning.

The Road to Serfdom
Hayek aficionados may express surprise that immediately after my discussion of the quite abstract and totally theoretical *The Pure Theory of Capital*, I

follow with a section on Hayek's most political and unabashedly polemical book. Interestingly, commentators on the economic calculation debate seldom mention this book and its arguments. *The Road to Serfdom* was written towards the end of World War II to warn those intellectuals who wished to retain the institutions of wartime planning in the period of peace (Moss, 1985). According to Hayek, what happened in Germany and Italy was neither an accident nor even a cultural aberration. Instead, he said that totalitarianism is what you get when impersonal market mechanisms are jettisoned for central planning (1944).

Hayek explained that totalitarianism does not come immediately. After a while it evolves as an unintended and unwelcome (but not unexpected) result of attempts to run the market system like a household. A pure-hearted statesman may set out to plan economic life within a framework of carefully articulated values including great respect for the dignity and autonomy of the individual. The statesman will learn that either his plans must be abandoned or else he must gradually become a totalitarian dictator to make certain that his plans reach fruition (Hayek, 1944, p. 135). A totalitarian dictator, according to Hayek, is one who casts aside morals and denies failure. All citizens become the means for the dictator to try to achieve his ends.

In Hayek's view the two central features of every collectivist system are the establishment of common group goals, and maximum power to achieve them. A planned economy must treat its members as the means to achieve those goals and ruthlessly punish or suppress behaviour that interferes or impedes the achievement of the wanted results. The individual, Hayek warns, becomes 'only a means to serve higher ends' (1944, p. 149).

The dictator must do what any patriarch needs to do. He must establish a hierarchy of values for his 'family.' The more intelligent the members of society and the more diverse their respective interests, the more arbitrary and impossible this task becomes (as any parent with teenagers at home soon discovers). That is why, Hayek explained, the totalitarian system will descend to lower and lower moral ideals and appeal to primitive instinct wherever possible. Racism, jingoism and fear rapidly become the currency of political power under the leadership of the dictator/patriarch. Hayek said of human nature that 'it is easier for people to agree on a negative program – on the hatred of an enemy, on the envy of those better off – than on any positive task' (Hayek, 1944, p. 139).

Hayek's strictures against central planning are of interest to us for several reasons. They show that when an economy is treated as if it were a single household then all individual members of that household lose their autonomy to the authority of the leader. That leader cannot allow 'individual conscience[s] free to apply [their] own rules' (Hayek, 1944, p. 146). The rules specify in detail goals individuals should pursue, and the great ideal of free societies, the so called 'rule of law,' is lost forever (Hayek, 1944, pp. 72–87; see also, Hayek, 1960).

Under the rule of law that accompanies the development of the market system, the rules are general and abstract; they are of the form, 'You shall not do this or that'. What should be done is left (mostly) to individual conscience. Thus, under a rule of law, cheating, stealing, torture, or betrayal of confidence is bad. Under a totalitarian regime, just about any means is acceptable so long as it furthers the plans of the leader. Thus, torture, disrespect for privacy, euthanasia of the sick and infirm and the elimination of all independence of mind are characteristics of totalitarian regimes (Hayek, 1944, pp. 147–8).

Hayek's political message is direct and straightforward. An economy run like a household would soon by the logic of household management, in the context of diverse self-interested agents, lead to an immoral and intolerable situation. I suspect that sometime between 1944 and 1967, when his article 'Confusion of Language in Political Thought' was published, Hayek had reached the conclusion that the household management model was fundamentally flawed as a representation of the market order.

The type of rationality provided by the market system is emphatically not the sort of rationality a patriarch applies to the management of a household (cf. Hayek, 1965; Hayek, 1968). This realization led Hayek to his most important contribution to understanding the economy.

Hayek's criticism of the household management metaphor

In the last decades of his life, Hayek unleashed a sustained and far-reaching attack on the household management metaphor, the cause of much confusion in economics.[7] He was bothered by the proposals that lay implicit in the planning models to manage the economy as if it were a gigantic household with a single end or neat hierarchy of ends in view. According to Hayek, the economy was a catallaxy and not a single organization to be managed by a single mind or small committee. In his 1968 essay, 'The Confusion of Language in Political Thought,' and also in his remarkable second volume to *Law, Legislation and Liberty* that appeared in 1976, Hayek linked that false search for social justice in economic affairs to this underlying misconception about the market system and its attendant institutions (Hayek, 1968; Hayek, 1976a). He criticized Aristotle for creating all the confusion in Book V of *Nicomachean Ethics* and thereby inaugurating the now centuries-old search for justice in exchange. The search for the 'just price' was a search for the precise rate of exchange that rewarded resource owners according to their social contribution to the nation, understood as an extended 'family'. Hayek declared that such a search was a chimera and would never bear fruit. It was based on a misunderstanding of what the market system is. Hayek explained:

What is commonly called a social or national economy is ... not a single economy but a network of many interlaced economies. Its order shares ... some formal characteristics [with a household economy] but not the most important one: its activities are not governed by a single scale or hierarchy of ends. ... While an economy proper is an organization in the technical sense in which we have defined that term, that is, a deliberate arrangement of the use of the means which are known to some single agency, the cosmos of the market neither is not nor could be governed by such a single scale of ends ... of all its separate members.

The confusion which has been created by the ambiguity of the word economy is so serious that for our present purposes it seems necessary to confine its use strictly to the original meaning in which it describes a complex of deliberately coordinated actions serving a single scale of ends, and to adopt another term to describe the system of numerous interrelated economies which constitute the market order. ... the order brought about by the mutual adjustment of many individual economies in a market. A catallaxy is thus the special kind of spontaneous order produced by the market through people acting within the rules of the law of property, tort, and contract. (1976a, pp. 108–9)

Already in *The Road to Serfdom*, but continuing in his 1968 essay, and again in *Law, Legislation and Liberty*, Hayek argued that household management is only possible in small groups such as families and perhaps primitive tribes (1944, p. 138; 1968, p. 89; 1976a, pp. 133–52; 1988, pp. 11–28). The group cannot grow large and culture cannot develop without personal tastes diverging. As the group grows larger the market order must be substituted for household management (Hayek, 1988, pp. 120–34). Unless this substitution takes place, a society of autonomous individuals cannot be maintained and at the same time be made to prosper.

In a market order or catallaxy, the individual members adopt general and abstract rules that are important because they increase the chances that any random individual can achieve his or her respective goals (Hayek, 1988, p. 131). The entire set of interrelated plans and experiences is coordinated not merely by the price system (as important as the price system is) but also by certain abstract rules that evolve and determine what needs to be priced and how. The abstract rules in the form of customs and laws help define what in fact is to be traded in accordance with what conditions (Hayek, 1988, pp. 66–88).

In his last book, *The Fatal Conceit*, Hayek explained that the market order becomes more effective not only when the group of participants expands in numbers but also when the population becomes ever more heterogenous with regard to particular skills and talents (Hayek, 1988, p. 122). I have dubbed this Hayek's 'law of increasing diversity' and it parallels his 1930s claims about the heterogeneity of capital goods as an obstacle in the way of economic planning (Hayek, 1935, pp. 188–9). The heterogeneity of labour that is occurring on a daily basis wreaks havoc in any listing of existing markets. As the number of markets expands, socialist attempts to develop a blueprint of the economy for the purpose of establishing the accounting prices must be revised. It is not simply a problem with solving many equations to get accounting prices; it is a matter of constantly having to revise the scope of what is traded by adding new equations. Attempts to plan and regulate will stifle the spontaneous adjustment associated with complex market orders.

Catallaxy and general equilibrium

If I am right in my claim that the key to a correct assessment of the impact of socialist thought on Hayek's scientific work is not a retreat from Walrasian economic modelling but rather a fundamental shift in thinking about the meaning of the type of coordination that is conceptualized by general equilibrium, then I should be able to point to examples in Hayek's later writings where the equilibrium approach is used despite his explicit adoption of the distinction between catallaxy and household. I shall draw attention to two such places but leave for another time an assessment of whether Hayek's use of these concepts is in all respects consistent with his view of the market system as a catallaxy.[8]

The first instance is in *Law, Legislation and Liberty* when Hayek asks us to think of the 'horizon of catallactic possibilities' as if it were 'represented by an n-dimensional surface' corresponding to n-goods (1976a, p. 119). Hayek goes on to show how the market system is capable of producing a maximum in only a limited technical sense. Since there is 'no agreed hierarchy of ends' we cannot speak of any global social maximum as we can in the economic management of a household. Again, general equilibrium analysis is not useless, it is simply silent on the broader questions involving social justice and ethics (1976a, pp. 109–15).

The second instance in which general equilibrium reasoning appears in the context of catallaxy is in *The Fatal Conceit* when Hayek credits the 'property rights school' with 'open[ing] new possibilities for future improvements in the legal framework of the market order' (1988, p. 36). The property rights school, headed by Ronald Coase, uses the maximization of output as the standard against which to evaluate changes in institutional rules such as property rights structures themselves (Moss, 1991). Can improvements in the market order be effected by an approach that likens the market order to a household bent on trying to maximize a single measure of output and presupposes a given hierarchy of ends by using market price as a measure of value?

The point is not to quarrel with Hayek, or even suggest that he himself was not entirely consistent in his own presentation of the catallaxy concept but simply to show that his encounters with the many faces of socialism did not chase him away from theoretical economics. Instead, it provided a much broader understanding of the economic problem that presages the development of a genuine calculus of coordination to replace the maximization of social product as the criterion for appreciating economic development.

Conclusion

I have demonstrated how Hayek's encounters with socialism, starting with the economic calculation debate in the 1920s and 1930s and culminating in his clear rejection of the dictator-household economics approach in *The Road to Serfdom* in 1944, were part of his lifelong battle against 'socialists of all parties'. These battles gave shape to Hayek's understanding of market order. In this search for the organizing principles of a modern capital-using economy, Hayek never faulted or in any way abandoned theoretical economics or the insights of general equilibrium. He did find fault with the socialists who misused a fictitious tool of analysis: namely, the single-agent household model, and therefore failed to appreciate the catallactic features of the market order.

I end with a note of some interest. Hayek's mentor, Mises, denied the logical possibility of economic calculation when the means of production had been nationalized. The socialists disagreed with Mises, setting off the economic calculation debate. During the course of that debate, Hayek sided with the socialists against Mises when he admitted the logical possibility of socialist planning. Ironically, Hayek realized decades later that central planning is indeed possible in small households and in primitive tribes where individual tastes are relatively homogenous. For other situations, such as those that are relevant to modern industrial economy, it is logically impossible for the economy to be planned by certain individuals within a framework respectful of the dignity and diversity of individual agents. In the end, Hayek joined Mises and denied the logical possibility of rational calculation under socialism. In Hayek's view the several faces of socialism all had one unfortunately grim expression when they tried to manage the market order.

Notes

1. Hayek (1976b), pp. 107–32. The history of the use of the term 'catallaxy' in economics remains to be written. Such a history would include references to this term as it was used by Whately (1976), and Mises (1949).
2. In the original essay, Mises emphasized the foolishness of believing that socialist managers could plan by using only technological criteria but there was also some discussion of the incentive problem (1920, pp. 116–22). In *Human Action*, Mises ridicules the socialists for their supposition that socialist managers can act as capitalist managers (1949, p. 707).
3. Lutz suggested that Hayek was attempting to 'dynamize' equilibrium analysis especially in *The Pure Theory of Capital* and came close to offering a version of 'period analysis' (1943, p. 309). According to Butos, Hayek was dissatisfied with the limitations of general equilibrium analysis and started to move away from that approach (1985, p. 341). Both Lutz's and Butos's respective positions deserve more attention that I can devote to them here. My immediate reaction (at least to Butos's article) is that even if it were true that Hayek found defects in the notion of equilibrium, it is more fruitful to interpret his economics as offering to make needed repairs to equilibrium economics and not declaring a fast and hasty retreat.
4. According to Lachmann, '...from Menger onwards [Austrians] have been skeptical about the general equilibrium model since the days of the school of Lausanne,' (1976, p. 60). See also Lachmann (1969, p. 89).

5. Modern Austrians are critical of general equilibrium analysis for three reasons: (1) it ignored the causal sequential approach that characterizes actual real world markets and adopts a logical or teleological approach; (2) it assumed that agents 'have full relevant knowledge' where Austrians in general and Hayek in particular were moving towards a more far-reaching understanding of the information problem; and (3) it assumes that there is a tendency for the economy to move towards equilibrium when it is rather the case that the economy consists of a 'perpetually evolving set of disequilibrium processes' (Colonna, 1990, p. 47). On the fundamental assumptions of general equilibrium see Weintraub (1985, p. 109) and Butos (1985, pp. 336–41).

6. If one lonely agent decided to sell present goods to obtain capital goods (that is, claims to future commodities) and this permitted a restructuring of the means of production so that a higher rate of community real income is maintained, then the one lonely agent has produced an externality. One agent has incurred the cost of giving up present consumption and everyone else is better off. Clearly, once the agent realizes that he incurs the entire cost but captures only a fraction of the benefit he will undertake less saving than would otherwise be optimal. This is sometimes referred to in the welfare literature as the case of the 'positive externality'.

7. I use the expression 'household management metaphor' as a synonym for Hayek's expressions such as 'dictator model' or 'model of a communist society' and so on. This expression is not to be found in Hayek's writings but I contend that this is the opposite construction to what Hayek calls the 'extended order' or the market system.

8. The challenge will be to decide if Hayek can establish a 'calculus of coordination' that does not simply parallel the existing utilitarian ideas about the maximization of output. Compare Eatwell and Milgate who suggested that Hayek wanted to have a radical defence of the market and did not want to rely on Pareto foundations. Their verdict is that Hayek failed in his attempt to offer an alternative conceptual framework for the load carried by the notion of 'perfect competition' (see Chapter 5 in Volume I of this series).

References

Arrow, K. (1971), *Essays in the Theory of Risk Bearing* Chicago: Markham.

Bator, F.M. (1957), 'The Simple Analytics of Welfare Maximization', *American Economic Review*, **47**(1), March, 22–59.

Bergson, A. (1967), 'Market Socialism Revisited', *Journal of Political Economy*, 75 (October), 655–73.

Böhm, S. (1986), 'Time and Equilibrium: Hayeks's Notion of Intertemporal Equilibrium Reconsidered', in Kirzner (ed.), (1986).

Butos, W.N. (1985), 'Hayek and General Equilibrium Analysis', *Southern Economic Journal*, 52 (October), 332–43.

Caldwell, B. (1988), 'Hayek's Transformation', *History of Political Economy*, **20**(4), Winter, 513–41.

Colonna, M. (1990), 'Hayek on Money and Equilibrium', *Contributions to Political Economy*, **9**, 43–68.

Hahn, F. (1973), 'The Winter of Our Discontent', *Economica*, **40**(August), 322–30.

Halm, G. (1962), *Economic Systems: A Comparative Analysis*, New York: Holt, Rinehart and Winston.

Hayek, F.A. von (1931), *Prices and Production*, London: Routledge & Sons. Second edition, 1935.

Hayek, F.A. von (ed.) (1935), *Collectivist Economic Planning*, London: Routledge and Kegan Paul.

Hayek, F.A. von (1937), 'Economics and Knowledge', *Economica*, new series, **4**(February), 33–54. Reprinted in Hayek (1949)

Hayek, F.A. von (1940), 'Socialist Calculation: The Competitive "Solution"', *Economica*, new series, **7**(May), 125–49. Reprinted in Hayek (1949)

Hayek, F.A. von (1941), *The Pure Theory of Capital*, London: Routledge and Kegan Paul.

Hayek, F.A. von (1944), *The Road to Serfdom*, Chicago: University of Chicago Press.

Hayek, F.A. von (1945), 'The Use of Knowledge in Society', *American Economic Review*, **35**(September), 519–30. Reprinted in Hayek (1949).

Hayek, F.A. von (1949), *Individualism and Economic Order*, London: Routledge and Kegan Paul.

Hayek, F.A. von (1960), *The Constitution of Liberty*, Chicago: University of Chicago Press.

Hayek, F.A. von (1963), 'The Legal and Political Philosophy of David Hume', *Il Politico*, **28**(December), 691–704. Reprinted in Hayek (1967).

Hayek, F.A. von (1964), 'Kinds of Order in Society', *New Individualist Review*, **3**(Winter), 3–12. Reprinted in *New Individualist Review*, Indianapolis: Liberty Fund Press, 1981, 455–66.

Hayek, F.A. von (1965), 'Kinds of Rationalism', *Economic Studies Quarterly*, 15(Tokyo). Reprinted in Hayek (1967).

Hayek, F.A. von (1966), 'Dr. Bernard Mandeville', *Proceedings of the British Academy*, 52. Reprinted in Hayek (1978).

Hayek, F.A. von (1967), 'Preface', in *Studies in Philosophy, Politics and Economics*, Chicago: University of Chicago Press.

Hayek, F.A. von (1968), 'The Confusion of Language in Political Thought'. Reprinted in Hayek (1978).

Hayek, F.A. von (1969), 'Competition as a Discovery Process', *Freiburgen Studien*. Reprinted in Hayek (1978).

Hayek, F.A. von (1976a), *Law, Legislation and Liberty*, 3 vols, Volume 2, *The Mirage of Social Justice*, Chicago: University of Chicago Press.

Hayek, F.A. von (1976b), 'The New Confusion About "Planning"', *The Morgan Guaranty Survey* (January). Reprinted in Hayek (1978).

Hayek, F.A. von (1978), *New Studies in Philosophy, Politics, Economics and the History of Ideas*, Chicago: University of Chicago Press.

Hayek, F.A. von (1988), *The Fatal Conceit: The Errors of Socialism*, W.W. Bartley (ed.), Chicago: University of Chicago Press.

Hurwicz, L. (1973), 'The Design of Mechanisms for Resource Allocation', *American Economic Review*, **63**(1), 1–30.

Kirzner, I. (1985), 'Prices, the Communication of Knowledge and the Discovery Process', in K.R. Leube and A.H. Zablinger (eds), (1985).

Kirzner, I. (ed.) (1986), *Subjectivism, Intelligibility and Economic Understanding*, New York: Macmillan.

Lachmann, L. M. (1969), 'Methodological Individualism and the Market Economy', in E. Streissler (ed.) (1969).

Lachmann, L. M. (1976), 'From Mises to Shackle: An Essay on Austrian Economics and the Kaleidic Society', *Journal of Economic Literature* **14**(March), pp. 54–62.

Lange, O. and F. Taylor (1956), *On the Economic Theory of Socialism*, B. Lippincott (ed.), New York: McGraw-Hill.

Lange, O. (1936/1937) 'On the Economic Theory of Socialism', 2 parts, *Review of Economic Studies*, (October/February), 53–71 and 123–42. Reprinted in Lange (1956).

Leube, K., and A.H. Zlabinger (eds) (1985), *The Political Economy of Freedom. Essays in Honor of F.A. Hayek*, Munich: Philosophia Verlag.

Liberty Fund (1981), *New Individualist Review*, collected reprinted edition of this journal, Indianapolis: Liberty Fund.

Lutz, F.A. (1943), 'Professor Hayek's Theory of Interest', *Economica*, **10**(November), 302–11.

Machlup, F. (1974), 'Hayek's Contribution to Economics', *Swedish Journal of Economics*, **76**(December), 498–531. Reprinted in Machlup (1976).

Machlup, F. (ed.) (1976), *Essays on Hayek*, New York: New York University Press.

Mises, L. von (1920), 'Economic Calculation in the Socialist Commonwealth', in F. A. Hayek (ed.), (1935).

Mises, L. von (1949), *Human Action*, New Haven: Yale University Press.

Moss, L.S. (1985), 'Reindustrialization and the Rule of Law', in K.R. Leube and A.H. Zlabinger (eds) (1985).

Moss, L.S. (1991), 'The Chicago Intellectual Property Rights Tradition and the Reconciliation of Coase and Hayek', *Eastern Economic Journal*, **17**(April–June), 145–56.

O'Driscoll, G. P. (1977), *Economics as a Coordination Problem: The Contributions of Friedrich A. Hayek*, Kansas City: Sheed and Ward.

Patinkin, D. (1965), *Money, Interest and Prices: An Integration of Monetary and Value Theory*, New York: Harper and Row.

Rothbard, M. N. (1962), *Man, Economy and the State*, 2 vols, Princeton, N.J.: Van Nostrand.

Rothschild, M. (1973), 'Models of Markets with Imperfect Information: A Survey, *Journal of Political Economy*, **81**(November/December), 1283–308.

Shubik, M. (1975), 'The General Equilibrium Model is Incomplete and Not Adequate for the Reconciliation of Micro and Macroeconomic Theory', *Kyklos*, **28**(3), 545–73.

Streissler, E. (ed) (1969), *Roads to Freedom. Essays in Honour of Friedrich A. von Hayek*, London: Routledge and Kegan Paul.

Taylor, F. (1929), 'The Guidance of Production in a Socialist State', *American Economic Review*, 19(March). Reprinted in O. Lange and F. Taylor (1956).

Vaughn, K. (1980), 'Economic Calculation Under Socialism: The Austrian Contribution', *Economic Inquiry*, **18**(October), 535–54.

Whately, R. (1831), *Introductory Lectures on Political Economy*, London: B. Fellowes. Reprinted by Augustus M. Kelley, 1966.

Weintraub, E.R. (1985), *General Equilibrium Analysis: Studies in Appraisal*, Cambridge: Cambridge University Press.

PART III

METHODOLOGY

6 Four theses on Hayek

*Bruce J. Caldwell**

I am currently engaged in a long-term research project, a book on Hayek's methodological thought. The central chapters will trace the evolution of his ideas from the 1920s through the 1950s. Though this in itself is a huge task, I also hope to do more. In the first chapters I want to examine the development of Austrian methodological thinking since Menger in order to place Hayek's theories in context. In the concluding chapters I would like to use what we have learned from studying Hayek's long and ironic tale as the basis for a meditation on the development of economics in the twentieth century. Given such ambitions, it is appropriate to characterize my project as a long-term one. But it is also appropriate to do so on historical grounds: I have been working on the project, in one form or another, since the mid-1980s.

The present paper updates themes explored in two earlier papers (Caldwell, 1988a, 1988b). Four theses on the development of Hayek's methodological thought are offered. They address the influence of Ludwig von Mises, the nature of Hayek's 'transformation' in the 1930s, the significance of his 'Scientism' essay, and the relationship between his ideas and those of Karl Popper. It will be obvious that some theses are more speculative than others, and though I am prepared to defend all of them, I also invite your criticism. Though I hope that none of my ideas are seriously wrong, I would prefer to be shown to be wrong now rather than later.

Mises as mentor

Ludwig von Mises had three great loves, academically speaking. The first of his mistresses was monetary theory. His 1912 book, *The Theory of Money and Credit*, applied marginal analysis to monetary issues and quickly established his reputation, though it was not enough to gain him a chair at the university.[1] Hayek studied psychology and economics at the University of Vienna, and took degrees in law (1921) and what today would be called political science (1923). While working on his second degree, he took a job in a temporary government office set up to settle prewar debts. Mises was

*Research for this paper was in part supported by the National Science Foundation under Grant No. SES90-09043. I would like to thank conference participants Meghnad Desai, Andrea Salanti, Stefano Zamagni, Erich Streissler, Jack Birner, Tony Lawson, Marielle Cauchy and Steve Fleetwood for their valuable comments, and especially Stephan Böhm for providing extensive oral and written comments. None of them are to blame for errors that remain.

one of the directors. Hayek recalls that Mises was then known for his book and for his unyielding liberalism, a stance which garnered little support in postwar Austria. His apparently prescient warnings about the dangers of inflation made an impression on the younger man.

Mises's second passion was the refutation of socialism. The year after Hayek started working with him, Mises published *Socialism*. Hayek conjectured that Mises wrote the book during the volatile postwar period and was responding, at least in part, to the utopian visions expressed by an earlier acquaintance of Mises from the days of Böhm-Bawerk's seminar, Otto Neurath. Hayek recalled the book's impact as follows: '...*Socialism* shocked our generation, and only slowly and painfully did we become persuaded of its central thesis' (1981, p. xxi).

The last of Mises's loves was methodology. His interest may initially have been sparked by the publication of Schumpeter's provocative 1908 book touting Pareto's positivist methodology (Lachmann, 1982, p. 34). It was doubtless revived during the brief period (the summer months of 1918) that Max Weber spent in Vienna; apparently the two debated methodological matters frequently. Mises's earliest goal may also have been to come up with a more adequate solution to certain problems raised by the *Methodenstreit*. For example, he attempted to clarify the relationship between history and theory, and he tried to fortify what he felt was Menger's incomplete subjectivism. He also felt that his more fully subjectivist standpoint, because it took agents' values as given, allowed praxeology to be 'value-free', thereby satisfying a key Weberian requirement for scientificity. Some of these positions (especially the extension of subjectivism) became mainstays of the Austrian programme, and others (such as the value-freedom thesis) gained even wider currency. What was uniquely Misesian, though, was his *a priorist* solution to the problem of the logical status of the axioms of praxeology. *A priorism* became a lifelong commitment for Mises. He first presented his claims in a paper published in the early 1930s. He elaborated on them in the opening chapters of *Human Action*, then returned to them in his last scholarly book in the early 1960s (Mises, 1960, ch. 1; 1949; 1962).

Even though he was not formally his teacher, Mises had a big influence on the direction of Hayek's economic research. Friedrich von Wieser was Hayek's teacher at the university. Hayek's 1923 dissertation was on the problem of imputation, a topic that Wieser had earlier contributed to, and that was then being pursued most prominently by Wieser's successor, Hans Mayer (Craver, 1986, pp. 8–11).[2] But after he began working with Mises, Hayek's economic interests quickly turned towards Mises's first love, monetary economics. The decision was reinforced by a fourteen-month trip to the USA that Hayek took immediately upon finishing his second degree. Armed with letters of introduction from Joseph Schumpeter, he met many of the most important American economists. Hayek later reported that he was disappointed with the state of theory in the States, but was intrigued by work investigating the ability of the Fed to control the business cycle. His knowledge of some simple statistical smoothing techniques that he had picked up while overseas made Hayek the obvious choice to head up the Austrian Business Cycle Institute, set up with Mises's help in 1927. The trip to the USA also set Hayek's direction as a monetary theorist. With the exception of one article on imputation, Hayek's earliest published research, parts of which have recently been translated, focused on monetary economics (McCloughry, ed., 1984). In 1929 the German version of *Monetary Theory and the Trade Cycle* was published. During this period he was also asked to provide a volume on money for an encyclopedic work originally edited by Max Weber. This project was later abandoned, but his long introduction on the history of monetary theory became the basis for his lectures in 1931 at the London School of Economics that ultimately gained him the Tooke chair. Hayek's move from the theory of value to monetary economics thus had a profound effect on his career (Hayek, 1983, pp. 406–7; 1984a, pp. 1–4; Craver, 1986, pp. 19–20).

Mises's second influence is also easy to establish. I suspect it will remain an open question just how long it actually took Hayek to be weaned from his apparent early enthusiasm for *Sozialpolitik*. But if we use his published work as a guide, his first mention of socialism occurs in his inaugural address, 'The Trend of Economic Thinking' (1933b). Soon after that, of course, the socialist calculation debate began, and thenceforth the refutation of socialism would become as important a topic for Hayek as it was for Mises.

Hayek, then, followed Mises's lead in terms of the direction of his economic research. He explicitly acknowledged Mises's role as mentor as follows: 'In my interests, I've been very much guided by him: both the interest in money and industrial fluctuations and the interest in socialism come very directly from his influence' (1983, p. 176). It is intriguing that there is no mention in this quote of Mises's third love, methodology. Though Hayek slowly came to articulate his own methodological vision, it is my thesis that Hayek never accepted Mises's *a priorism*. Indeed, it is a testimony to his diplomatic abilities that this never caused a rift between them. Hayek was careful never to criticize Mises's methodological views directly while Mises was alive.[3] Because of his diffidence, some interpretation of the evidence will be necessary.

We can begin by noting that there was plenty of opportunity for an interest in methodology to be nurtured. Hayek reports that, due to the work of Max Weber and Ernst Mach, methodological issues were a common subject of debate among intellectuals in postwar Vienna. Hayek had even hoped to go to Munich to study under Weber after finishing his degree, but Weber died in 1920. Hayek and Herbert Fürth organized a circle in 1921 that included Felix

Kaufmann and Alfred Schütz. Kaufmann was very familiar with the work of Husserl, and Schütz became known among Austrians as Weber's best interpreter. Mises's own particular views were often discussed in his *Privatseminar*, which Hayek joined upon his return from the USA in 1924 (Hayek, 1983, pp. 30–40, 249; Craver, 1986, pp. 16–17).

Given this background, it is interesting that there is no methodology to be found in any of Hayek's earliest published research. The first hint of a concern with methodology comes in his 1928 paper on intertemporal price equilibrium (Hayek, 1984b). This blossoms into a full methodological argument in *Monetary Theory and the Trade Cycle*, published in German in 1929. But there is no *a priorism* to be found in his argument. Rather, we find the standard Austrian position (standard since the *Methodenstreit*) that theory must take precedence over empirical work, which seems in this instance to be directed against the enthusiasm for empiricism that Hayek had encountered among some economists in the States. There is also the typical Austrian emphasis on the centrality of relative price movements. Finally, there is the claim that any adequate theory of the cycle must be consistent with the 'equilibrium theory' result that all markets clear. This last claim (one that later macroeconomists would pick up, more about this below) was not justified, as one might expect, by invoking the *a priorist* foundations of equilibrium theory. In fact, it was not justified by Hayek at all; it was simply asserted. His failure to make use of Mises's claims at this critical juncture in his argument, a place where they would have fitted perfectly, suggests an early hesitancy on Hayek's part to embrace Mises's *a priorism*. Absence of justification apparently seemed less suspect to Hayek than grounding his argument on inadequate foundations.

In the next decade Hayek twice mentions *a priorism* and appears to incorporate an *a priorist* stance into his system. I have dealt with these instances in earlier papers (Caldwell, 1988a, 1988b), so I will simply summarize my response here. In 'Economics and Knowledge' (1937) Hayek states that the 'pure logic of choice' is tautological and therefore is *a priori* true. In 'The Facts of the Social Sciences' (1943) he argues that we know *a priori* that the structure of the human mind is the same for all people. My response to these apparent endorsements of Mises's position is that though Hayek uses the term *a priori* in these two instances, he does not use them in the same way that Mises did. In the first case, the sense of the term is similar to 'analytical', whereas in the second it means something like 'known to humans by introspection'. These meanings of *a priori* are quite different from Mises's usage. Mises claimed that the *a priori* true axioms of praxeology though untestable are apodictically certain, and that all logically valid derivations from such axioms carry the same certainty. Hayek never used the term in this way. Indeed, Hayek makes a point of emphasizing in 'Economics and Knowledge' that the tautologies of the pure logic of choice, which apply to the equilibrium of an individual decision maker, do not carry over to societal equilibrium, which for him was the most important question. But Mises never seems to have picked up on his hint (Hayek, 1983, pp. 57–8).

Mises was Hayek's mentor in terms of economics. And as we shall soon see, Hayek (as well as all later Austrians, to varying degrees) endorsed at least one crucial Misesian methodological position, namely, the belief that subjectivism must play a central role in analysing the behaviour of agents. But as far as his *a priorism* is concerned, it is incorrect to think that Hayek once followed Mises, then changed course sometime in the 1930s. Hayek never accepted the *a priorist* elements of Mises's approach, so there was nothing for him to give up.

Hayek's transformation

If it was not a turning away from Misesian *a priorism*, what was the nature of Hayek's transformation in the 1930s? Since this was the principal subject of an earlier (1988a) paper, my claims will only be summarized here.

Hayek's transformation involved a turning away from equilibrium theory. He did so because equilibrium theory assumes that all agents have the same, objectively correct knowledge. Actual agents have access to different bits of knowledge (knowledge is dispersed) and, because knowledge claims are based on subjective perceptions, some agents are mistaken in their beliefs. By assuming perfect knowledge, equilibrium theory ignores the central problem of the social sciences, how such dispersed and subjectively held claims come to be coordinated. His first step, taken in 'Economics and Knowledge', was to redefine equilibrium in terms of the compatibility of agents' expectations. But by the war years Hayek despaired of analytically solving the problem of how such an equilibrium was to be reached. Instead, he turned to the more pragmatic task of examining institutions with the hope of identifying those that would least hinder the coordination of agents' plans.[4] Since Hayek had earlier virtually defined economics as the discipline that makes use of equilibrium theory, he was by this move turning away from (at least the general equilibrium variant of) economics and towards a more broadbased study of social institutions.

I stand by my interpretation of the nature of Hayek's transformation. I would like to qualify, however, my discussion of the causes of his change.

In the introduction of my earlier paper I included the following disclaimer: 'Though I will not claim that his participation in the [socialist calculation] debate *caused* Hayek's transformation, a knowledge of his role will be helpful in understanding why events unfolded as they did' (1988a, p. 516, emphasis in the original). This hedge was somewhat disingenuous. True enough, in the article I mention a number of other contributing factors that help explain

Hayek's change in direction: his failure to put his new equilibrium concept to use, his debates with Cambridge economists, and his research on Menger. Nonetheless my discussion in the last part of the paper might lead one to conclude that the socialist calculation debate was the primary cause of his transformation.

In any event, were I writing the paper today I would provide a much fuller treatment of the multitude of things that contributed to Hayek's transformation. I would emphasize how Hayek's failure to come up with an analytically tractable model of the Austrian theory of the cycle pushed him to seek out an alternative way of presenting the Austrian insights. I would be more specific about Menger's influence, discussing both his causal–genetic theory of institution formation and his emphasis on the extension of knowledge as a corollary of 'the progress of civilization'. Hayek's famous endorsement of subjectivism in the statement that '... every important advance in economic theory during the last hundred years was a further step in the consistent application of subjectivism' (1942–44, p. 52) would be identified as Hayek's acknowledgement of what he thought was right in Mises's methodological thought.[5] I would identify the sources of his interest in expectations, and include among them his debate with Myrdal. Finally, though Morgenstern's 1928 book is mentioned in my (1988b) paper as a possible source of the idea of dispersed knowledge, I did not then realize that Morgenstern had published a paper in 1935, itself cited by Hayek (1937, p. 42, n. 7), that directly anticipates many of the most important themes in 'Economics and Knowledge'[6].

I still think that it is correct to say that, if one looks at the episode in retrospect, the causal factor that eventually emerged as most important was his battle with the market socialists. The debate laid the groundwork for so much of Hayek's future work: his continuing criticism of interventionism, his search for a set of defensible liberal institutions, even his reading of intellectual history. These are the topics that Hayek would take up, rather than, say, the study of expectation formation, or, as Lachmann and Shackle were to do, a tracing of the implications of the extension of subjectivism. But this is different from saying that his battle with the socialists was the main cause at the time that Hayek's transformation was actually taking place. No single cause stands out.

The second qualification involves correcting a possible misunderstanding of my thesis. When I said that Hayek turned away from economics, I did not mean to imply that he was never again to discuss economic issues. I meant only that he stopped doing the kind of theoretical economics associated with equilibrium theory. Hayek would continue to write about economics throughout his life: he was in his seventies, for example, when he proposed a plan for the denationalization of money. What he would no longer do is to try to develop a formal model of the economy.

Linking methodology with ontology

My third thesis is that the 'Scientism' essay is Hayek's most important piece of methodological work. There are two reasons for its centrality. First, nearly all of Hayek's subsequent methodological views (sometimes in nascent form, in other instances more fully developed) can be found in the essay. As such, Hayek's methodological thinking was in its broad outlines substantially complete by the early 1940s. I defend this reading in some detail in an earlier (1988b) paper and shall not repeat my arguments here. Instead, I shall focus on the second reason why I think 'Scientism' is so important: in it Hayek attempts to link methodology with ontology. The ontological claims are familiar ones: the social world is composed of individual agents whose knowledge is dispersed and subjectively held. The essay's main theme is that scientism, defined as the 'slavish imitation' of the method and language of the natural sciences, is wrong-headed in the social sciences precisely because the *subject matter* of the latter differs fundamentally from that of the natural sciences. Hayek then uses his ontological claims to justify certain methodological choices (the individualist, compositive method; and the view that explanation of the principle, rather than point predictions, is the most that can be reasonably expected in the social sciences) and to reject others (objectivism, collectivism and historicism). One does not have to agree with Hayek's methodological conclusions to see that he has taken a big step.

Indeed, this is a radical departure even from his own methodological stance in *Monetary Theory and the Trade Cycle*. There Hayek practised methodology by assertion: any legitimate science *must* use theory; any adequate explanation of the trade cycle *must* be consistent with equilibrium theory; changes in relative prices *must* play a role within the theory. There is no attempt to defend these methodological choices, except perhaps with the vague notion that 'this is how real science is done'. There may have been an ontology underlying Hayek's methodological choices, but he certainly did not make it explicit.

As noted above, the approach of this earlier, more scientistic Hayek is not unique among economists, few of whom attempt to ground their methodological prescriptions. Indeed, certain modern macroeconomists looking to justify their methodological preferences for equilibrium modelling cite the early Hayek. This move appears to be doubly appropriate: not only do these economists share with Hayek the same specific methodological commitments regarding equilibrium theorizing; they also share a distaste for providing ontological underpinnings for their methodological preferences.

In reality, though, the whole attempt fails, and on a number of different levels. First, the invocation of Hayek is nothing more than an argument from authority. Worse, it is not even a very good argument from authority, since the 'authority' in this instance is an Austrian whose views on other matters would normally be suspect. As such, the use of Hayek would better be labelled 'an argument from antiquity'. But alas, it turns out not to be a very good argument from antiquity, either, since Hayek was soon to abandon both ontology-free methodology and his commitment to equilibrium theorizing. And even were this not the case, the sort of equilibrium theory that Hayek was defending has little in common with the dynamic optimization models of the new classical economists.[7]

In any event, the step to link up methodological with ontological claims is evident in the essay. His decision to take ontology more seriously may also explain why Hayek resurrected his unpublished essay on psychology, *The Sensory Order*. This was written during his student days in the early 1920s, but not published until 1952. The timing suggests that the essay may be Hayek's attempt to provide an empirical grounding for his ontological claims. I must confess that I do not know quite what to make of *The Sensory Order*. I do not know whether it is a good move to try to ground one's ontology in a psychological theory, nor do I know how to go about assessing the specific theory that he offers. It does seem to be an Austrian predilection (Menger had it too, and Mises had it in reverse), be it an affliction or a virtue, to be fascinated with psychology. If anyone knows why this is so, I would be interested in finding out.

I think that the move to tie one's methodology to a specific description of the world is important, but for reasons different from Hayek's. I think that were economists to be more explicit about their ontological commitments, we would get closer to understanding the nature of the many differences that separate economists into rival research traditions. This, in turn, would allow debate across paradigms to focus on substantive rather than on secondary issues. My reasoning is as follows.

As mentioned above, most economists today do not try to ground their chosen methodologies in a specific ontology. Put another way, many of the methodological commitments that economists embrace are ontologically neutral: they can be held by individuals whose views of the world are diametrically opposed. Consider, for example, the two most ubiquitous methodological commitments of economists, the use of maximization procedures and of equilibrium models. Neither one is *inherently* tied to any particular ontology. Of course, such models can be and often are used to support one or another set of metaphysical presuppositions. This occurs as soon as one specifies the content of the objective function to be maximized and asserts the universalizability of the content, or when one asserts that some equilibrium configuration accurately mirrors some real economic process. Economists differ as to what that content or process might be. This is why individuals with such divergent views of economic reality as Sen, Roemer and Varian are able to employ models in which agents maximize; why neoclassicals and Sraffians can both use equilibrium models.

Why should the absence of ontological commitment matter? The first reason is that it is easy, especially for the average, non-methodologically astute economist, to get confused. Let me give an example. A neoclassical economist is confronted by a student who suspects that his teacher's model must somehow be ideologically tainted. The instructor retorts that his tools are demonstrably ideologically neutral. He then shows the student that one can define the contents of the objective function in any way that one wants. Other people's preferences can be added, or a taste for virtue. The student (and maybe the instructor) goes away with the feeling that the tools of economists are 'value-free'; that they are, to use the word, 'scientific'. And they would be right: the tools are value-free as long as no ontology is specified. But usually an ontology *is* specified, but hidden (as is the case, for example, when we assume that agents' preferences are independent). The danger is that one may wrongly infer that results that depend on a particular ontological commitment are themselves value-free.

Such confusions aside, there is another reason to bring our ontological commitments into the foreground. Simply put, it is typically disagreements over ontology, over our descriptions of underlying social reality, that give rise to rival research traditions. Yet even so, it is very difficult to identify exactly where the crucial differences among us lie. Though ontological commitments refer to the world, they generally are not empirically determinable. They are based on individual perceptions, and these are coloured by values, past experiences, who one's teachers were, and so on. Such influences are not easy to pinpoint, much less to discuss with someone whose perceptions differ. Furthermore, many of us harbour the feeling, held over from the positivist era, that the metaphysical underpinnings of science (since they depend on things like values) are not proper topics for scientists to discuss. But entertaining this positivist prejudice has brought with it a huge cost. If one refuses to discuss ontology, one bans from the domain of legitimate discourse many of the most important questions economists face.

Some will respond that such discussions do take place in economics, and that they have thus far been fruitless. Neoclassicals and Sraffians have debated the nature of reality, after all. One group thinks exchange is fundamental, the other thinks production is. Where does one go from there? What can one do when the opponents have such radically different, even incommensurable visions of the nature of reality?

There is much validity in this objection: talking about ontology is anything but easy. But this is precisely why Hayek's contribution is such a valuable one. For the ontology that he proposes has been embraced in its broad outlines by (some, not all) economists from two very different groups in economics, the Austrians and the post-Keynesians. Members of these two groups differ radically on a number of points: in their value commitments, in their view of typical human nature, in their assessments of the efficacy of markets and of their effects on the human condition, on their policy recommendations, and so on. But they seem to share at least certain elements of a common ontology. As such, a debate between them might help clarify exactly where their other differences lie.[8]

In summary, I am advocating that the discussion of ontological commitments be not just permitted, but encouraged. Let me be clear about expected payoffs: I do *not* think that this will resolve debates among the rival groups. But the nature of the differences between them will be *clarified*, and such clarification is one of the goals of methodology.

In any case it promises to be an improvement over the (by now rather tired) sort of methodological discussion one often encounters among Austrians and post-Keynesians, namely attacks against general equilibrium theory and the rationality assumption. When Austrians and post-Keynesians endlessly repeat that these constructs are 'unrealistic', part of what they are saying is that the constructs should be ontologically grounded. This has no effect on advocates of general equilibrium theory or the rationality assumption, for they (good heirs of positivism) find discussions of ontology 'unscientific'. Austrians and post-Keynesians would be better off confronting each other rather than bashing those who do not share their commitment to ontological grounding.

A few more points before moving to my next thesis. First, some post-Keynesians will balk at being dubbed ontological Hayekians. If they choose to call themselves by some other name instead, I will not object. Next, there is obviously another way to try to resolve debates between post-Keynesians and Austrians, or any such groups, and it does not involve talking about something so unscientific as ontological commitments. One can simply 'let the facts decide'; that is, turn to empirical work. This is the solution embraced by the vast majority of economists when they confront conflicting theories. I shall simply state without supporting argument that Hayek's ontology, if we accept it, provides a powerful argument to suggest why there has been so little progress towards resolving these kinds of issues on empirical grounds. And the absence of empirical progress, in turn, suggests why economists tend to measure progress in their discipline in terms of improvements in their theoretical tools. Finally, it is doubtful that Hayek saw all the implications of the position he was espousing. He was trying to construct a case against socialism and planning. Observers will differ on how successful they think he was in this endeavour. What cannot be disputed is that along the way he made some provocative contributions to methodology, contributions whose importance have yet to be fully realized.

Disregarding Popper

My fourth thesis is again simple to state: Popper had little influence on the development of Hayek's methodology. There is scant evidence of any Popperian influence in the 1930s, when Hayek's transformation first began. There are no citations of Popper in 'Scientism'. If one accepts my argument in the last section that this essay contains all of the important elements of Hayek's subsequent methodological thought, then clearly Popper did not play a crucial role in its development.

Hayek's citations of Popper's work become numerous in the 1950s and 1960s, but this produces no discernible shifts in his thinking. For example, had Hayek known of Popper's treatment of explanation, his confused discussion of the topic in the second chapter of 'Scientism' would have been greatly improved. His later widely acknowledged acceptance of Popper's views, however, appears to have carried with it no consequences. For example, his endorsement of the view that theoretical sciences are structured as 'hypothetico-deductive' systems, or that 'prediction and explanation are merely two aspects of the same process', seem little more than window-dressing, a matter of changing one's language to reflect current philosophical usage (1955, pp. 4, 9). In particular, one does *not* find Hayek correcting past errors, or trying to formulate his own explanations to conform to the model, or arguing for the symmetry thesis when he talks about prediction. In another instance, Hayek thanks Popper for showing him that the methods of the natural sciences that social scientists try so slavishly to mimic are not, in fact, followed in the natural sciences themselves (1967, p. viii). This is an addition to Hayek's knowledge. But it concerns his perception of what goes on outside his discipline, and had little discernible effect on his characterization of economics. Nor is there any evidence that Popper's 'Three Worlds' ontology made any difference to Hayek's work. Of course, what advocates of the Popperian thesis are most impressed with is Hayek's frequent advocacy of falsifiability as the demarcation criterion between science and non-science. But as I demonstrate in another paper (1992), a careful examination of each of Hayek's citations shows that in every case his praise of falsifiability is back-handed.

There is only one place where I would modify my earlier arguments concerning the relationship between Popper and Hayek. In a deliberate attempt to be provocative I once said that, though Hayek was no Popperian, Popper might well be described as a Hayekian (1988b, p. 81). My rationale was that since Popper's situational analysis was a generalization of the methodology of economics, presumably he got it from Hayek. Though I am still attracted to its twist, I now think that this argument is wrong. Popper's situational logic owes much more to Max Weber than it does to Hayek. It has to do with the logic of choice, a topic that Hayek avoided.

But there is still a way to end on a provocative note. Mises, like Popper, started from Weber and eventually produced a logic of choice, though their versions of it could not be more different. One reason that Hayek may have avoided the topic initially was that he did not want to have to confront Mises, with whose *a priorism* he apparently disagreed. Later on he may not have wanted to have to choose between them. In any event, since Hayek never explored the logic of choice, in this matter Mises and Popper, the *a priorist* and the falsificationist, shared more in common with one another than they did with Hayek. Popper is no Hayekian, but both he and Mises may well be post-Weberians![9]

Notes

1. There has been much discussion about why Mises remained a *Privatdozent* and was never offered a full faculty position in Austria. Erich Streissler told me that from one perspective, there is little to explain. Mises was third on the list for Wieser's chair, after a full professor at Munich (who turned the job down) and Hans Mayer (who took the offer), the latter also a full professor and seven years Mises's senior. As for other appointments, he was again usually on the list. But problems were posed by the fact that Mises, who was making good money at his existing job, insisted on jumping directly to the position of full professor to avoid the sizeable cut in salary that passing through the intermediate 'extraordinary professor' rank would entail.

   Less innocent explanations have also been offered. Lionel Robbins puts the matter with his usual delicacy: Mises was 'excluded by sectarian animus from the position in the University of Vienna which on intellectual merits was his due... [because] he was neither a Catholic nor a Social Democrat...' (1971, p. 107). Earlene Craver is more blunt: Mises was passed over four times for an appointment because '(i) he was too conservative, that is, an unreconstructed "liberal" in an age when liberalism of the old style was going out of vogue; (ii) he was a Jew, in a society that had rigid social requirements for the integration of Jews, and less and less place for them; and (iii) he was difficult to the point that many people thought him "personally obnoxious"' (1986, p. 5). Hayek noted that Jewish capitalists (that is, businessmen) were common enough in Vienna, and so were left-wing Jewish intellectuals. A Jewish intellectual who opposed socialism, on the other hand, was viewed as something of 'a monstrosity' (1983, p. 404).

2. Jack Birner noted that Wieser's influence might be seen in Hayek's *The Pure Theory of Capital*; the structure of the argument in that book is reminiscent of that in Wieser's *Natural Value*.

3. Hayek occasionally did express his disagreement after Mises had died. See, e.g. (1983, pp. 57–8).

4. When I speak in terms of institutions that would 'least hinder' coordination (rather than those that would 'best assure' it), my awkward phrasing is intentional. Hayek's vision is essentially pessimistic. The Austrians disdain the optimism that informs the world view of social planners, of course. But they also reject the language of neoclassical economists: 'maximization' and 'optimization' carry decidedly ambitious connotations.

5. Note that the sentence endorsing subjectivism taken from the 'Scientism' essay carries a long footnote that begins, 'This is a development which has probably been carried out most consistently by Ludwig von Mises, and I believe that most peculiarities of his views which at first strike many readers as strange and unacceptable trace to the fact that in the consistent development of the subjectivist approach he has for a long time moved ahead of his contemporaries' (p. 52). I suspect that the origins of Hayek's sometimes incautious subjectivist claims in this essay were two: a desire to show solidarity with his mentor on some methodological issues, and a desire to make as strong a case as possible against doctrines like behaviourism or operationalism, for which only the observable mattered. I

was unable to follow up on Marielle Cauchy's trenchant observation that Husserl's influence seems evident in parts of Hayek's 'Scientism' essay. Given Hayek's earlier association with Kaufmann, the thesis is a plausible one.

6. Morgenstern's paper was brought to my attention by Böhm (1992). It was also mentioned in a detailed letter from Nicolai juul Foss (16 March 1989) commenting on 'Hayek's Transformation.' Foss also argued that the neglected Scandinavian debates were an impetus for Hayek's investigation of expectations, as foreshadowed in Hayek (1933b).

7. I owe the last observation to Kevin Hoover.

8. The new journal *Review of Political Economy* is a welcome venue for this kind of exchange. The similarity in their thought is what motivated Stephan Böhm and me to invite a number of post-Keynesians to serve as critical discussants of papers in a volume on Austrian economics. Cf. Böhm (1989), Caldwell (1989), Caldwell and Böhm (eds) (1992).

9. I will not defend here the claim that Popper and Mises began from Weber. Two pertinent citations are Weber (1947, pp. 87–118; 1975). I thank Stephan Böhm for alerting me to the latter article.

References

Böhm, S. (1989), 'Subjectivism and post-Keynesianism: towards a better understanding', in J. Pheby (ed.), *New Directions in Post-Keynesian Economics*, Aldershot: Edward Elgar.

Böhm, S. (1992), 'Austrian economics between the wars: some historiographical problems', in B. Caldwell and S. Böhm (eds).

Caldwell, B. (1988a), 'Hayek's transformation', *History of Political Economy*, **20** (4), Winter, 513–41.

Caldwell, B. (1988b), 'La méthodologie de Hayek: description, évaluation et interrogations', *Politique et Economie*, **9**, 71–85.

Caldwell, B. (1989), 'Post-Keynesian methodology: an assessment', *Review of Political Economy*, **1**, 43–64.

Caldwell, B. (1992), 'Hayek the falsificationist? A refutation', *Research in the History of Economic Thought and Methodology*, **10**, 1–15.

Caldwell, B. and S. Böhm (eds) (1992), *Austrian Economics: Tensions and New Directions*, Boston: Kluwer Academic.

Craver, E. (1986), 'The emigration of the Austrian economists', *History of Political Economy*, **18** (2), Spring, 1–32.

Hayek, F.A. von (1933a), *Monetary Theory and the Trade Cycle*, New York: Kelley Reprints, 1966.

Hayek, F.A. von (1933b), 'The trend of economic thinking', *Economica*, **13**, May, 121–37.

Hayek, F.A. von (1933c), 'Price Expectations, Monetary Disturbances, and Malinvestment'. Reprinted in F.A. Hayek, *Profits, Interest and Investment*, New York: Kelley Reprints, 1970.

Hayek, F.A. von (1937), 'Economics and knowledge'. Reprinted in Hayek (1948).

Hayek, F.A. von (1942–44), 'Scientism and the study of society'. Reprinted in F.A. von Hayek, *The Counter-Revolution of Science*, Glencoe, Ill.: The Free Press, 1952.

Hayek, F.A. von (1943), 'The facts of the social sciences'. Reprinted in Hayek (1948).

Hayek, F.A. von (1948), *Individualism and Economic Order*, Chicago: University of Chicago Press, Midway Reprint, 1980.

Hayek, F.A. von (1952), *The Sensory Order: An Inquiry into the Foundations of Theoretical Psychology*, Chicago: University of Chicago Press, Midway Reprint, 1976.

Hayek, F.A. von (1955), 'Degrees of explanation'. Reprinted in Hayek (1967).

Hayek, F.A. von (1967), *Studies in Philosophy, Politics and Economics*, Chicago: University of Chicago Press.

Hayek, F.A. von (1981), 'Foreword', in L. von Mises, *Socialism*, Indianapolis: Liberty Fund.

Hayek, F.A. von (1983), 'Nobel prize-winning economist'. Transcript of an oral history interview conducted in 1978 under the auspices of the Oral History Program, University Library, UCLA. Copyright 1983, Regents of the University of California.

Hayek, F.A. von (1984a), 'Introduction', in McCloughry (ed.) (1984).

Hayek, F.A. von (1984b), 'Intertemporal Price Equilibrium and Movements in the Value of Money', in R. McCloughry (ed.) (1984).

Lachmann, L. (1982), 'Ludwig von Mises and the Extension of Subjectivism', in Kirzner (ed.), *Method, Process, and Austrian Economics: Essays in Honor of Ludwig von Mises*, Lexington, Mass.: D.C. Heath, 31–40.

McCloughry, R. (ed.) (1984), *Money, Capital, and Fluctuations: Early Essays*, Chicago: University of Chicago Press.

Mises, L. von (1934), *The Theory of Money and Credit*, Indianapolis: Liberty Fund, 1980.

Mises, L. von (1949), *Human Action: A Treatise on Economics*. Revised ed., Chicago: Henry Regnery, 1963.

Mises, L. von (1960), *Epistemological Problems of Economics*, Princeton, NJ.: Van Nostrand.

Mises, L. von (1962), *The Ultimate Foundations of Economic Science*, 2nd ed., Kansas City: Sheed, Andrews and McMeel, 1976.

Morgenstern, O. (1935), 'Perfect foresight and economic equilibrium', in A. Shotter (ed.), *Selected Economic Writings of Oskar Morgenstern*, New York: New York University Press, 1976.

Weber, M. (1947), *The Theory of Social and Economic Organization*, Translated by A.M. Henderson and Talcott Parsons. New York: Oxford University Press.

Weber, M. (1975), 'Marginal utility theory and "the fundamental law of psychophysics"', *Social Science Quarterly*, **56**, June, 21–36.

7 Realism and Hayek: a case of continuing transformation

*Tony Lawson**

If it is by now commonplace to observe that Hayek's essay 'Economics and Knowledge' signalled a transformation in his thinking (a transformation that Hayek himself acknowledged some thirty years later on, Hayek, 1965, p. 91) there is less agreement about the precise nature of the change that occurred. Perhaps the only agreed feature of existing commentaries (although no commentators put it quite as starkly as this) is that, at least at the level of methodology, the noted change represented for Hayek a more or less clean break with the past coupled with a move to a perspective that would remain reasonably fixed throughout his future writings.

It is this 'agreed feature' that I want to question here. Specifically by focusing on his most explicit and influential methodological contribution written about the time of the noted essay, namely his three-part 'Scientism and the Study of Society' (1942–44), I want to argue that this latter contribution is flawed; that its errors follow directly from Hayek's having failed fully to escape from precisely the perspective which he is attacking; and that only in his contributions of about twenty years on does Hayek in any clear way begin to overcome the problems identified earlier. If this interpretation is correct Hayek's course is better portrayed as one of *continuing* transformation rather than a once and for all change of track.[1]

The term *realism* figures in the title of this paper to signal a concern throughout for explicit ontological elaboration, a concern to elaborate the *nature* of the objects of natural and social science. The reason for this orientation is that it is primarily Hayek's ontological presuppositions, and specifically their path of evolution or transformation, that, or so I shall suggest, constitute the central issue here, an orientation rendered all the more appropriate by Hayek's explicit intention, in his 'Scientism' essay, of criticizing economists precisely for failing to tailor their methods to the nature of the objects of the social realm.

*The discussion which follows is highly influenced by the writings of realist philosophers and especially those of Roy Bhaskar. I am also indebted to numerous discussions with various participants of the Cambridge Workshop on Realism and Economics, especially Steve Fleetwood, Pat Northover, Steve Pratten and Jochen Runde. For very useful comments on an earlier draft I am similarly in gratitude to Stephan Böhm, Bruce Caldwell and Uskali Mäki.

Discussions of theories of ontology are not yet a common feature of economic contributions. Let me, then, briefly prepare the ground at the outset by contrasting at a rather general or abstract level two theories of ontology that provide significant points of reference not only for understanding the recent course of debates in the philosophy of science in general, but also, and more specifically, for tracing Hayek's own particular path of development.

The first such theory can, in its most general form, be labelled *transcendental realism*.[2] According to transcendental realism the world is constituted not only by *experience*, and the *actual* objects of experience such as events and states of affairs, but also by (irreducible) *structures*, powers, and mechanisms and so on that may not be directly perceivable but which underlie the events of experience and govern them. Thus not only are there, for example, actual (de)formations which occasionally emerge on the skin, which we experience as spots, but underlying them and governing them are such agents as viruses. Similarly such phenomena as falling leaves, movements in iron filings, productivity changes in the UK, and so on, are governed by such structures or mechanisms as gravity, magnetic fields, systems of industrial relations, and so on. According to transcendental realism, then, there are three levels or domains of reality that must be distinguished, corresponding to such items as experiences, events and governing mechanisms, respectively. These can be referred to as the domains of the *empirical*, the *actual* and the *non-actual* or (metaphorically) '*deep*'. All three domains are real. Moreover, and crucially, these three domains must be recognized as 'unsynchronized' or 'out of phase', as it were, with one another. Thus, while experiences are out of phase with events, allowing contrasting, as well as the possibility of revising, experiences of a given event, so events are typically unsynchronized with the mechanisms that govern them. On the latter structure/event non-correspondence, for example, autumn leaves are not in phase with the 'pull' of gravity for the reason that they are also subject to aerodynamic, thermal and other tendencies. Indeed it is because the underlying structures are not straightforwardly manifest in events (or 'appearances'), according to transcendental realism, that science has its non-trivial objective, namely to identify and understand the structures and mechanisms that govern the phenomena that we experience.

According to transcendental realism, then, the world is composed, in part, of objects that are structured and (to use Bhaskar's term) intransitive – *structured* in the sense of their being irreducible to the events of experience, *intransitive* in the sense of their existing and acting independently of their identification. Once an intransitive dimension is constituted, of course, it is possible to understand how a changing knowledge of (possibly) unchanging objects is possible. But what can be said about the manner in which knowledge is obtained? If discovery is to be possible, clearly the discovered objects can not be previously known. But if this is so, and if knowledge is not to arise out of nothing, then it is equally necessary to recognize (to employ Bhaskar's term once more), a *transitive* dimension to science. That is, it is necessary to acknowledge a dimension of *transitive* objects of knowledge, including facts, observations, theories, hunches, intuitions, speculations and so on which facilitate, and come to be transformed in, the active labour of science. In short, according to transcendental realism, the objects of knowledge exist and act to a significant extent independently of our knowledge of them, while the knowledge we possess always consists in historically specific social forms, as items continually transformed in the social and laborious process of science. Just as making sense of science requires attention to an intransitive realm of objects of investigation so it also requires acknowledgement of a transitive realm of cognitive objects or materials, as well as human scientific social activities and capabilities.

In contrast to, and in competition with, transcendental realism are various philosophical positions that can be collected under the heading of *empirical realism*. Behind this perspective lies the acceptance of an empiricist ontology constituted by the category of experience. Hume encouraged this position by denying that the world is composed of objects that (in terminology employed here) are structured and intransitive. Instead all we have are impressions or experiences. It is these items that constitute the world. Now from the transcendental realist perspective so far elaborated the very notion as well as conception of an empiricist ontology involves certain philosophical mistakes of which two are crucial. The first lies in the use of the category of experience to define the world. This entails giving an epistemological category an ontological task and in doing so commits what Bhaskar refers to as the 'epistemic fallacy'. This 'fallacy' consists in the view that statements about being can be reduced to, or analysed solely in term of, statements about knowledge, that matters of ontology can always be translated into epistemological terms. It presupposes, in other words, that the transitive dimension/intransitive dimension distinction can be dissolved. The second error consists in the view that being experienced, or being open to possible experience, is an essential feature of reality. It neglects, in other words, the causal criterion for ascribing something as real, acknowledging as real only what is experienced. And a consequence of these errors, according to transcendental realism, is an inevitable failure, or inability, to distinguish the conditions under which experience is in fact significant to science (a point to be developed below).

Of course, it is never possible to banish an intransitive dimension altogether, to dissolve completely any conception of being, of a real ontology. For, following Hume, by focusing upon perceptions or impressions, an implicit ontology consisting of the objects of those perceptions or impressions, i.e. an ontology of events and states of affairs, is thereby resurrected. The result is that such events, because given in experience, are taken to constitute all that is real, and experience, because in effect constitutive of the world, is taken to be certain. And if the world consists only in the events given in experience, then the only possible job for science and general knowledge is to detect relationships between these events. Causal laws on this conception then are, and can be nothing more than, constant conjunctions of the events of experience. Now whatever their guiding presuppositions, their motives and points of entry, the empiricist and the Kantian wings of positivist philosophy have tended to agree on this point. Both have uncritically accepted the doctrine, implicit in the empirical realist dissolution of ontology, that causal laws or 'significant results' consist in empirical regularities, in constant conjunctions of events. Anything else, any 'surplus element' for the Kantian tradition is then treated only as a construction of the mind, couched solely in terms of 'creations' or 'constructions'.

In sum, whereas according to transcendental realism the world is structured and intransitive and the goal of science is to intervene in nature in order to identify, or reveal, the structures that govern the events of experience, according to empirical realism the world is composed only of the events of experience, and the objective of science is to record their constant conjunctions, to elaborate generalities of the form 'whenever event X then event Y'. Any labour involved in the latter exercise is merely intellectual effort restricted to the production of a 'surplus element', conceptual entities that are simply constructions of the mind.

How then do we choose between these competing accounts? In fact, it is easy to demonstrate relative support for the transcendent realist account by examining the conditions in which empirical regularities actually occur in science. Consider first the situation in the natural sciences. Particularly relevant here are two observations the significance of which has been well brought out by Bhaskar (1975). The first of these is that most of the constant conjunctions of events that constitute significant substantive results of science in fact *only* occur in experimental situations – in general they are not spontaneously occurring. The second observation is that the results or 'laws' supported in experimental activity are frequently successfully applied outside the experimental situation.

Now these observations raise certain problems for Humean accounts which tie laws to constant conjunctions of events. For, if scientific laws, or significant results, only occur in such restricted conditions as experimental set-ups then a (rather inhibiting) implication is that science and its results, far from being universal, are effectively fenced off from most of the goings on in the world. In other words, most of the accepted results of science are not of the form 'whenever event X then event Y always follows' after all, but are of the form 'whenever event X then event Y always follows, as long as conditions E hold', where conditions E typically amount to the specification of the experimental situation. A further rather counterintuitive implication is that any actual regularity of events that a law of *nature* supposedly denotes appears not to occur independently of human intervention. But, in addition to such problems and at least as seriously, the constant conjunctions view of laws leaves the question of what governs events outside experimental situations not only unanswered but completely unaddressed. And, in doing so it also leaves the fact that experimentally obtained results *are* successfully applied outside experimental situations without any valid explanation.

In order to render Bhaskar's observations intelligible it is necessary to abandon the view of nature as consisting of event regularities and to accept, instead, the transcendental realist account of the objects of the world as intransitive and structured. That is, experimental activity and results, and the application of experimentally determined knowledge outside experimental situations, can be accommodated only through invoking the transcendental realist ontology of generative structures, powers, mechanisms and necessary relations, that lie behind and govern the flux of events in an essentially open world. The fall of an autumn leaf, for example, does not typically conform to an event regularity, and precisely because it is governed, in complex ways, by the actions of different juxtaposed and counteracting mechanisms. As noted above, not only is the path of the leaf governed by gravitational pull, but also by aerodynamic, thermal, inertial and other tendencies. On this transcendental realist view, then, experimental activity can be explained as an attempt to intervene in order to close the system, that is to insulate a particular mechanism of interest by holding off all other potentially counteracting mechanisms. The aim is to engineer a closed system in which a one-to-one correspondence can obtain between the way a mechanism acts and the events that eventually ensue. In other words, experimental activity can be rendered intelligible *not* as creating the rare situation in which an empirical law is put into effect but as intervening in order to bring about those special circumstances under which a non-empirical law, a power, or tendency, or way of acting of some structure, or mechanism, can be empirically identified. The law itself, of course, is always operative – if the triggering conditions hold, the mechanism is activated whatever else is going on. On this transcendental realist view, for example, a leaf is subject to the gravitational tendency even as I hold it in the palm of my hand. Through this sort of reasoning then, transcendental but not empirical realism can render intelligible the application of scientific knowledge outside experimental situations. The context or *milieu* under which any mechanism will be operative is irrelevant to the law's specification. Once activated the mechanism is operative whatever empirical pattern ensues.

In short, although the traditional conception of science is the seeking of constant conjunctions of events, in practice such event regularities that have been elaborated have been restricted in the main to situations of experimental control. Transcendental realism, unlike empirical realism, can render this situation intelligible. And it follows from the transcendental realist perspective that the traditional Humean conception rests upon an inadequate analysis, and illegitimate generalization, of what is found to be a special case – wherein a single and stable (set of) aspect(s) or mechanism(s) is physically isolated and thereby empirically indentified.

Most of the discussion so far has referred implicitly to the situation in the 'natural' sciences. However it is not difficult to see that the transcendental realist arguments hold more generally, and specifically with regard to the social realm. At least this follows if we note the absence of non-trivial event regularities in the social realm and accept the widespread intuition that human beings have real choice. For it is analytic to the concept of human choice that any human agent could always have acted otherwise; and it is a necessary condition for the possibility of choice and action that the world is open in the sense that events really could have been different. At the same time, the reality of choice entails that human actions must be intentional under some description, necessitating that social objects, the social conditions of these acts, must pre-exist these very actions and be sufficiently enduring that an adequate (choice facilitating) knowledge of them be obtained. Accepting then, that human choice is real, then if there is a social world it must be open and structured – obvious examples of conditioning social structure being rules, relations, positions and so forth. In consequence, any possible economic laws must typically be statements of tendencies, and not empirical regularities, and the Humean project in its economic or social science guise must be regarded as misguided more or less in its entirety.

Transcendental, but not empirical, realism, then, can render significant aspects of scientific results and practices and human capabilities intelligible and, in consequence, can be accepted as the more adequate philosophical theory. I now want to argue that Hayek erroneously starts out accepting a position akin to empirical realism as a theory of ontology appropriate to the natural realm, and that it is in explicit reaction to this position that he elaborates a theory of a social ontology in his most famous and influential essay, 'Scientism and the Study of Society'. I shall suggest, however, that the social ontology that Hayek develops is not sustainable, and that the reason for this is precisely that the contrast he is attempting to draw presupposes the inadequate ontology of empirical realism for the natural sphere. What is then achieved is not a transcendence of empirical realism and its associated positivist account of science but merely a displacement of this position, a sideways shift, as it were – in effect a subjectivized version. Only in later years does he achieve more than this when he begins to take on board some of the insights of transcendental realism. Let me now examine how this all takes place.

'Scientism and the Study of Society': the background

In his essay 'Economics and Knowledge' (1937) Hayek is concerned with elaborating the conditions under which economic equilibrium, in the sense of the mutual compatibility of different people's plans, can be expected to come about. He observes that in the 'traditional treatment of equilibrium' various difficulties of obtaining such compatibility are 'avoided by the assumption that the data... will be equally given to all individuals and that their acting on the same premises will somehow lead to their plans becoming adapted to each other' (p. 38) and notes numerous problems with this 'solution'. Specifically, among other things, Hayek draws attention to the fundamental problem of what is to be meant by certain data being *given*:

> The confusion about the concept of a datum is at the bottom of so many of our difficulties in this field that it is necessary to consider it in somewhat more detail. Datum means of course something given, but the question which is left open, and which in the social sciences is capable of two different answers, is to whom the facts are supposed to be given. Economists appear subconsciously always to have been somewhat uneasy about this point, and to have reassured themselves against the feeling that they did not quite know to whom the facts were given by underlining the fact that they *were* given – even by using such pleonastic expressions as 'given' data. But this does not solve the question whether the facts referred to are supposed to be given to the observing economist, or to the persons whose actions he wants to explain, and if to the latter, whether it is assumed that the same facts are known to all the different persons in the system, or whether the 'data' for the different persons may be different.
>
> There seems to be no possible doubt that these two concepts of 'data', on the one hand in the sense of the objective real facts, as the observing economist is supposed to know them, and on the other in the subjective sense, as things, known to the persons whose behaviour we try to explain, are really fundamentally different and ought to be kept carefully apart. And, as we shall see, the question why the data in the subjective sense of the term should ever come to correspond to the objective data is one of the main problems we have to answer. (Hayek, 1937, p. 39)

Hayek never finds any answer to this problem, he never advances any reason to suppose that 'the data in the subjective sense of the term should ever come to correspond to the objective data', and this triggers a significant change of direction in his thinking. For, if subjective beliefs do not correspond to what Hayek terms objective facts of the external world, then, given that it is the actual (i.e. subjective) conceptions of lay agents that guide their actions, there arises the question of what this observation entails both for the nature of the social order that apparently attains, including its relationship to the formalist notion of economic equilibrium, and for the possibilities that follow for social science. Having attempted to understand and having examined all possible routes of justifying the notion of economic equilibrium, and recognizing its dependence on specifications about the nature and dispersion of knowledge, Hayek is forced to become more explicit about the real possibilities for knowledge in a complex, decentralized society.[3] In short, a turn to philosophy is necessitated – and 'Scientism and the Study of Society' is the first significant outcome of this seemingly compulsory endeavour.

Hayek's 'Scientism and the Study of Society': a case of hermeneutic foundationalism

Hayek's starting point in 'Scientism and the study of society', (1942–44) then, is the observation that, in general, human beliefs and opinions are not reducible to any given 'objective facts' about the external world. And his important inference in this essay is that even when there are grounds to question the relationship of these 'subjective views' to any external reality, these human beliefs, opinions, and attitudes and so on are nevertheless essential to, and indeed in some way productive of, social life. In consequence, or so Hayek argues, the starting-point for substantive social science can have nothing to do with 'given data', with 'objective facts', but rather turns on the quite different point that the social realm faces the would be social scientist as preinterpreted, as cognitively prepared as it were, before any scientific investigation of it. The preinterpreted nature of social life, of course, is the great insight of the hermeneutic tradition, and once grasped explicitly by Hayek it is an insight that significantly informs his writing thereafter.

Having emphasized and drawn attention to the significance to social science of this situation, however, Hayek, in the fashion of hermeneutic writers quite widely, then proceeds to overstate the subjectivist or hermeneutic case by suggesting, in effect, that social life must consist *only* in those concepts in which agents perceive their existence. In other words, in addition to highlighting the concept-dependent nature of social life, Hayek, most of the time at least, argues as if social life is concept-determined, as if it is exhausted by individual conceptions and attitudes, so that the latter constitute all that is of relevance to the study of society and economy:

> What is relevant in the study of society is not whether these laws of nature are true in any objective sense, but *solely* whether they are believed and acted upon by people...
> ...What is true about the relations of men to things is of course even more true of the relations between men, which for the purposes of social study cannot be defined in the objective terms of the physical sciences but *only* in terms of human beliefs. (Hayek, 1942–44, pp. 51–2, italics added)

It follows that, for social scientists, their subject-matter must be understood exclusively according to the subject-matter's own definitions. Thus to describe an item as an 'instrument', a 'medicine', a 'word' or a 'sentence', to distinguish an act as 'crime' or 'punishment', depends only on how such things or acts are understood within the form of life under study. In similar fashion social wholes, such as society, the economy, language, and so on are constituted only through, and only in terms of, individual opinions and attitudes, and can be understood by the social scientist solely in reference to them:[4]

> Not only man's actions towards external objects but also all the relations between men and all the social institutions can be understood only by what men think about them. Society as we know it is, as it were, built up from the concepts and ideas held by the people; and social phenomena can be recognised by us and have meaning to us only as they are reflected in the minds of men. (pp. 57–8)

The same moreover is true of human needs. These, for social science, according to Hayek, are just what individuals believe they are – in effect, merely subjective preferences. Thus, for Hayek, when other 'objectivist' economists make their 'frequent statements about the objective needs of the people… [the term]…*objective* is merely a name for somebody's views about what the people ought to want' (p. 92).

Society then is conceptual in nature consisting, or rooted, in the opinions, beliefs and attitudes of individual agents. It is certainly the case for Hayek that lay conceptions include fallible accounts of the 'external' world. However, this does not detract from the view that they are nevertheless constitutive of society. Nor does it provide any obstacle to social scientific investigation. For whether lay conceptions are right or wrong it is always possible for the scientist to access lay conceptions, to understand them and indeed to interpret the phenomena of the world in identical fashion, due to a common structure of all human minds.

> The… fact that different men do perceive different things in a similar manner which does not correspond to any known relation between these things in the external world, must be regarded as a significant datum of experience which must be the starting point in any discussion of human behaviour. (p. 37)

> We take it for granted that other men treat various things as alike or unlike just as we do, although no objective test, no knowledge of the relations of these things to other parts of the external world justifies this. (p. 43)

> …the facts of the social sciences are merely opinions, views held by the people whose actions we study. They differ from the facts of the physical sciences in being beliefs or opinions held by particular people, beliefs which as such are our data, irrespective of whether they are true or false, and which, moreover, we cannot directly observe in the minds of the people but which we can recognise from what they do and say merely because we have ourselves a mind similar to theirs. (p. 47)

Given these ontological premises, then, Hayek's epistemological conclusions follow. Specifically, because the social realm, the subject matter of social science, is constituted by the manner in which lay agents conceptualize the world around them, by the way in which they interpret their existence, social scientific knowledge proceeds precisely through accessing these lay conceptions, by understanding or grasping the way in which individuals understand or grasp their existence:

> In the sense in which we here use the contrast between the subjectivist approach of the social sciences and the objectivist approach of the natural sciences it says little more than what is commonly expressed by saying that the former deal in the first instance with the phenomena of individual minds, or mental phenomena, and not directly with material phenomena. They deal with phenomena that can be understood only because the object of our study has a mind of a structure similar to our own. (p. 47)

And in accepting social science's primary objective of elaborating social wholes the social scientist can proceed by, albeit only by, tracing through the conceptual connections rooted in the base elements, the individual subjective opinions. Thus, while the significance of particular combinations of human attitudes and so on may not be immediately obvious, and may remain unrealized by individual agents, the social wholes can nevertheless be elaborated by the social scientist through building upon individual concepts and beliefs:

> The structure of men's minds, the common principle on which they classify external events, provides us with the knowledge of the recurrent elements of which different social structures are built up and in terms of which we can *alone* describe and explain them. While concepts or ideas can, of course, exist only in individual minds, and while, in particular, it is only in individual minds that different ideas can act upon another, it is not the whole of the individual minds in all their complexity, but the individual concepts, the views people have formed of each other and of the things, which form the true element of social structure...
>
> While we can recognise these elements of human relationships only because they are known to us from the working of our own minds, this does not mean that the significance of their combination in a particular pattern relating different individuals must be immediately obvious to us. It is only by the systematic and patient following up of the implications of many people holding certain views that we can understand, and often even only learn to see, the unintended and often uncomprehended results of the separate and yet interrelated actions of men in society. That in this effort to reconstruct these different patterns of social relations we must relate the individual's action not to the objective qualities of the persons and things toward which he acts, but that our data must be man and the physical world as they appear to the men whose actions we try to explain, follows from the fact that *only* what people know or believe can enter as a motive into their conscious action. (pp. 58–9, italics added).

In sum, interpretive understanding or, in effect, *Verstehen* (a term, however, which Hayek at this stage never uses) becomes necessary for social scientific explanation and, when complemented by the mental tracing through of relations between individual conceptions (or 'compositive analysis'), sufficient for it. In short, Hayek's position is an account of subjectivist or hermeneutic foundationalism.

The limitations of Hayek's hermeneuticism
Hayek's hermeneuticist or subjectivist position, then, is that lay opinions and beliefs uniquely and completely differentiate the social world, so that it is only and sufficiently by reference to such beliefs that the social world can be understood. The problem with this position is that, first, the social realm is not in fact exhausted by its conceptual aspects while, second, relevant conceptual aspects, typically, are not immediately available to consciousness (and so accessible by the social scientist) while the latter may in some way that is significant for social science be false.

On the first point Hayek is no doubt correct that social life is conceptually (as it is linguistically) mediated – so that *Verstehen* (or the grasping of subjective interpretations) is necessary for social science. Indeed the explananda of economics and other social sciences depend upon or consist in intentional human agency so that reference to beliefs, opinions, interpretations, attitudes and other conceptual matter is, in general, clearly necessary for any adequate social explanation (see, e.g. Bhaskar, 1979). But this attention to conceptual matters will not in general be sufficient. For human action always has a material aspect which cannot be reduced to its conceptual one. To an individual agent, being unemployed, on strike, living in poverty, and so on is not just (and sometimes perhaps not at all) possessing a particular idea of what one is doing: it involves being physically separated from the means of 'earning a living'; being party to industrial conflict, and being separated from (adequate) forms of health care, shelter and nutrition, with all the material problems which that involves. Indeed, social reality is inescapably embedded in, and internally related to, the material/physical basis of reality. If we consider Hayek's favourite examples of various instruments such as hammers or barometers (1942–44, p. 44) it is not in general the case, as Hayek supposes, that 'a definition which is to comprise all instances of the class will not contain any reference to its substance, or shape, or other physical attribute' (p. 45). Nor is it the case, even, that an 'ordinary hammer and a steamhammer, or an aneroid barometer and a mercury barometer, have nothing in common except the purpose for which men think they can be used' (p. 45). Again contra Hayek, the point is *not* 'that they are abstractions from *all* the physical attributes of the things in question and that their definitions must run entirely in terms of mental attitudes of men toward the things'

(p. 46). Rather, what the various tools, the varieties of hammer or of barometer, have in common is an intrinsic physical/material structure which facilitates the purpose intended. It is true that this physical structure may vary from one example of a hammer, say, to another. But physical structure is not thereby absent or irrelevant. Typically, when objects have become classified as hammers and so on it is because they have been found to do the job. They are called hammers not merely because of the *a priori* purpose for which they are designed/maintained/desired, but because *ex posteriori* they have been found suitable for that purpose, to possess an appropriate physical/material constitution, or set of properties/facilities. It is not because I label a snowflake a hammer that I succeed in constituting it as one. Similarly, to suggest, as Hayek does, that what 'is relevant in the study of society is not whether... laws of nature are true in any objective sense, but *solely* whether they are believed and acted upon by the people' (italics added) is to overstate the case once more – to overemphasize the conceptuality of society. It is not because gravity is (or is not) correctly perceived that individual agents (or earthbound things in general) are or are not propelled into outer space. And it is not merely beliefs about whether or not the earth is flat that determine whether or not people fall over an edge. Of course agent conceptions concerning gravity and the constitution of the earth always make a difference to their actions and so to the society that they help reproduce, but it can never be that their conceptualizations constitute all that is of relevance to society and so to social science.

In short, we intervene in, we both manipulate and are conditioned by, nature in all our causal interactions with the world, including those with other human agents. The social realm is not a dislocated redescription (or misspecification) of nature. Rather it is embedded within and in continuous dynamic causal interaction with the rest of nature – as the increasing incidence of worldwide poverty on the one hand and human-aided ecological disaster on the other clearly testify.

Now just as human action consists in something more than the concept under which the action falls, i.e. there is always a material dimension, so most human action, though not taking place independently of some concept, occurs independently of its adequate concept. By this, of course, I do not mean merely that agents' conceptions of 'external' or physical reality are fallible – a point that Hayek openly admits. I mean also that the immediate own intentions of agents and the meaning of their own acts may be opaque to themselves – frequently at the level of everyday interaction, and systematically at the level of the explanations and descriptions of the reasons motivating their contributions to such interaction. Thus, social science may reveal, as a necessary real condition of some actual social activity, a level or aspect of reality which, although not existing independently of agents' conceptions, may itself be quite unknown, or at least inadequately, including perhaps misleadingly, comprehended. Such a feature or level of reality may consist in real relations, or processes, or structural complexes that are really productive of social life but unavailable to direct access by the senses. It may also consist in an aspect of knowledge or motivation that is not consciously reflected upon. Hayek emphasizes that the 'social sciences...are concerned with man's conscious or reflected action, actions where a person can be said to choose between various courses open to him...' (p. 42). But it is not thereby the case that social science deals *only* with 'conscious or reflected', i.e. discursively decided upon, action. It is the case of course, that real choice, the ability to have acted otherwise, involves (presupposes) not only the transformational capacity of being able to 'make a difference' but also, to a greater or lesser extent, that the action is under the agent's control. In other words, human action is characterized by intentionality, it is caused by reasons, i.e. beliefs grounded in the practical interests of life, so that it is always directed towards some end. But the pursuit of ends cannot be understood as some simple, unitary, always discursive, activity. The complexity of human beings appears to be such that human powers include not only those (also possessed by other animals) of initiating changes in purposeful ways and monitoring and controlling performances, but also those of monitoring the monitoring of performances, of assessing one's own state of awareness during the course of activity, and of passing commentary upon, i.e. communicating information about, it. Now the economic life and social activity that each agent reflexively monitors is an ongoing flow – the individual's own acts, the doings of others, the socially constituted appropriateness of forms of conduct in specific settings, and so on. In consequence, the reflexive monitoring of activity must itself occur as a continuous flow rather than a discrete series of acts. But if the monitoring of conduct is an ongoing process then it must be largely *tacit* – a continuous discursive commentary appears infeasible. Only rarely is the discursive identification of acts attempted – and then usually in response to an explicit (internal or external) demand for clarification. The faculty of reflexive monitoring of activity, in short, presupposes not only a discursive consciousness but also the level of tacit consciousness. Now if the reflexive monitoring of conduct is largely tacit so too must be the reasoning and decision taking that occurs on a continuous basis. The underlying motives or needs that stimulate or prompt action, and the overall plans that may be formulated in line with them, tend to have direct bearing or purchase only in relatively unusual circumstances – such as in moments of significant changes in possibilities and constraints. Such motives and needs, in short, bear on the reasons for action rather than the manner or modes in which it is chronically carried out. But much day-to-day conduct is concerned precisely with the questions of possible modes in which relevant conduct can be carried out and thus will only be tacitly determined.

In addition to tacit consciousness, furthermore, a level of *unconscious* motivation can be recognized as bearing upon human praxis. If it is correctly observed by Veblen (and the later Hayek) that we are creatures of habit; by Keynes that, especially in conditions of uncertainty, we fall back on the 'convention' of supposing that the existing state of affairs will continue (until there are definite reasons to suppose otherwise); and by Giddens that agents chronically engage in the performance of routines, then some explanation is called for. But as human agents are typically not only unaware of the substantially routinized nature of their daily lives but are observed, even when pressed, to be unable to explain it, then a recognition of a level of unconscious motivation seems warranted. Of course, the unconscious motivations at work in the case of routines – i.e. the by now well researched, unconscious need to control anxiety through reproducing conditions of stability, sameness and continuity – though a feature of human subjectivity of significant consequence for praxis, is but one example of such a feature. For present purposes, however, one such is sufficient to indicate that, in their actions, human agents draw upon not only discursive thought but, in addition to tacit and unacknowledged skills, unconscious needs and motivations.

Thus, contra Hayek of the 'Scientism' essay, social life, the subject-matter of social science, has a material aspect and human conceptions are corrigible in a manner that is relevant to social science. In other words, the essential and productive role of human beliefs, opinions, wants and needs in social life must be recognized without lapsing into hermeneutic foundationalism whereby such items are treated as discursive, incorrigible and the sole constituents of society. Of course, because they are, in part, productive of society the conceptions that agents hold cannot be ignored. But total agreement between lay accounts and social science is not a condition for understanding all that is going on and, in particular, for identifying and understanding the actions through which society is reproduced. Rather, although indeed starting with lay concepts of what is going on, the social scientist must transform these insights into whatever account appears most explanatorily adequate – whether or not this proves to be particularly charitable to initiating (of social science) conceptions that lay agents hold. (Of course, Hayek implicitly presupposes precisely this by his very attempt to critique 'scientism' as he finds it within economics.)

Explaining Hayek's position

If Hayek's hermeneuticist reasoning is fallacious, what explains it? For at times Hayek writes as if supposing only that social life is concept-dependent (rather than concept-determined), and he surely recognized the complexity of the human mind and, specifically, the fact of different levels of consciousness? Yet his most sustained and apparently most influential account of methodology in the social sciences is full of explicit statements to the contrary. Although Hayek presents his account of social science as being contrasted to, and in competition with, positivist or 'collectivist' contributions, his problem, I now want to argue, lies ultimately in a failure to escape fully from positivist influence. Specifically, I want now to argue that Hayek's (effectively neo-Kantian) orientation rests on an essentially positivist perspective on natural science or at least, and more generally, on an implicit empiricist ontology. Once this is recognized Hayek's theory of social ontology and account of social science, if erroneous, are rendered comprehensible.

Consider first Hayek's account of natural science. Positivism turns on the Humean theory that laws, or significant results in science are, or depend upon, constant conjunctions of events or states of affairs, where the latter are interpreted as the objects of actual or possible experience. As noted above it is underpinned by, or presupposes, an empiricist ontology and an individualist account of human beings, that is by a perspective on reality as constituted by given and atomic facts or events, and a view of human beings as passive recorders of their constant conjunctions. The achievement of the programme is a viewpoint whereby whatever is given in experience is taken to constitute *all* that is real while because experience is thereby effectively constitutive of the world, it is in consequence held to be certain.

Now Hayek's account of natural science is easily recognizable as a (neo-Kantian) variation on these positivist themes. Hayek accepts that the aim of science is to seek out empirical regularities, to elaborate constant conjunctions of events or states of affairs, where the events so conjoined are the objects of actual or possible experience. His neo-Kantian development or gloss on this is merely to argue that in the process of elaborating empirical regularities science provides a classification of 'external stimuli' different from that immediately provided by our senses.[5] Thus, for example, while we might first of all classify all white powders together precisely because we immediately perceive them as powdery and white, science comes to reclassify any substances in question according to the sort of events that ensue when the substance is placed in alternative states or conditions, i.e. according to the event regularities with which they are thought to be associated.

Now in this process of reclassifying the objects of perception through seeking event regularities, non-perceivable entities such as, for example, 'atomic structures' or 'electromagnetic fields' are sometimes mentioned. But, significantly, Hayek avoids any acknowledgement of their existence or reality, referring to them only as 'constructs', or 'creations'. The purpose of such constructions, it seems, is merely to facilitate a 'rule' or a 'key' whereby the 'world of our senses' or 'sense perceptions' – perceptions in terms of which such constructs are themselves defined – are found to be related. In short, for Hayek, natural science is conceived of as the search for event regularities, and for the natural realm, an empiricist ontology is accepted. His contribution to the usual Humean account is to augment the conception of the scientist as a passive recorder of constant conjunctions by allowing in this a role for mental labour in producing the surplus elements that facilitate the elaboration of event relations, but which remain only constructions of the mind:

> This process of reclassifying 'objects' which our senses have already classified in one way, of substituting for the 'secondary' qualities in which our senses arrange external stimuli a new classification based on consciously established relations between classes of events is, perhaps, the most characteristic aspect of the procedure of the natural sciences. The whole history of modern science proves to be a process of progressive emancipation from our innate classification of the external stimuli till in the end they completely disappear so that 'physical science has now reached a stage of development that renders it impossible to express observable occurrences in language appropriate to what is perceived by our senses. The only appropriate language is that of mathematics'[6] that is, the discipline developed to describe complexes of relationships between elements which have no attributes except these relations. While at first the new elements into which the physical world was 'analyzed' were still endowed with 'qualities', that is, conceived as in principle visible or touchable, neither electrons nor waves, neither the atomic structure nor electromagnetic fields can be adequately represented by mechanical models.
>
> The new world which man thus creates in his mind, and which consists entirely of entities which cannot be perceived by our senses, is yet in a definite way related to the world of our senses. It serves, indeed, to explain the world of our senses. The world of Science might in fact be described as no more than a set of rules which enables us to trace the connections between different complexes of sense perceptions. But the point is that the attempts to establish such uniform rules which the perceptible phenomena obey have been unsuccessful so long as we accepted as natural units, given entities, such constant complexes of sense qualities as we can simultaneously perceive. In their place new entities, 'constructs', are created which can be defined only in terms of sense perceptions obtained of the 'same' thing in different circumstances and at different times – a procedure which implies the postulate that the thing has in some sense remained the same although all its perceptible attributes may have changed.
>
> In other words, although the theories of physical science at the stage which has now been reached can no longer be stated in terms of sense qualities, their significance is due to the fact that we possess rules, a 'key', which enables us to translate them into statement about perceptible phenomena'. (1942–44, pp. 32–4)

For Hayek, then, if to repeat, it appears that to be is to be perceivable, that empirical realism is the ontology implicitly subscribed to, and that natural science reduces to the search for event regularities, for constant conjunction of events, couched in terms of purely hypothetical conceptions or constructions.

From positivism to hermeneuticism

It was observed above that Hayek's insight is to recognize that individual subjective conceptions, opinions and beliefs are in some sense essential to social life. It has now also been noted that Hayek maintains an essentially positivist account of natural science – his empiricist ontology, i.e. his failure to recognize that science accepts a causal as well as a perceptual criterion for ascribing reality, prevents him from transcending positivism as in transcendental realism, but facilitates only its reworking in a particular neo-Kantian form.

It is this conceptual couple of society as concept-dependent and natural science as positivistic that, I suggest, accounts for Hayek's hermeneuticist foundationalism as an account of social science. For this combination clearly encourages a further reworking of positivism, or at least of many of its themes, resulting this time in an essentially subjectivized version. Thus, whereas in positivism in its original form, facts are given in sense perception and, being constitutive of reality, are certain while the scientist is, in essence, their passive autonomized recorder, in Hayek's subjectivist or hermeneutic key we find lay conceptions or opinions that are given to social science, and are inexplicable and so incorrigible by it, while the role of the social scientist is then passively to arrange these 'data', these interpretations, in orderly fashion[7]. In short, the brute facts of positivism are in effect transformed into the brute opinions, beliefs, attitudes and interpretations of hermeneuticism; the self-evidence of the empirical world in positivism is reflected in the self-characterization of the social world in hermeneuticism; the empiricist foundations of positivist natural science translated into conceptual foundations in Hayek's hermeneuticized scienticism.

Moreover, just as, in positivism, the objects of experience are atomistic, or externally related, so too are the beliefs, opinions or attitudes and so on that, for Hayek, comprise the base elements for, and constituents of, society. In consequence, then, the social wholes whose investigation is regarded by Hayek as the primary object of social science, are similarly atomistically constituted'.[8] In consequence, there can be no question of the internal-relatedness of structures, no category of totalities with properties irreducible to the parts and capable of sustaining endogenous change. The only obstacle to prediction, it appears, is the possible complexity of any such atomistically connected 'whole'. Thus whereas in the natural science the elaboration of event regularities constitutes the objective, this may be impossible in the social realm due to, but it seems only to, the degree of complexity to be found there, i.e. the 'number of separate variables' upon which any such regularity will depend:

> While the astronomer aims at knowing all the elements of which his universe is composed, the student of social phenomena cannot hope to know more than the types of elements from which his universe is made up. He will scarcely ever know

even all of the elements of which it consists and he will certainly never know all the relevant properties of each of them. The inevitable imperfection of the human mind becomes here not only a basic datum about the object of explanation but, since it applies no less to the observer, also a limitation on what he can hope to accomplish in his attempt to explain the observed facts. The number of separate variables which in any particular social phenomenon will determine the result of a given change will as a rule be far too large for any human mind to master and manipulate them effectively. In consequence our knowledge of the principle by which these phenomena are produced will rarely if ever enable us to predict the precise result of any concrete situation. (p. 73)

Perhaps the most interesting transposition of positivist themes, however, relates to the reputed reality, the existence, of social 'wholes'. In positivism the attempted dissolution of ontology, along with its resurrection in the notion of the empirical world, entails that only the perceivable is real. Thus, any non-directly perceivable 'entities' referred to in the elaboration of constant conjunctions of events are regarded as mere constructions or creations with no independent, real, existence. And with the collapse of the intransitive dimension under the influence of the epistemic fallacy, such generalities as are recorded, i.e. those connecting sensory items, are not considered to exist independently of their investigation. Transposed to a hermeneutical mode with the empiricist ontology argued to include thought itself, the 'wholes' whose elaboration, according to Hayek, constitutes the primary objective of social science, are equally conceived of as having no existence independently of their investigation:

> These 'wholes', in other words, do not exist for us apart from the theory by which we constitute them, apart from the mental technique by which we can reconstruct the connections between the observed elements and follow up the implications of this particular combination. (p. 125)

According to Hayek, then, things are either given to us in perception, in observation, as 'definite objects', or they are constructions of the mind which, with the privileged exception of thought itself, have no real existence, or at least none apart from the theory in which they are conceptualized.

It is worth dwelling on this point for a moment. Notice that on the one hand, and as just noted, with the dissolution of an intransitive dimension Hayek cannot, as transcendental realism can, allow without strain that such wholes, whose investigation constitutes the primary and legitimate objective of science, exist independently of their investigation. As such, such wholes cannot be *expressed* in social theories. For Hayek the 'theories of the social sciences ... are not *about* the social wholes as wholes' (Hayek, 1949, p. 72). Their task instead is to constitute those wholes. On the other hand, however, if social wholes are constituted in theory, and in that sense can be said to exist for us, Hayek cannot allow that the mere construction of any theory thereby constitutes, i.e. brings into existence for us, any whole that is conceptualized within it. Certainly, if such a *conceptual realism* (of which Hayek is so critical[9]), were accepted it is not obvious what distinguishing role social science could fulfil. Any claimed elaboration of a social whole would be as good as any other. In the end, then, Hayek has to maintain both that the constitution of any 'wholes' necessitates an adequate or 'correct' theory, while at the same time it is only through that theory that the whole is constituted:

> [Such wholes] can be studied only by following up the implications of the particular combinations of relationships. In other words, the wholes about which we speak exist only if, and to the extent to which, the theory is correct which we have formed about the connection of the parts which they imply, and which we can explicitly state only in the form of a model built from those relationships.
>
> The social sciences, thus, do not deal with 'given' wholes but their task is to *constitute* these wholes by constructing models from the familiar elements – models which reproduce the structure of relationships between some of the many phenomena which we always simultaneously observe in real life. (p. 98)

The issue then arises as to the criterion by which a theory is interpreted as being 'correct'. In the natural sciences, for Hayek, 'constructs' are persevered with when the event generalizations they underscore are found to be empirically adequate. In social science, in contrast, where social wholes are not objects or phenomena that can be perceived,[10] and the base elements are not empirical 'facts' but subjective opinions and attitudes, the adequacy of any elaborated connections can be assessed, it seems, *only* in the working of the mind.

Transcendental realism and the social realm

Once, then, it is recognized that Hayek fails to escape from various central features or themes of positivism but succeeds only in providing a hermeneuticized version, it is easy enough to see how the insight that social phenomena are concept-dependent encourages the oversight that concepts are exhaustive of society and economy. Behind it all lies Hayek's implicit, if augmented, empiricist ontology (with an acceptance of the associated epistemic fallacy) along with its presupposition of the relatively passive agent of science and society. Once it is acknowledged, however, that science properly employs a causal, in addition to the perceptual, criterion of existence, and that, as indicated by the analysis of the experimental situation in the natural realm and human choice and intentionality in the social, the world is structured and intransitive, then the basis is laid for the errors of positivism to be, as in transcendental realism, not merely displaced but effectively transcended.

It does not follow from all this, of course, that Hayek's account of social science is completely incorrect, or that there are no differences between natural and social science. But by maintaining a flat, atomistic, ontology Hayek is prevented from establishing the real significance of the subjectivist/ hermeneuticist insights while, by essentially abandoning natural science to positivism, he is prevented from locating the real natural/social scientific distinctions.

According to transcendental realism, as argued at the outset, natural and social realms are both structured and intransitive. Now in observing this the hermeneutic insights emphasized by Hayek, and particularly the recognition of the concept-dependent nature of social material, must not be overlooked. But just as it is an error, one characteristically committed in determinism, to reduce agency to structure, so it is equally an error, one often found in voluntarism and here taking on a hermeneuticist/subjectivist guise, to reduce structure to agency. Both reductionisms are equally to be avoided. For without the pre-existence of social structure intentional agency would be impossible, and without human beings social structure would not exist at all. Structure and agency, then, each presuppose the other, although neither can be reduced to, identified with, or explained completely in terms of, the other. What is required is not a conception whereby agency *creates* or constitutes structure, or vice versa. Rather instead of *creation* the relevant conception is *transformation*. Human activity does not *create* social structure for it is presupposed by that very activity. Instead individual agents draw upon social structure as a condition for acting, and through the action of individuals taken in total the structures are *reproduced* or *transformed*. The transformation of social structure, however, is rarely (although it may sometimes be) the reason that agents have for acting the way they do – although they will always have some conception of what they are doing in their activity. In addition, of course, there can be no *a priori* presumption that such conceptions will be discursively available, rather than, as will the rules of grammar, be tacit or, as with the control of anxiety and with other needs, be unconscious.

In the light of this transformational conception of social activity, then, social science must be recognized as concerned not only to determine the unintended consequences of action but equally to identify their unacknowledged conditions, including material requirements, tacit skills and unconscious motivations and needs. In short, the task of social science is to describe what social process must be going on in total for some manifest phenomenon to be possible.

As for understanding social wholes, including society, Hayek is, of course, correct, as against positivism in its pure form, that such wholes are never a mass of separable events and sequences available merely to perception. But if they cannot be read straight off from our experiences nor, typically, can they be constructed straight out of our self-interpretations. Rather any such whole may, in principle, be a complex, as well as causally efficacious, totality, subject to the possibility of endogenous as well as exogenous change, whose concept, though constructed in theory, must be continually subjected to empirical checks and assessment.[11]

After the 'Scientism' essay: from hermeneuticism to transcendental realism

In his preface to *Studies in Philosophy, Politics and Economics*, first published in 1967, Hayek acknowledges that, in the previous twenty to thirty years, he had spent significant effort in qualifying himself for the discussion of the problems of philosophy of science and of politics that arose from his earlier work in economics. In his 1965 essay entitled 'Kinds of Rationalism' – in which Hayek explicitly acknowledges the essay on 'Economics and Knowledge' as the beginning of his move from technical economics to questions of a philosophical kind – Hayek also notes that it was 'still a long way' from his earlier (1937) insights to his current position; a road which apparently involved, among other things, 'a re-examination of the age-old concept of freedom under the law, the basic conception of traditional liberalism, and of the problems of the philosophy of law which this raises' (p. 92). In various writings in this later period Hayek also acknowledges the influence of various named philosophers, most notably Popper, among others.

Now, I do not propose here to attempt to trace the particular path trodden by Hayek, nor become embroiled in such debates as those currently prominent about whether Hayek was really influenced by Popper, and if so in what way. Of course, to be influenced by someone does not necessitate that their position be adopted unamended – and in the light of his biographical notes in 'Two Types of Mind' (Hayek, 1975) a straightforward adoption of an alternative viewpoint appears particularly unlikely in Hayek's case. The point I want to emphasize here is merely that on his own admission, Hayek, by the mid-1960s at least, had undertaken significant philosophical reflection and re-training so that it is only to be expected that his earlier position might have been significantly amended. By focusing very briefly and schematically on one or two essays of that period, and particularly those collected together in *Studies in Philosophy, Politics and Economics* (1967a), I want to indicate the nature of his change and particularly his later, at least embryonic, acceptance of something like a transcendental realist ontology.[12]

Now a first point to note about Hayek's later writings is that, at the level of the situation facing any individual, the language of 'opinions' and 'attitudes' that predominates in his early 'Scientism' essay is replaced by that of 'rules that govern action', 'rules that people obey' and so on. That rules are irreducible to actions leads Hayek to investigate the conditions under which rules will be most strictly observed:

> The knowledge of some regularities of the environment will create a preference for those kinds of conduct which produce a confident expectation of certain consequences, and an aversion to doing something unfamiliar and fear when it has been done. This establishes a sort of connection between the knowledge that rules exist in the objective world and a disinclination to deviate from the rules commonly followed in action, and therefore also between the belief that events follow rules and the feeling that one 'ought' to observe rules in one's conduct. (p. 79)

Second, this acceptance that the social realm is structured, i.e. the recognition that certain structures, and specifically rules, exist and are irreducible to action (the event-analogue of the social realm) encourages a serious consideration of (or perhaps follows from a revision in Hayek's beliefs about) the manner in which social objects are known. Specifically discursive, tacit and unconscious levels of knowing or observing are now entertained. In his 1937 essay economic orthodoxy was (correctly) criticized for assuming that agents hold perfect knowledge or some such, when in fact, according to Hayek, each agent is only aware of segments of knowledge, when no one agent is capable of knowing it all. By the 1960s, the orthodox rationalist conception of agency is now criticized further for its neglect of the fact that much of what people know or observe is not even available to their conscious reasoning. Thus we find Hayek suggesting that we learn as children to use language 'according to rules we do not explicitly know' (p. 87); and that in interpreting the world and acting appropriately we draw upon 'rules that will guide us though we have never explicitly formulated them' (p. 87). In the end Hayek acknowledges that there is perhaps an element of non-discursive rule reliance in *all* our thinking and action: 'The fact to which I have just referred probably means that in all our thinking, we are guided (or even operated) by rules of which we are not aware, and that our conscious reason can therefore always take account only of some of the circumstances that determine our actions' (p. 87).

Third, with a gap opened up between individual conscious reflection and social structure, with a recognition that individuals, typically, are unable adequately to conceptualize all the conditions of their actions, the *focus* of the analysis now moves away from individual conceptions, and falls significantly more upon actions. The point of social science, in effect, becomes precisely to explain human actions – to identify and illuminate the conditions, internal and external, acknowledged or unacknowledged, that provide the basis upon which individual acts are performed.

> The concrete individual action will always be the joint effect of internal impulses, such as hunger, the particular external events acting upon the individual

(including the actions of other members of the group) and the rules applicable to the situation thus determined. The rules upon which different individual members of a group will at any moment act may therefore be different either because the drives or external circumstances acting upon them make different rules applicable, or because different rules apply to different individuals according to age, sex, status, or some particular state in which each individual finds himself at the moment. (p. 68)

It is important always to remember that a rule of conduct will never by itself be a sufficient cause of action but that the impulse for actions of a certain kind will always come either from a particular external stimulus or from an internal drive (and usually from a combination of both), and that the rules of conduct will always act only as a restraint on actions induced by other causes. (pp. 68–9)

Yet, though the whole of economic theory (and, I believe, of linguistic theory) may be interpreted as nothing else but an endeavour to reconstruct from regularities of the individual actions the character of the resulting order, it can hardly be said that economists are fully aware that this is what they are doing. The nature of the different kinds of rules of individual conduct (some voluntarily or even unconsciously observed and some enforced), which the formation of the order presupposes, is frequently left obscure. (p. 72)

Fourth, with the social order now recognized as dependent on human conceptions but no longer reduced to them, and with the possible inadequacy and non-discursive nature of agent conceptions acknowledged, the compositive method of mentally tracing relationships between individual conceptions or beliefs, no longer receives attention. At one point, indeed, Hayek suggests that 'a particular *order* of actions can be observed and described without knowledge of the rules of conduct of the individuals which bring it about' (p. 68). Focusing specifically on the methods of history, compositive theory is now replaced by 'conjectural history', which is retroductive in method, giving rise to theories which can be empirically 'tested', which are assessed, in essence, according to their relative explanatory power:

Conjectural history in this sense is the reconstruction of a hypothetical kind of process which may never have been observed but which, if it had taken place, would have produced phenomena of the kind we observe. The assumption that such a process has taken place may be tested by seeking for yet unobserved consequences which follow from it, and by asking whether all regular structures of the kind in question which we find can be accounted for by that assumption. (p. 75)

Fifth, with social objects of knowledge such as rules and now processes apparently recognized as intransitive, i.e. acknowledged as existing independently, at least in part, of the knowledge that individuals have of them, Hayek is now able to countenance explaining how rules of individual conduct change:

Such systems of learnt rules will probably nevertheless be more flexible than a system of innate rules and a few more remarks on the process by which they may change will be in place…One factor influencing it will be the order of dominance of the individuals within the group. There will be, on the one end of the scale, a greater margin of tolerance for the young who are still in the process of learning and who are accepted as members of the group, not because they have already learnt all the rules peculiar to the group, but because as natural offspring they are attached to particular adult members of the group. On the other end of the scale there will be dominant old individuals who are firmly set in their ways and not likely to change their habits, but whose position is such that if they do acquire new practices they are more likely to be imitated than to be expelled from the group. The order of rank is thus undoubtedly an important factor in determining what alterations will be tolerated or will spread, though not necessarily in the sense that it will always be the high-ranking who initiate changes. (pp. 78–9)

In short, Hayek's ontological presuppositions and his consequent formulation of the possibilities for social science have undergone a radical change. In place of hermeneutic foundationalism an embryonic transcendental realist account is accepted. In emphasizing this I do not wish to imply that all that Hayek concludes in the course of his later writing is somehow entailed by his adopting a transcendental realist perspective. In particular, such a general perspective implies no automatic support for Hayek's often functionalist emphasis in his evolutionary theory, nor for his reduction of social reality to an essentially rule-constituted social ontology. Nor does it follow that Hayek's well known conclusions concerning the supposed superiority of the existing social order in comparison to feasible alternatives are in any way necessitated or compelling.[13] Transcendental realism is susceptible to various specific forms of elaboration (one example is the version recently systematized as *critical realism* – see for example Bhaskar, 1975, 1979, 1989; Lawson, 1989a, 1989b, 1994a, 1994d). But a transcendental realist account Hayek's later contribution appears to be. The flat ontology of empirical realism is in some measure replaced by a differentiated ontology of structured, intransitive objects, while the nature of human agency and the character of social science are accordingly reassessed[14] – a move which, however tentative, marks something of a transformation in Hayek's thought.

Conclusion
Hayek's social theorizing is often interpreted as radically 'subjectivist' and in this guise has proven to be influential. However, if the arguments of this paper are correct such a position, stylized here as hermeneutic foundationalism, represented only a stage on his course of philosophical transformation. It was an important stage, providing the content for 'Scientism and the Study of Society' which is probably his most sustained philosophical work. But it was no more than a stage, and an untenable one at that. In parallel with the

positivist reduction of physical reality to experience, Hayek merely reduced society to interpretation – a foundationalism that appears to have given way in later years as, in effect, a transcendental realist perspective came to be elaborated.

Notes

1. Hutchison (1981) for example distinguishes 'Hayek I (–1936)' and 'Hayek II (1937–)' claiming that, although there is some constancy in Hayek's writings, 1936 provides a 'vital turning point' or 'U-turn' or 'fundamental shift' (p. 215) in Hayek's methodological position. Hutchison interprets Hayek I and Hayek II as, in effect, two internally consistent if opposed bodies of thought. Bruce Caldwell (1988, 1989, 1992) in a series of papers on Hayek's transformation agrees 'that the publication of "Economics and Knowledge" constitutes an important turning point for Hayek' (1992), but takes issue with Hutchison's interpretation of what was involved. Even Caldwell, however, encourages the view that Hayek's methodological views remain fairly fixed after the 'turning point' noted. Thus, while assessing Hayek's 'Scientism' essay, Caldwell (1989) argues, for example, that '... virtually all of Hayek's later writings on methodology simply extend themes found in this essay; little of importance was added in the intervening years'. See also Paqué (1990, p. 282) amongst others.
2. For further discussions of transcendental realism see Bhaskar (1978, 1979, 1986, 1989) and Lawson (1989a, 1989b, 1992, 1994a, 1994b).
3. In saying this I do not wish to deny a degree of continuity in Hayek's philosophical position especially regarding his (initially largely implicit) theory of knowledge. For an excellent contribution which indeed emphasizes an 'essential unity underlying Hayek's thought on knowledge over the course of half a century' see Böhm (1989).
4. Uskali Mäki (1990) has noted the possibility of giving a subjectivist interpretation to the following passage but questions it. More precisely Mäki suggests that the passage be 'interpreted suitably' meaning *not* after all in the subjectivist manner I am proposing. Mäki's reasoning is that it 'would not seem to be compatible with the reconstruction of Austrian explanation suggested [by Mäki] to adopt the view that the domain of economics has a subjective (ideal, mental, conceptual) character all down the line' (pp. 335, 336). Now Mäki's reconstruction of Austrian explanation is essentially a version of the form of explanation that, above, I have collected under the general heading of transcendental reasoning. Mäki, accepting Hayek as within the Austrian tradition, finds it hard to reconcile Hayek's comments in his Scientism essay with his interpretation of Austrianism. But my point is precisely that Hayek is not consistent, or constant, through time. Only much later (i.e. several years after writing his Scientism essay – see below) does Hayek's reasoning approach Mäki's interpretation of Austrian explanation, a position here generalized as transcendental realism. For further evidence of Hayek's 1940s' subjectivism 'all down the line' see below.
5. This distinction relates to his contrast drawn in *The Sensory Order* between the phenomenal and the physical world. Here Hayek employs 'the pair of terms "phenomenal" and "physical" to describe the order of events perceived in terms of sensory qualities and the order of events defined exclusively in terms of their relations respectively' (1952, p. 4).
6. The quotation marks within this statement denote the fact that the relevant phrase is being borrowed, by Hayek, from Stebbing (1939).
7. Hayek puts it as follows: 'It is important to observe that in all this the various types of individual beliefs or attitudes are not themselves the object of our explanation, but merely the elements from which we build up the structure of possible relationships between individuals. In so far as we analyse individual thought in the social sciences the purpose is not to explain that thought but merely to distinguish the possible types of elements with which we shall have to reckon in the construction of different patterns of social relationships. It is a mistake, to which careless expressions by social scientists often give countenance, to believe that their aim is to *explain* conscious action. This, if it can be done at all,

is a different task, the task of psychology. For the social sciences the types of conscious action are data and all they have to do with regard to these data is to arrange them in such orderly fashion that they can be effectively used for their task' (1942–44, p. 68).

8. Hayek, for example, writes: 'The physicist who wishes to understand the problems of the social sciences with the help of an analogy from his own field would have to imagine a world in which he knew by direct observation the inside of the atoms and had neither the possibility of making experiments with lumps of matter nor the opportunity to observe more than the interactions of a comparatively few atoms during a limited period. From his knowledge of the different kinds of atoms he could build up models of all the various ways in which they could combine into larger units and make these models more and more closely reproduce all the features of the few instances in which he was able to observe more complex phenomena. But the laws of the macrocosm which he could derive from his knowledge of the microcosm would always remain a 'deductive'; they would, because of his limited knowledge of the data of the complex situation, scarcely ever enable him to predict the precise outcome of a particular situation; and he could never confirm them by controlled experiment – although they might be disproved by the observation of events which according to his theory are impossible' (1942–44, p. 72).

9. Hayek writes: 'The naïve realism which uncritically assumes that where there are commonly used concepts there must also be definite "given" things which they describe is so deeply embedded in current thought about social phenomena that it requires a deliberate effort of will to free ourselves from it. While most people will readily admit that in this field there may exist special difficulties in recognizing definite wholes because we have never many specimens of a kind before us and therefore cannot readily distinguish their constant from their merely accidental attributes, few are aware that there is a much more fundamental obstacle: that the wholes as such are never given to our observation but are without exception constructions of our mind' (p. 96).

10. As Hayek writes at one point: '[Natural Scientists] are used to seek first for empirical regularities in the relatively complex phenomena that are immediately given to observation, and only after they have found such regularities to try and explain them as the product of a combination of other, often purely hypothetical, elements (constructs) which are assumed to behave according to simpler and more general rules. They are therefore inclined to seek in the social field, too, first for empirical regularities in the behaviour of the complexes before they feel that there is need for a theoretical explanation. This tendency is further strengthened by the experience that there are few regularities in the behaviour of individuals which can be established in a strictly objective manner; and they turn therefore to the wholes in the hope that they will show such regularities. Finally, there is the rather vague idea that since "social phenomena" are to be the object of study, the obvious procedure is to start from the direct observation of these "social phenomena," where the existence in popular usage of such terms as *society* or *economy* is naïvely taken as evidence that there must be definite "objects" corresponding to them' (p. 94).

11. I have considered Hayek's 'Scientism and the Study of Society' at length here because it is, I think, Hayek's best known, most influential methodological contribution. However, I do not wish to imply that it is the only contribution of its period in which an essentially hermeneutic foundationalist orientation shines through. Indeed in other contributions his position is often more compact and direct as, for example, in the following passage from 'The Facts of the Social Sciences': 'This is all the theories of the social sciences aim to do. They are not *about* the social wholes as wholes; they do not pretend to discover by empirical observation laws of behaviour or change of these wholes. Their task is rather, if I may so call it, to *constitute* these wholes, to provide schemes of structural relationships which the historian can use when he has to attempt to fit together into a meaningful whole the elements which he actually finds. The historian cannot avoid constantly using social theories in this sense....

There are two important consequences which follow from this and which can here be only briefly stated. The first is that the theories of the social sciences do not consist of "laws" in the sense of empirical rules about the behaviour of objects definable in physical terms. All that the theory of the social sciences attempts is to provide a technique of reasoning which assists us in connecting individual facts, but which, like logic or mathematics, is not about the facts. It can, therefore, and this is the second point, never be verified or falsified by reference to facts' (Hayek, 1943, pp. 72–3).

12.   A result, of course, of treating as a relative fixed line of thought one that is in continuous transformation is not only a variety of interpretations, but instances of central points in some appearing as anomalies in others. Thus, for example, while Caldwell (1989) endorses certain of Hayek's comments as designed 'to undercut a belief that has little currency today, at least amongst economists: namely, the notion that collectivities have an independent existence' (p. 14), Peacock (1991), in contrast, explicitly adopting a critical realist perspective, observes of Hayek's remarks: 'However, Hayek... on some occasions, has the unfortunate habit of describing social wholes and structures as nothing more than theoretical constructs' (p. 32).

13.   In other words, if Hayek's eventual position may be appropriately characterized as a transcendental realism it remains relatively impoverished both in nature and the extent of its elaboration. In particular it does not, I think, compare with recent developments in the transcendental realist project systematized under the heading of *critical realism* (Bhaskar, 1975, 1979, 1989; Lawson 1989a, 1989b, 1994a). Although this is a topic that cannot be entered into here, a brief comment should perhaps be made on the question of rational societal change. It is well known, of course, that Hayek, throughout his career, and as just noted above, implied superiority for the existing social–economic order over any conceivable alternative. Although his argument was based on the criterion of making efficient use of decentralized and dispersed local knowledge, in truth such a conclusion was built into his early philosophical presuppositions. For with the flat, undifferentiated, ontology of empirical realism, whether in pure or transposed form, real change becomes impossible (just as science becomes too easy).

Transcendental realism, however, does allow of significant change, of structural transformation (see Lawson, 1994d). It is thus significant that with his implicit acceptance of transcendental realism in the later years Hayek tends to play down the potential for changes by reducing the content of structure, most of the time, to rules, while encouraging the view that the objective of policy is to change rules in ways in which we are all equally and beneficially affected.

In contrast, the perspective systematized under the heading critical realism entails a conception of structure that is not limited to rules. Indeed, it supports, primarily, a *relational* conception of the social, including a central concern for the relationally defined positions into which agents essentially slot, with their associated, relationally defined, positioned practices, rights, tasks, obligations, prerogatives and so on. In other words, rules in current society are seen to be, as with much else, differentiated and tied to definite interests, power structures and resources in the position-practice system that characterizes the existing, market-economy based, social order. In consequence, among other things, any assessment of the desirability of the existing order must focus on issues of relative freedoms in addition to the efficient use of knowledge.

In similar fashion, the viable alternatives to the present order are conceptualized differently on the critical realist perspective. Notably, they consist neither in the possibility of an all-knowing dictatorship nor, as some 'scientific socialists' would have it, in an economy or society without determination. Rather, an alternative social order would, for example, be of a kind in which unwanted, unneeded, and restrictive modes of determination are replaced by wanted, needed and emancipatory ones. To emphasize all this, of course, is not to deny that Hayek's concerns, i.e. the use of knowledge, or on the nature of rules, in society would not be central issues to any alternative social conception. It is just, to make the obvious point, that unless at least the natures both of the existing social order and the alternative real possibilities are adequately elaborated, any claim concerning the possible superiority/inferiority of either cannot be seriously assessed.

14.   The characterization of social science may have changed but even here I think the improvement should not be exaggerated. Indeed, I think it can be argued that Hayek perhaps never fully or in any consistent, non-ambivalent way, relinquishes the view that

science, including the study of society, ought really to be, or be analogous or in parallel to, the seeking out of constant conjunctions of events.

References

Bhaskar, R. (1978), *A Realist Theory of Science*, Sussex: Harvester Press, 2nd ed. (1st ed., Leeds: Leeds Books Ltd, 1975).

Bhaskar, R. (1979), *The Possibility of Naturalism*, Sussex: Harvester Press.

Bhaskar, R. (1986), *Scientific Realism and Human Emancipation*, London: Verso.

Bhaskar, R. (1989), *Reclaiming Reality*, London: Verso.

Böhm, S. (1989), 'Hayek on Knowledge, Equilibrium and Prices: Context and Impact', *Wirtschaftspolitische Blätter*, **36**(2), 201–13.

Caldwell, B.J. (1988), 'Hayek's Transformation', *History of Political Economy*, **20**(4), Winter, 513–41.

Caldwell, B.J. (1989), 'Hayek's Methodology: Explication, Analysis, and Questions', mimeo in English, University of North Carolina (page references are to this); French version published in G. Dostaler and D. Ethier (eds), *Fredrich Hayek: Philosophie, économie et politique*, Paris: Economica.

Caldwell, B.J. (1992), 'Hayek the Falsificationist? A Refutation', *Research in the History of Economic Thought and Methodology*, **10**, 1–15.

Hayek, F.A. von (1937), 'Economics and Knowledge', *Economica*, **IV**, 33–54. Reprinted in Hayek (1949), (page references to the latter).

Hayek, F.A. von (1943), 'The Facts of the Social Sciences', *Ethics*, **LIV**, 1–13. Reprinted in Hayek (1949) (page references to the former).

Hayek, F.A. von (1942–44), 'Scientism and the Study of Society', *Economica* (various issues). Reprinted in *The Counter-Revolution of Science*, Indianapolis: Liberty Press (page references to the latter).

Hayek, F.A. von (1949), *Individualism and Economic Order*, London and Henley: Routledge and Kegan Paul.

Hayek, F.A. von (1952), *The Sensory Order: An Inquiry into the Foundations of Theoretical Psychology*, London: Routledge and Kegan Paul.

Hayek, F.A. von (1965), 'Kinds of Rationalism', *The Economic Studies Quarterly*, Tokyo, **XV**, 3, republished in Hayek (1967a) (page references to the latter).

Hayek, F.A. von (1967a), *Studies in Philosophy, Politics and Economics*, London: Routledge and Kegan Paul.

Hayek, F.A. von (1967b), 'Notes on the Evolution of Systems of Rules of Conduct', published as Chapter 4 of Hayek (1967a).

Hayek, F.A. von (1975), 'Two Types of Mind', *Encounter*, **45**, reprinted with additions in Hayek (1978).

Hayek, F.A. von (1978), *New Studies in Philosophy, Politics, Economics and the History of Ideas*, London, Melbourne and Henley: Routledge and Kegan Paul.

Hodgson, G., M. Tool and W. Samuels (eds), (1994), *The Elgar Companion to Institutional and Evolutionary Economics*, Aldershot, Edward Elgar.

Hutchison, T.W. (1981), *The Politics and Philosophy of Economics: Marxians, Keynesians, and Austrians*, Oxford: Basil Blackwell.

Lawson, T. (1989a), 'Abstraction, Tendencies and Stylised Facts: A Realist Approach to Economic Analysis', *Cambridge Journal of Economics*, **13**(1), March, 59–78. Reprinted in T. Lawson, G. Palma and J. Sender (eds) (1989), *Kaldor's Political Economy*, London and San Diego, Calif: Academic Press. Also reprinted in P. Ekins (ed.) (1992), *Real-life Economics: Understanding Wealth Creation*, London, New York: Routledge.

Lawson, T. (1989b), 'Realism and Instrumentalism in the Development of Econometrics', *Oxford Economic Papers*, **41**(1), 236–58. Reprinted in N. De Marchi and C. Gilbert (eds) (1990), *The History and Methodology of Econometrics*, Oxford: Oxford University Press.

Lawson, T. (1992), 'Realism, Closed Systems and Friedman', *Research in the History of Economic Thought and Methodology*, **10**, 149–69.

Lawson, T. (1994a), 'Realism, Philosophical', in Hodgson et al. (1994).

Lawson, T. (1994b), 'Methodology', in Hodgson et al. (1994).
Lawson, T. (1994c), 'Econometrics, The Limits of', in Hodgson et al. (1994).
Lawson, T. (1994d), 'Critical Realism and the Analysis of Choice, Explanation and Change', *Advances in Austrian Economics*, **1**, 3–30.
Mäki, U. (1990), 'Scientific Realism and Austrian Explanation', *Review of Political Economy*, **2**(3), 310–44.
Paqué, K.M. (1990), 'Pattern Predictions in Economics: Hayek's Methodology of the Social Sciences Revisited', *History of Political Economy*, **22**(2), 281–94.
Peacock, M. (1991), 'Realism in Economics', mimeo, Sussex University.
Stebbing, L.S. (1939), *Thinking to Some Purpose*, Harmondsworth, Middlesex: Pelican Books.

8 Hayek and knowledge: some question marks
Stephan Böhm*

To say that 'knowledge', or 'the problem of knowledge', strikes at the heart of Hayek's social philosophy in general and his characteristic version of economic theory in particular is both a commonplace and an understatement.

It is a commonplace because whenever the informational economy of a market-price system is informally discussed – encapsulated in some slogan such as: 'how little the agents steered, or guided, by the price system need to know in order to take "correct" decisions' – footnotes to Hayek's early forays into the economics of knowledge invariably abound.[1] What has been less appreciated in the general commentaries,[2] though, is the extent to which Hayek's line of inquiry follows an entirely different path from the one mapped out in what was to emerge as 'the economics of information'.

To anticipate in brief, whatever Hayek's notion of knowledge may be, it cannot simply be subsumed within 'information' as conceptualized in the economics of information literature. For Hayek, then, 'knowledge' is emphatically not simply an $n + 1$ traded commodity which can be acquired at some specified resource cost. Such commodities (called 'pure Arrow–Debreu commodities'), as is well known, are characterized by their complete technical description, the time and place of their availability, and (for contingent commodities) the event of their delivery (see Allen, 1990, for a lucid recent statement). But Hayek is most concerned with knowledge that cannot directly be obtained at *any* cost, knowledge that is not marketable like any other commodity.[3] It is therefore not particularly illuminating, if not downright misleading, for Jagdish Bhagwati to call attention to Hayek's 'then [in the 1930s and 1940s] novel views that information is an *input* in the functioning of an economic system' as pointing to '*the source of inefficiency under socialism*' (Bhagwati, 1992, p. 38; emphasis added). The language used by Bhagwati accords well with what George Shackle identified as the standard treatment of 'knowledge as a *stuff*, obtainable in measurable quantities for a known expenditure, and guaranteed to produce effects knowable in advance' (Shackle, 1972, p. 114; emphasis added).

*For helpful discussions, comments and reactions I am grateful, in one way or another, to Jack Birner, Bruce Caldwell, Lord (Meghnad) Desai, Steve Fleetwood, Tony Lawson and Andrea Salanti. The usual caveat applies.

To say that concern with 'knowledge' is at the centre of Hayek's thinking is to indulge in an understatement because there are not many other economists, if any at all, who immersed themselves in broadly epistemological issues to such an extent as he did. 'Hayek is at all times an epistemologist, especially when doing technical economics, and even in his historical and popular writings' (Weimer, 1982, p. 263). It should, in particular, be noted that it was his epistemological stance that provided Hayek with the intellectual ammunition and sustained him in his lifelong crusade against socialism, or more correctly, anything and everything that smacks of central planning or global interventionism.

In what follows I wish to consider two sets of arguments pertaining to my broad theme, famously indicated by the (deliberate) ambiguity of the title of Hayek's essay on 'Economics and Knowledge' (Hayek, 1937). As he sets out, its 'main subject is ... the role which assumptions and propositions about the knowledge possessed by the different members of society play in economic analysis'. But as Hayek is quick to point out, there is also the related question which might be raised under the same heading, i.e. 'to what extent formal economic analysis conveys any knowledge about what happens in the real world' (Hayek, 1937, p. 33).

A Hayekian economics of knowledge perspective

The central question according to Hayek

As a point of entry into this circle of ideas, let me latch on to Hayek's programmatic pronouncement concerning the *division of knowledge* as 'the really central problem of economics as a social science' (Hayek, 1937, p. 50). The paramount importance Hayek attaches to the problem of the division of knowledge in society is clearly motivated by his enduring intellectual enterprise: to explain how the interactive adaptations of individual agents following general rules, each drawing on different bits of, possibly contradictory, knowledge, generate a state of affairs which could be deliberately instituted only by someone having access to the combined bits of knowledge dispersed among members of society. This is, in Hayek's words, the 'central question of all social sciences, how the combination of fragments of knowledge existing in different minds can bring about results which, if they were to be brought about deliberately, would require a knowledge on the part of the directing mind which no single person can possess' (Hayek, 1937, p. 54).

Taken at face value, there are several issues emerging from this passage that, if not running counter to distinctly Hayekian tenets, strike me at least as worth pondering and calling for clarification. Hayek's phrasing of the 'central problem' of economics as a social science suggests, in the first place, that the notion of knowledge as being bound up with – that is, as not being available independently of – the social process of its generation may be dispensed with. But as Hayek himself insisted, knowledge is not simply 'out there' for the taking. Knowledge is a social institution: it cannot be acquired in splendid isolation, except on the presupposition that knowledge is solely grounded in experience provided by the senses (this would, of course, also hold for any would-be Descartes seeking to erect the edifice of knowledge on the secure foundation of reason). Neither does knowledge come in bits and pieces; it is embedded in the social practices of a particular community.

Secondly and closely related to the first point, Hayek conveys the impression – and again on Hayekian grounds (see, for instance, Hayek, 1946, p. 103) he would be mistaken to hold such a view – that the outcomes of competitive market transactions are independent of the processes generating them. And in this sense his programmatic declaration veers perilously close towards the Arrow–Debreu conception of the perfectly competitive economy in which an equilibrium state is decidedly not the outcome of some social mechanism generating it. Indeed, it has become a standard complaint against the Arrow–Debreu model of general equilibrium that it poses the allocation of resources as a once-and-for-all decision problem, thus abstracting from the introduction of new production technology and new products and the constant emergence of new market participants (see, for example, Stiglitz, 1989, p. 7).

Thirdly, and most irritatingly, Hayek can be read – whether the account is charitable is a moot question – as intimating that the spontaneous ordering processes have a preassigned *telos* – some definite configuration, equilibrium or otherwise, towards which they are presumed to converge. This way of thinking sits somewhat uneasily with the asserted open-endedness and essential unpredictability of specific market outcomes and, above all, the notion of the market as a creative process – as facilitating 'a voyage of exploration into the unknown, an attempt to discover new ways of doing things better than they have been done before' (Hayek, 1946, p. 101). In neglecting the creative role of individual choice, any anthropomorphic understanding of the market order as teleological is misconceived. As James Buchanan and Viktor Vanberg have recently urged, 'If the market is genuinely perceived as an open-ended, nondetermined evolutionary process in which the essential driving force is human choice, any insinuation, however subtle, of a "telos" toward which the process can be predicted to move must be inherently misleading' (Buchanan and Vanberg, 1991, p. 180).

The basic point to grasp, according to Buchanan and Vanberg, is that whatever the market order may consist in, the 'order' constitutive of it – that is, a specific allocative outcome – cannot be defined independently of the process generating it. That is to say, without the voluntary exchange interactions, there cannot be any 'order'. The order is defined as it were in its emergence (Buchanan, 1982). To liken the order emanating from market adjustments to the order that would ensue if designed and engineered by an omniscient mind gives the game away all too easily, i.e. by encouraging the notion that an omniscient master planner would in principle not face any difficulties in mimicking market outcomes.

But there is a catch here: in order for such an exercise in welfare economics to be conceivable at all, it needs to be based on the presupposition that prior to the act of choosing agents are endowed with well behaved preference functions. If, on the other hand, markets are primarily construed as 'an environment for preference development' (McPherson, 1983, p. 119), an arena for the expression of autonomy (rather than as instruments at the disposal of the central planner for satisfying existing wants supposedly perfectly known to him), as has been the wont of economists with an Austrian mind-set to emphasize, the notion of an omniscient master planner catering to preferences as yet to be revealed through future choices is nothing short of bizarre.

To be sure, on the basis of such a dubious juxtaposition the relative superiority of market arrangements on informational grounds may easily be argued for. What is missing, though, from such considerations, as Buchanan and Vanberg remind us, is an appreciation of the limitations that a non-teleological understanding of market processes imposes on the analyst. The deeply flawed conception of 'the market economy' with its teleological moorings, derived on the analogy of a military unit as an entity with a clearly defined hierarchy of objectives of its own, runs foul of the basic subjectivist tenet that the outcomes of market transactions cannot in their very nature be gauged against a benchmark severed from individual choices that could have been different. 'There is no "external," independently defined objective against which the results of market processes can be evaluated' (Buchanan and Vanberg, 1991, p. 181).

Hayek's rendering of the 'central question' *may* further lend itself to the reading – and again it would run counter to the drift of his thinking – that if there were an omniscient, directing mind, the combination of fragments of knowledge existing in different minds, to use his locution, could deliberately be brought about as results that would otherwise obtain. But as Buchanan and Vanberg (1991, p. 180) rightly emphasize, any conceptualization of an omniscient, directing mind – even if only alluded to in the negative – is misleading because it implies a *telos* defined independently of the market participants' creative choices.

It is precisely this sort of reading that prompted Frank Hahn's comment, in his Fred Hirsch Memorial Lecture, on Hayek. Having noted Hayek's recognition of the significance of the highly decentralized nature of much economically relevant knowledge, Hahn comments:

Indeed, it is quite clear that such specialised knowledge and information is commonplace. Now one of the claims made for the price system by Hayek was that it successfully aggregates this information so that the economy behaves as if there had been no specialised knowledge in the first place. Hayek did not prove this to be so and it is only very recently that we have understood the circumstances in which the claim made is correct. (Hahn, 1982, p. 16)

That Hahn presupposes here in standard fashion that the results of market processes can be evaluated against a well defined standard formulated independently of the choosing process of market participants is further underscored when he goes on to say, 'The economising of information and the utilisation of widely dispersed information is one feature of a market economy which has only recently been studied with the seriousness it deserves. It is already evident that *the outcome will not always be as good as it could have been if an all-knowing agent were in control*' (Hahn, 1982, p. 17, italics added).

The destination of the path Hahn is treading is preordained. It is hardly surprising, therefore, to find him arguing that what he calls 'the pure theory of the invisible hand' should be taken prescriptively: 'That is, the task of the planners is to make the invisible hand work as the textbook says it does: for instance, by instructing functionaries to follow marginal cost pricing rules or to attain some prescribed rate of return in their investment plans' (ibid.).

Now, the point at issue is not whether Hahn's reading of Hayek is adequate, but rather how easily what purports to be an invisible hand theory lends itself to a transformation into a design theory. For the question that immediately suggests itself (if the planner is held to be in a position to instruct Hahn's 'functionaries') is why, put at its starkest, one should bother with markets in the first place, and – following the argument to its logical conclusion – why one should not take recourse to directing the production and distribution of commodities and services *ex cathedra*.

Against the background of the canonical efficiency theorems of Paretian welfare economics the standard argument, very briefly, runs along the following lines. According to the 'second fundamental theorem' of welfare economics, which is of sole concern here, it is possible to prove the following proposition: every Pareto-efficient feasible allocation of resources is attainable as a perfectly competitive market equilibrium allocation given the appropriate distribution of wealth.[4] This then suggests at first blush an attractive, irresistible opportunity for economic policy. A policy maker who finds the welfare distribution implied by a given market equilibrium disagreeable should, according to the theorem, not interfere with the competitive market mechanism but rather change the initial distribution of resources directly. Thereby is claimed a neat separation between the workings of markets and the sphere of political interference. We are invited to conceive of the market mechanism as an efficient resource allocation machine, on the analogy of a sausage machine: first feed in the appropriate distribution of resources, then let the unfettered market mechanism churn away, and out comes the desired distribution of welfare.

Since well aired caveats about this proposal abound, there is no need here to dwell on them. A couple of points must suffice. First, if the desired distribution of resources requires a large-scale redistribution of ownership bordering on a political revolution, then the case for the supposedly depoliticized market mechanism is thoroughly undermined. In that sense, the 'second fundamental theorem' certainly belongs to the 'revolutionary's handbook' (see Sen, 1985, p. 11).[5] Furthermore, if the government wishes to engage in a redistribution of initial endowments, through a mixture of lump-sum taxes and subsidies in order to maximize the criterion of social welfare, before allowing perfectly competitive markets to do their bit, the information it would need to have about individual tastes and productivities, and technological possibilities – disregarding for the moment the very serious issue of how to persuade agents to reveal the required information, is such that one may wonder why it should take recourse to the price mechanism in the first place. If the government knows as much about personal characteristics and resource constraints as the 'second fundamental theorem' invites it to know, why should it not enforce the full optimum directly by command? Indeed, on strictly consequentialist, 'welfarist' grounds (that is, evaluating states of affairs by utility information only), why not? So we have come full circle to the structure of Hahn's argument: the question then presents itself whether there is much to choose between the price mechanism and the command system for attaining the full welfare optimum. The upshot of the matter is that economists' appeal to the 'second fundamental theorem', which is usually seen as bolstering the role of markets (suggesting as it does that governments in pursuit of the *optimum optimorum* ought to rely on markets), is singularly ill-suited to make the case for relying on markets because it considers circumstances in which they become superfluous. As Partha Dasgupta concedes tellingly, 'I have no explanation for this paradox' (Dasgupta, 1986, p. 31).

Having completed this minor detour it is time to revert to Hayek. In Buchanan and Vanberg's account Hayek's thoughts on the matter are not mentioned in any detail, but obviously his work was very much on their minds in drafting the essay. Tucked away in a short footnote (1991, p. 183, n. 33), they refer to Hayek's considerations in his essay on 'Competition as a Discovery Procedure' (Hayek, 1978a) as a striking example of the ambiguities surrounding the notion of the market as a process of discovery. In the following comments, some of the more noteworthy passages in Hayek's essay will be taken up in turn.

In the first instance, it should be noted that Hayek in effect provides a rejoinder to the apparent 'paradox' identified by Dasgupta when he argues that it seems difficult to defend economists in general against the charge to have analysed market competition under conditions such that it can be wholly dispensed with. Hayek, as is well known, deems competition valuable because and only in so far as no one could deliberately have brought about its results. This aspect also makes for its peculiar character: in those instances where its role is significant its performance cannot be tested, because once it is granted that we do not know beforehand what we want to find out by recourse to competition, there is no way in which we could ascertain how successful competition has been in its allotted task.

The ambiguity creeps in when Hayek points to the confusion generated by mistakenly applying criteria devised for evaluating the performance of an 'economy' (that is, an organization in which there is somebody exclusively in charge of running the business of allocating resources according to a given hierarchy of ends) to the analysis of a market order, or 'catallaxy', as Hayek prefers to call it – one of the chief differences understood as being that in the latter needs are not attended to in strict order of priority established by 'public opinion'.

The distinction between a 'catallaxy' and an 'economy in the strict sense' stands Hayek in good stead when it comes to warding off claims to 'social justice' – a notion that is held to be meaningless when applied to the former, but perfectly legitimate when pertaining to the latter. When he is concerned with assessing the performance of the market order, however, Hayek doesn't seem to be able to make up his mind. On the one hand, he adopts a non-teleological stance in arguing that the market order as an instance of a spontaneously formed order not having been made for a specific purpose cannot properly be said to *have* particular purposes.[6] Although the specific outcomes of a discovery procedure are in their nature unpredictable, the catallaxy nonetheless 'produces in some sense a maximum or optimum' (Hayek, 1978a, p. 183).

Now, if this were merely to mean that the chances for randomly taken individuals to pursue their ends 'as effectively as possible will be very high – even if it cannot be predicted which particular aims will be favoured', it would sound innocuous enough although serious doubts are in order as to how one would have to go about establishing such a claim. If the expectation of improving the chances for unknown people is all there is to 'the adoption of an effective discovery procedure', one may indeed rest content with exploring the abstract features of the order, or pattern, conducive to it (Hayek, 1978a, p. 184). But Hayek goes much further than that (see pp. 185–6): not only does the market order achieve a mutual adjustment of plans; in addition, whatever the commodity output mix being produced, 'as much will be produced as we know to bring about by any known method'. Especially coming from someone who has castigated the economics profession for the question-begging manner in which it has treated such issues as the acquisition and dissemination of knowledge, this is a startling statement. Besides, who is 'we'?

Hayek continues in an even stranger way, 'It [commodity output] will of course not be as much as we might produce if all the knowledge anybody possessed or can acquire were commanded by some one agency, and fed into a computer (the cost of finding out would, however, be considerable)' (ibid.). Unfortunately, this line of reasoning flies in the face of Hayek's own harsh strictures against central planning. In fact, the argument amounts to what a devoted (that is, uncritical) Hayekian would probably hold up as an example of a standard ('neoclassical') caricature of Hayek. But it also illustrates – and this is the point at issue – the fatal misconception Buchanan and Vanberg are rallying against: the idea of pitting market outcomes against what an (idealized) omniscient planner could accomplish.

It should at once be added, however, that Hayek, of course, displays an awareness of the minefield he has just entered when he immediately reins himself in by conceding that market outcomes should not be judged 'from above', as it were, by pitting them against 'an ideal standard which we have no known way of achieving'. Yet having said that, he balks again: the insight does not prevent him from contending that the market order is to be credited with securing an approach towards some point on the n-dimensional (for n goods) production possibility surface (or, what in the case of two goods is more familiar as the 'transformation curve'), indicating the range of Pareto-efficient combinations of goods. What is again remarkable here is that a few pages earlier (Hayek, 1978a, p. 181) Hayek takes issue with 'economic theory' because of its assumption of a '"given" supply [*sic*] of scarce goods'. He demurs on the grounds that the issues of which things are goods; which goods are scarce goods; and the degree of their scarcity are something for competition to discover.

In taking recourse to what he elsewhere calls 'the horizon of catallactic possibilities' (Hayek, 1976, pp. 118–9), Hayek himself may be accused of labouring under the *synoptic delusion*, that is, 'the fiction that all the relevant facts are known to some one mind' (1973, p. 14) – a view which he attributes as characteristic to all variants of constructivist rationalism. 'A mind knowing all the facts could select any point he liked on the surface and distribute this product in the manner he thought right. But the only point on, or tolerably near, the horizon of possibilities *which we know how to reach* is the one at which we shall arrive if we leave its determination to the market' (Hayek, 1978a, p. 186, emphasis added). If there is no agreement concerning the hierarchy of ends, it is no longer possible to adjudge which combination of goods corresponding to the horizon of catallactic possibilities is larger than any other. Yet there is a distinct, limited sense in which the notion of a 'maximum' may legitimately be retained: 'The so-called "maximum" which we thus reach naturally cannot be defined as a sum of particular things, but only in terms of the chances it offers to unknown people to get as large a real equivalent as possible for their relative shares, which will be determined partly by accident' (ibid.). And again Hayek warns against gauging the results of a catallaxy as if they were the results of an economy proper.

To sum up, then, what all this suggests: the emblematic feature of a catallaxy at issue here, in contradistinction to an economy in the strict sense, is seen to derive from the circumstance that its constituent elements – that is, agents – do not submit to a common hierarchy of ends. Although Hayek conceives of catallaxy as a game whose outcome is 'determined partly by skill and partly by chance', he nonetheless doesn't hesitate to ascribe to the real equivalent each player is expected to receive from taking part in this mixed game of chance and skill the property of 'a true maximum' (1976, p. 119).

One may well wonder whether, and if so how, Hayek's views tie in with the main findings of mainstream welfare economics as encapsulated in the familiar efficiency theorems. Considering the relevant passages from 'Competition as a Discovery Procedure' and *The Mirage of Social Justice*, the link seems much more pronounced than one may be entitled to expect from studying some of Hayek's other pertinent deliberations. In this vein, Robert Sugden has sought to relate Hayek's concerns to mainstream welfare economics (see Sugden, 1992). He invites us to consider the homely setting of an exchange economy in which a finite number of homogeneous commodities are traded in a Walrasian auction, and prices are adjusted by an auctioneer in a standard *tâtonnement* process. Traders are assumed to know their own preferences and the prices cried out by the 'secretary of the market'; the latter is assumed to know the total quantities of all commodities supplied and demanded at alternative prices, but not traders' preferences. Given the appropriate stability conditions, a Pareto-efficient equilibrium state is guaranteed. According to Sugden, 'within its own restricted framework' the model can accommodate what Hayek takes to be 'the central problem of economics as a social science'. Unlike Buchanan and Vanberg, Sugden has no qualms about the assumption of 'given' preferences. The economist–planner does not necessarily fall prey to synoptic delusion when she pretends to know individual preferences in setting up the model. All she does is to assume certain general properties (such as convexity) about them and then to show that for any given preferences complying with those general properties the *tâtonnement* process will lead to Pareto-efficient outcomes. Moreover, as Sugden maintains, this strategy would not be compromised by any considerations on how much or how little the model tells us about the division, acquisition and dissemination of knowledge.

According to Sugden, then, 'the Walrasian model' may be seen as 'an example of how to theorize about spontaneous order': first, one makes very general assumptions about the properties of the system under discussion, not worrying about the specifics of the particular circumstances which may affect outcomes; secondly, one takes account of how alternative specifications of the particular circumstances would affect outcomes. Now, I don't think Sugden is riding that particular Walrasian horse too hard. What is more, his proposal may claim an even closer affinity with Hayek than he seems to be aware of. It should be recalled that on several occasions Hayek has held up the Walras–Pareto system of simultaneous equations as an example of a description of the abstract order, or pattern, that will form itself under certain specifiable conditions. The description of the general character of the pattern does not rest on the knowledge of the particular circumstances, such as preferences and actors' knowledge, which the theorist would have to ascertain in order to be able to calculate the prices and quantities of all goods and services sold. The description of the general kind of pattern obtaining under certain conditions can never be translated into a prediction of its particular manifestations (see, for example, Hayek, 1967a, pp. 35–6; 1967b, pp. 261–2; 1978b, pp. 27–8.)

Hayek's concept of knowledge

Hayek's 'knowledge problem' is often presented merely as a problem concerning the need for knowledge of (current and future) prices. But this involves only a small segment in his account of the general problem of how different commodities can be obtained and used, and under which conditions they are actually obtained and used (see Hayek, 1937, p. 51). Since this is an area where misunderstandings abound, it may be instructive to consider briefly the kind of knowledge yielded by market prices according to Hayek.

Straight textbook advice suggests that equilibrium prices convey perfect information:[7] agents consult costlessly provided equilibrium prices and then take 'correct' decisions confronted, or constrained, by those prices. In the perspective adopted by Hayek, this would, of course, be question-begging. In Hayek's understanding of the market as an 'epistemic institution'[8] prices do not primarily constrain market participants; rather, they enable and encourage them to draw on knowledge of whose 'possession' they may not have any clue whatsoever. Hayek's point is not simply that prices as such convey knowledge, let alone infallible knowledge, but rather that they *enable* us to make use of knowledge that is 'ignorant of itself'. The knowledge yielded by market prices is knowledge generated through the operation of the market order – that is, it cannot be generated in any other way – and is available to *all* market participants, but to none of them individually. Since the knowledge embodied in market prices is not possessed, and cannot be appropriated, by any one market participant, it has rightly been described as '*systemic or holistic knowledge*, knowledge unknown and unknowable to any of the elements of the market system, but given to them all by the operation of the system itself' (Gray, 1986, p. 38; emphasis in original).

In the more familiar terminology of 'information', the matter may be put thus. The explicit, articulate information provided by the scalar of market prices presupposes and needs to be supplemented by a framework. That is, the information conveyed by, or summarized in, market prices is in itself worthless unless it is related to a wide background of inarticulate knowledge. Contrary to devices such as telephones storing telephone numbers, or answering machines receiving, retaining and transmitting information, cognitive subjects such as human beings are capable in varying degrees to draw on background information about that information in order to assess and process it. While Hayek stressed that market prices permit decision makers to adjust to changes in relative scarcities of goods and services without any awareness, except on the part of a few market participants, of the circumstances which might have contributed towards them, it does not follow that he considers prices to be the only means of communication in a market order. Prices acquire meaning to those who calculate with them only against the background of shared, usually unarticulated assumptions about the general properties of priced goods and services. For example, even though most consumers would be hard pressed to specify the features of most goods they consume, a slight change in their unspecified attributes might alter the demand for them substantially. Likewise, the rules guiding a producer in using a particular method of production are to a large extent not articulated; the role of prices here is not to supply producers with instant and unambiguous positive information about the least-cost technique of production, but rather to narrow down significantly the technologically feasible production methods to the most likely economically viable ones (see Lavoie, 1986, pp. 13–16). In short, the knowledge of how to use prices is never contained in the information provided by those prices.

There is a noteworthy, important change of tack – no doubt under the impact of the socialist calculation debate (see Caldwell, 1988) – between the two 'knowledge papers' (Hayek, 1937; 1945). In the earlier statement Hayek held out the prospect of an economic theory of knowledge as a theory of how people come to know what they do. On this conception, then, it may be argued that a theory of knowledge is severed from its philosophical moorings; it belongs to that subfield of psychology called learning theory (Lehrer, 1990, p. 5).[9] This may, for example, be gleaned from Hayek's characterization of the 'empirical element in economic theory' as consisting in 'propositions about the acquisition of knowledge' (Hayek, 1937, p. 33); from his conception of the equilibration process as a process of learning; and from his outline of 'the wider aspect of the problem of knowledge' as 'the general question of why the subjective data to the different persons correspond to the objective facts' (pp. 51–2). 'Knowledge', as the word is used here, denotes much more than merely the 'skills' with which someone engages in production and trade; rather, 'in order to be able to say anything about the processes in society' we need to have 'knowledge of alternative possibilities of action of which he makes no direct use' (p. 51 n. 17).

In Hayek's 1945 essay, however, the underlying philosophical theory of knowledge is conceived primarily as a conceptual or linguistic exercise by enquiring into the meaning of 'knowledge' and semantically related epistemic concepts. This links up with a substantive change of topic in that the research enterprise announced in 1937 – an empirically testable theory of expectation formation and learning – had been dumped for the rather different investigation of the use of fragmented, or dispersed, knowledge under different institutional arrangements. In standard philosophical jargon, 'to know' basically means to be acquainted with things or persons, to have 'knowledge by acquaintance'. Hayek points out the distinction between two kinds of knowledge: scientific and economic knowledge. The latter differs from the former in that it is 'unorganized', that it does not obey general rules. It is 'knowledge of the particular circumstances of time and place', of 'people, of local conditions, and of special circumstances', of 'temporary opportunities'; it is specialized knowledge of 'circumstances of the fleeting moment not known to others', and of 'facilities of communication and transport' (Hayek, 1945, pp. 80–81).

In later work, from the 1950s onwards, Hayek (see, for example, 1956; 1962; 1973) elaborates upon the concept of knowledge introduced in his 1945 essay. What he is concerned with is primarily practical knowledge, incorporated in competences, skills, practices, habits and dispositions. Such knowledge is in the main non-scientific, non-technical, non-theoretical, non-propositional, non-deductivist and non-justificationist. Much of the 'practical knowledge'[10] Hayek is talking about is inarticulate, that is, not available to the discursive awareness of actors, a somewhat pretentious way of saying that it is not easy or even possible to communicate. It is, in Gilbert Ryle's phrase, 'knowledge how' rather than 'knowledge that' (Ryle, 1949/1990, ch. 2). Knowing a lot of details about English football is not the same thing as knowing how to play football. Neither does one need to talk about what one is doing in order to be able to play it. Speaking a language is itself a familiar example of knowing how. In order to speak a language properly, an individual needs to know a vast range of syntactical, idiomatic and other rules of language use. Supposing she speaks the language knowledgeably, if she were pressed to give a discursive account of what it is that she knows in knowing these rules, the chances are that she would have a difficult time indeed, although she does 'know' them, that is, know how to use them. And this equally holds for many other practices which constitute our daily social routine activity. Knowledge about the conditions of our actions is not limited to what we can discursively say about them.

Hayek makes much of the fact that many of the rules on which the market order depends for its operation are followed tacitly, to use Michael Polanyi's expression (see, for example, Polanyi, 1966) – that is, the existence of rules is not contingent upon explicit canonical formulations serving as a performance standard for conduct. The role of tacit knowledge is quintessential for Hayek's mature position in the socialist calculation debate (see Lavoie, 1986). It is his significant contribution in this area and goes well beyond Mises's original argument concerning calculation. For Hayek, the market is an epistemic institution which serves to economize on the scarcest of all resources – knowledge. The epistemological impossibility of central economic planning stems primarily from the peculiar character of the knowledge economic actors are supposed to be endowed with. It is in the main not theoretical or quantifiable knowledge, but local knowledge embodied in skills, practices and entrepreneurial hunches. This sort of knowledge is in its very nature impervious to being passed on to, and collected by – in statistical, concentrated form – a central planning bureau. The epistemic role of markets may be construed as making available the widely scattered fund of traditional and local knowledge. It is prices that enable market participants to draw on this knowledge pool. The inarticulate and inarticulable nature of this sort of knowledge imposes insuperable limitations on comprehensive attempts at computer market simulation, because people know much more than they can say – or in other words, they are ignorant of much of what they know.

One problem with this view of the role of markets that Hayek does not seem to address is whether there might be any reluctance on the part of market participants to exploit their practical knowledge and to make it publicly available. It may well be very true that relative to central planning markets succeed much better in marshalling dispersed knowledge. But surely the matter cannot rest there. Consider technical know-how. It may be the very essence of market competition to withhold such, possibly vital, knowledge. To the extent that it is impossible to articulate such knowledge the patent system would not be of any help whatsoever.

Knowledge of economics
In the remainder of this chapter I wish to broach the issue whether, according to Hayek, economic-theoretical knowledge, or rather social scientific knowledge in general, may contribute towards our understanding of the real world.

There is in philosophy what only at first blush seems to be a neat separation between ontology and epistemology. The epistemologist raises questions about how we know, the ontologist about what it is that we know when we know. Questions of existence and questions of knowledge have traditionally vied for the dominant position in the history of philosophical inquiry. Ever since the times of Descartes and Kant, in particular, philosophy has been characterized by an 'epistemological turn', holding the question 'What can I know?' to be of primary importance. The high point was reached with the advent of logical empiricism, and philosophical movements sympathetic to it, which virtually eliminated the ontological dimension of theories. According to logical empiricism, only those things exist that are susceptible of direct verification. The test of reality is epistemological. According to this view, scientific theories are epistemological structures, or systems, rather than descriptions of the nature of things.

What are then the ontological commitments of Hayek's social theory? A casual approach to this issue suggests that Hayek's social theory is strongly antimetaphysical. He poses a kind of Kantian question: how are the social sciences possible at all? He shares the Kantian view that we can only have knowledge of phenomena; knowledge of noumena, or 'things-in-themselves', is impossible. We do not have access to the world as it is; and we cannot hope ever to be in a position to be able to uncover the Aristotelian nature of things. So perhaps Hayek's position is a full-blown Kantian one, combining transcendental idealism and empirical realism (see Hacking, 1983, p. 96)? As Tibor Machan (1979, pp. 280–81) observes, it is a somewhat curious irony that the self-confessed arch enemy of positivism in all its manifestations shares with the positivists a common philosophical debt to Kant in their rejection of metaphysics.

Hayek's Kantian theory of knowledge comes out quite clearly in his work on theoretical psychology (Hayek, 1952), whose 'basic idea', according to the preface, he had already conceived as a student in Vienna in the early 1920s.

One important strand of *The Sensory Order* is a view of mind not as a passive receptacle of sensations received from the external world, but as an active classificatory apparatus of sense perceptions. Hayek accentuates the variability of mind and its cognitive structure, contending that the mental framework by which we categorize the world is not universal; that it is sensitive to the environment in which we happen to live; and that it is subject to change in an evolutionary fashion. He insists that 'experience is not a function of mind or consciousness [...] mind and consciousness are rather products of experience' (Hayek, 1952, p. 166). This is tantamount to saying that owing to the variability of the cognitive structure of mind objective knowledge is impossible.

As highlighted by Miller (1979), this is in stark contrast to Hayek's diatribe against historical relativism in 'Scientism and the Study of Society' where he charges, 'Consistently pursued historicism necessarily leads to the view that the human mind is itself variable ...' (Hayek, 1942–44, p. 133). And in discussing the issue of the 'constancy of the human mind', he argues: 'Whether the human mind is ... constant can never become a problem – because to recognize mind cannot mean anything but to recognize something as operating in the way as our own thinking' (p. 135). Further on we are told, 'Through the theory of the variability of the human mind, to which the consistent development of historicism leads, it cuts, in effect, the ground under its own feet: it is led to the self-contradictory position of generalizing about facts which, if the theory were true, could not be known' (p. 137).

To complete this confusing picture, there are also strong indications in *The Sensory Order* that Hayek wishes to hold on to the notion that science can present us with a reliable account of the objective world. Consider the following passage:

> [W]e must assume the existence of an objective world (or better, of an objective order of the events which we experience in their phenomenal order) towards the recognition of which the phenomenal order is merely a first approximation. The task of science is thus to try and approach ever more closely towards a reproduction of this objective order – a task which it can perform only by replacing the sensory order of events by a new and different classification. (Hayek, 1952, p. 173)

This smacks of a position that one may describe as 'epistemological', 'hypothetical', or 'conjectural', realism.[11] For the ontological, or metaphysical, realist this would still stop short of the real thing: worries about the hypothetical status of our knowledge are epistemological worries and have nothing to do with the ontological status of the world (see Trigg, 1989, p. 218). From this perspective, to qualify realism in such a way is akin to being 'a bit pregnant'.

Concluding remarks

Two suggestions for deeper probing emerge from these brief considerations of Hayek's views on knowledge. On the one hand, Hayek is concerned with the limitations of the mind in its quest for knowledge. This is the sceptical Kantian side to Hayek. The argument from ignorance is deployed to bolster a regime of economic liberty entailed by the market order.

But there is another strand in Hayek which eschews a conception of knowledge as representing the world altogether and takes recourse to tradition and relativism. Knowledge no longer represents the world; it is a means of coping with the world. Faintly reminiscent of a certain brand of pragmatism, Hayek asserts, 'Knowledge of the world is knowledge of what one *must* do or not do in certain kinds of circumstance' (Hayek, 1973, p. 18, emphasis added). What one must do is dictated by tradition. It is by no means assured that the appeal to submission of the authority of practical knowledge will not undermine the foundations of the open society – a tendency that Hayek, as will be recalled, associated with the idolatry of theoretical knowledge.

Notes

1. Frank Hahn, who has on other occasions been known to be quite scathing about Hayek's contribution to economics, has recently referred to Hayek's 1937 essay on 'Economics and Knowledge' as a 'profound paper', in which it had been argued that 'the allocation of resources in the textbook manner was not the only role of prices: they also transmitted information' (Hahn, 1990a, p. 238). For Hahn's more recent pronouncements on Hayek, see also Hahn (1989) and, in particular, Hahn (1990b), where he even brings himself to say some good words about *The Road to Serfdom*.
2. Grossman (1989) is representative of the mainstream reading of Hayek's work on the informational role of prices.
3. There is, it may be argued (and I am indebted to Meghnad Desai for drawing my attention to it), some analogy here between the Hayekian notion of knowledge and the Marxian notion of labour power. Although labour power appears as a commodity for sale on the market, it is unlike other such commodities in that, in order to use it, its buyer, the capitalist, has to enter into a whole series of other relationships with the seller, the worker. It is not the purchasing of labour power itself which generates wealth but the consumption of it. Likewise, according to Hayek, market exchanges facilitate the use of knowledge that would otherwise be untapped; the creation of wealth is not due to the production and sale of knowledge as such but to the transformational social activity from previously existing knowledge, as exhibited in market processes.
4. It should be noted that the theorem is based on stringent convexity requirements for both consumers and producers.
5. No wonder it loomed large in the historical debate on market socialism between the wars. In what amounts to an off-the-cuff remark, Stiglitz candidly observes that 'the perspective provided by the Lange–Lerner–Taylor theorem, suggesting an equivalence between socialist and market economies, provides a dramatic example of how traditional approaches can lead one far astray' (Stiglitz, 1989, p. 29, n. 27).
6. Bearing in mind Hayek's insistence on the distinction between 'purposeless', spontaneous orders and 'purposive', made orders, or organizations, the following quotation is quite remarkable: 'I've come to believe that *both the aim of the market order, and therefore the object of explanation of the theory of it*, is to cope with the inevitable ignorance of everybody of most of the particular facts which determine this order' (Hayek, 1983, p. 19; emphasis added).
7. In fact, in a perfect information, general equilibrium model prices do nothing of the sort; they are efficient rates of exchange separating agents in such a way that there is no need for them to act strategically.
8. As far as I am aware, this coinage is due to John Gray.
9. To what extent epistemology should be psychologistically oriented, to what extent it should draw on inputs from cognitive science, is a heated topic among philosophers; see, for example, the remarks in Goldman (1986, pp. 1–9).
10. On this issue, compare the almost contemporaneous work of Michael Oakeshott (1947, p. 12), who draws attention to two sorts of knowledge, distinguishable but inseparable, which are held to be at all times involved in any scientific, artistic or practical endeavour. According to Oakeshott, the chief differences between the two sorts of knowledge are those which derive from the divergent ways in which knowledge can be expressed or formulated, and from the divergent ways in which it can be learned or acquired. 'Technical knowledge', or 'knowledge of technique', is susceptible of being expressed in rules, principles, or more generally, in propositions which may be consciously learned, remembered and put into practice, and in principle it is capable of being precisely formulated.

Technical knowledge can be written down in a book; it can be learned and taught. 'Practical knowledge', on the other hand, exists only in use and is neither reflective nor susceptible of being formulated in rules or prescriptions. Considering the manner in which this sort of knowledge comes to be shared, it might also be called 'traditional knowledge'. It can neither be taught nor learned, but only imparted and acquired by continuous contact with someone ('the master') who is practising it. On Oakeshott, see the recent book-length appraisal by Franco (1990), which also considers the links between Hayek's and Oakeshott's thought.

11.   Bartley (1987, p. 98, n. 8) holds that Hayek is a hypothetical realist.

References

Allen, B. (1990), 'Information as an Economic Commodity', *American Economic Review* (Papers and Proceedings), **80** (2), May, 268–73.

Bartley, W.W. (1987), 'The Division of Knowledge', in G. Radnitzky (ed.), *Centripetal Forces in Society*, vol. 2, New York: Paragon House.

Bhagwati, J. (1992), 'Democracy and Development', *Journal of Democracy*, **3** (3), July, 37–44.

Buchanan, J.M. (1982), 'Order Defined in the Process of Its Emergence', *Literature of Liberty*, **5** (4), Winter, 5; a slightly altered version is reprinted in his *Liberty, Market and State: Political Economy in the 1980s*, Brighton: Harvester Wheatsheaf, 1986.

Buchanan, J.M., and V. Vanberg (1991), 'The Market as a Creative Process', *Economics and Philosophy*, **7** (2), October, 167–86.

Caldwell, B.J. (1988), 'Hayek's Transformation', *History of Political Economy*, **20** (4), Winter, 513–41.

Dasgupta, P. (1986), 'Positive Freedom, Markets and the Welfare State', *Oxford Review of Economic Policy*, **2** (2), Summer, 25–36; reprinted in Helm (ed.) (1989).

Franco, P. (1990), *The Political Philosophy of Michael Oakeshott*, New Haven, Conn.: Yale University Press.

Goldman, A.I. (1986), *Epistemology and Cognition*, Cambridge, Mass.: Harvard University Press.

Gray, J. (1986), *Hayek on Liberty*, 2nd edn, Oxford: Blackwell.

Grossman, S.J. (1989), *The Informational Role of Prices*, Cambridge, Mass.: MIT Press.

Hacking, I. (1983), *Representing and Intervening: Introductory Topics in the Philosophy of Natural Science*, Cambridge: Cambridge University Press.

Hahn, F. (1982), 'Reflections on the Invisible Hand', *Lloyds Bank Review*, 144, April, 1–21.

Hahn, F. (1989), 'On Market Economies', in R. Skidelsky (ed.), *Thatcherism*, Oxford: Blackwell.

Hahn, F. (1990a), 'Expectations', in J.D. Hey and D. Winch (eds), *A Century of Economics: 100 Years of the Royal Economic Society and the Economic Journal*, Oxford: Blackwell.

Hahn, F. (1990b), 'On Some Economic Limits in Politics', in J. Dunn (ed.), *The Economic Limits to Modern Politics*, Cambridge: Cambridge University Press.

Hayek, F.A. von (1937), 'Economics and Knowledge', *Economica*, new series, **4**; page numbers refer to reprint in Hayek (1949).

Hayek, F.A. von (1942–44), 'Scientism and the Study of Society' (in three parts), *Economica*, new series, **9–11**; page numbers refer to reprint in Hayek (1952/79).

Hayek, F.A. von (1945), 'The Use of Knowledge in Society', *American Economic Review*, **35**; page numbers refer to reprint in Hayek (1949).

Hayek, F.A. von (1946), 'The Meaning of Competition', Stafford Little Lecture delivered at Princeton University; page numbers refer to reprint in Hayek (1949).

Hayek, F.A. von (1949), *Individualism and Economic Order*, London: Routledge and Kegan Paul.

Hayek, F.A. von (1952), *The Sensory Order: An Inquiry into the Foundations of Theoretical Psychology*, London: Routledge and Kegan Paul.

Hayek, F.A. von (1952/79), *The Counter-Revolution of Science: Studies on the Abuse of Reason*, 2nd edn., Indianapolis, Ind.: Liberty Press.

Hayek, F.A. von (1956), 'Über den "Sinn" sozialer Institutionen', *Schweizer Monatshefte*, **36**, 512–24.

Hayek, F.A. von (1962), 'Rules, Perception and Intelligibility', reprinted in *Studies in Philosophy, Politics and Economics*, London: Routledge and Kegan Paul, 1967.

Hayek, F.A. von (1967a), 'The Theory of Complex Phenomena', in *Studies in Philosophy, Politics and Economics*, London: Routledge and Kegan Paul.

Hayek, F.A. von (1967b), 'The Economy, Science, and Politics', in *Studies in Philosophy, Politics and Economics*, London: Routledge and Kegan Paul.

Hayek, F.A. von (1973), *Law, Legislation and Liberty: A New Statement of the Liberal Principles of Justice and Political Economy*. Vol. 1: *Rules and Order*, London: Routledge and Kegan Paul.

Hayek, F.A. von (1976), *Law, Legislation and Liberty: A New Statement of the Liberal Principles of Justice and Political Economy*. Vol. 2: *The Mirage of Social Justice*, London: Routledge and Kegan Paul.

Hayek, F.A. von (1978a), 'Competition as a Discovery Procedure', in *New Studies in Philosophy, Politics, Economics and the History of Ideas*, London: Routledge and Kegan Paul.

Hayek, F.A. von (1978b), 'The Pretence of Knowledge', in *New Studies in Philosophy, Politics, Economics and the History of Ideas*, London: Routledge and Kegan Paul.

Hayek, F.A. von (1983), *Knowledge, Evolution, and Society*, London: Adam Smith Institute.

Helm, D. (ed.) (1989), *The Economic Borders of the State*, Oxford: Oxford University Press (Clarendon Press).

Lavoie, D. (1986), 'The Market as a Procedure for Discovery and Conveyance of Inarticulate Knowledge', *Comparative Economic Studies*, **28**, 1–19.

Lehrer, K. (1990), *Theory of Knowledge* (Dimensions of Philosophy Series), Boulder, Col.: Westview Press.

Machan, T. (1979), 'Reason, Morality, and the Free Society', in R.L. Cunningham (ed.), *Liberty and the Rule of Law*, College Station: Texas A & M University Press.

McPherson, M.S. (1983), 'Want Formation, Morality, and Some "Interpretive" Aspects of Economic Inquiry', in N. Haan, R.N. Bellah, P. Rabinow and W.M. Sullivan (eds), *Social Science as Moral Inquiry*, New York: Columbia University Press.

Miller, E.F. (1979), 'The Cognitive Basis of Hayek's Political Thought', in R.L. Cunningham (ed.), *Liberty and the Rule of Law*, College Station: Texas A & M University Press.

Oakeshott, M. (1947), 'Rationalism in Politics', *Cambridge Journal*, vol. I; page numbers refer to reprint in *Rationalism in Politics and Other Essays*, new edn, Indianapolis, Ind.: Liberty Press (1991).

Polanyi, M. (1966), *The Tacit Dimension*, New York: Doubleday.

Ryle, G. (1949/1990), *The Concept of Mind*, Harmondsworth: Penguin.

Sen, A. (1985), 'The Moral Standing of the Market', *Social Philosophy and Policy*, **2** (2), Spring, 1–19; a slightly altered version is reprinted in Helm (ed.) (1989).

Shackle, G.L.S. (1972), *Epistemics and Economics: A Critique of Economic Doctrines*, Cambridge: Cambridge University Press.

Stiglitz, J.E. (1989), 'Incentives, Information, and Organizational Design', *Empirica* (Austrian Economic Papers), **16** (1), 3–29.

Sugden, R. (1992), 'Commentary on Hamlin: Austrian Prescriptive Economics', in B.J. Caldwell and S. Boehm (eds), *Austrian Economics: Tensions and New Directions*, Boston: Kluwer Academic.

Trigg, R. (1989), *Reality at Risk: A Defence of Realism in Philosophy and the Sciences*, 2nd edn, Brighton: Harvester Wheatsheaf.

Weimer, W.B. (1982), 'Hayek's Approach to the Problems of Complex Phenomena: An Introduction to the Theoretical Psychology of *The Sensory Order*', in W.B. Weimer and D.S. Palermo (eds), *Cognition and the Symbolic Processes*, vol. 2, Hillsdale, N.J.: Lawrence Erlbaum.

9 Rational processes: markets, knowledge and uncertainty

Omar F. Hamouda and Robin Rowley

The long professional career and liberal views of Friedrich von Hayek present several difficulties for current historians of economic thought and for anyone interested in the methodology of economics. He fully deserves the attention that we expect him to receive following his recent death. The strong ebb and flow of recognition for his particular views (from both governmental and professional circles), during the 60 years after he moved to the London School of Economics, was quite extraordinary. Three peaks are clear – the interwar period in Britain, when he was briefly seen as, perhaps, the most effective competitor to Keynes; the subsequent period in Britain when he was the leading opponent of governmental planning, the scourge of 'scientism', and the promoter of liberal causes; and the more recent period when he became a significant figurehead for some important neoconservative and libertarian movements, especially in the United States of America and Britain. During these three peaks, his personal influence was profound, both directly through his lucid books and his involvement with the Mont Pelerin Society and, indirectly, through the impact of his views on many conservative constituents of the powerful US 'Counter-Establishment' (Blumental, 1986; Smith, 1989). Overall, the persistence of Hayek's firm arguments against much governmental interference and his robust promotion of more market freedom were clearly rewarded. For many conservatives and libertarians, Hayek's efforts exerted a dominant and widespread influence 'strengthening the moral and intellectual support for a free society' (Friedman, 1976, p. xxi).

Exploration of Hayek has not removed our initial exasperation with the haphazard understanding and incomplete promotion of his views. He often seems to be hidden in the shadows as similar views expressed by his friends, disciples, and fellow-travellers (such as Popper, Buchanan, Campbell, and Friedman for example) attract much greater attention in popular discourse, especially through the flood of publications from some influential organizations like the Heritage Foundation, the Hoover Institute, the American Enterprise Institute and the Fraser Institute. However, Hayek remains the standard reference for many discussions of economic knowledge and of the rational working of individual markets; he shares with Adam Smith the dubious honour of being frequently cited but seldom read. Given the clarity and consistency of his writing, this neglect is unfortunate.

One difficulty with Hayek stems from the feeling that his message is so simple that it surely does not need more repetition. Another difficulty arises from his unfashionably firm rejection of most mathematical formulations of economic models, as reflected in the excessive use of axiomization and theories based on individual optimality. Here he often seems markedly out of step, even with newer theoretical developments in the economics of decentralized information and research. Consequently, his broad visions of real economic phenomena are particularly compressed and distorted to fit within formal theoretical bounds that he must have found quite distasteful. Otherwise, the same visions are just ignored because of the inherent hazards that they will associate with some popular requirements for the attributes of economic theories, including those of predictability and mathematical precision.

Our current objective is to consider other difficulties which arise from Hayek's interest in knowledge, especially as expressed in his focus on the rational processes of market participants and the attention that he gives to both cognitive limitations and to evolutionary shifts in the presence of uncertainty and changing circumstances. With this backdrop, we begin by identifying some important features of his theoretical framework (including the inherent complexity of economic phenomena and actions, quantitative biases, subjectivism and individualism) as implemented both in his own treatment of markets, knowledge (or ignorance) and uncertainty, and also in a few relevant comments drawn from other reviewers of his efforts. Clearly, by beginning here, we ignore the alternative and earlier visions, illustrated by Hayek (1931) and the translated essays in Hayek (1984), that preceded his dramatic 'transformation' (Caldwell, 1988) from a narrow 'pure' theorist to a composite of political philosopher, historian, scientific methodologist and liberal 'applied' economist. This historical break was incomplete and some particular changes can be exaggerated, but there do seem to be significant changes in focus which occurred after the move to London (perhaps a 'flowering' of hidden interests made possible by the additional freedom of a secure academic life).

After briefly considering some aspects of these theoretical features, we follow the path of scholarly common-sense that was advocated by Hayek (1937, p. 54), namely, 'from time to time it is probably necessary to detach one's self from the technicalities of the argument and to ask quite naively *what is it all about*.' With this sensible advice in mind, we look at three particular areas of current significance: predictions, explanations and the dynamic nature of theory and theorizing; data, testing and econometrics as basic summaries of aggregate information and as the necessary components of the methodological engine of progress for 'scientific' economics; and the reappraisal by economists of information sharing and the value of competition, due to the growth of agglomeration in capitalist economies and to the emergence of the successful Japanese model (involving the interfirm connections of the *keiretsu* and the business–government cooperation of 'Japan, Inc.'). Various aspects of knowledge and notions of rationality are central to any reasonable discussion in these areas. Many of the potential constraints on method and evolutionary challenges to stationary economic models, that were consistently raised by Hayek during the last 60 years, remain pertinent. However, as may be expected, we have to amend some of his personal judgements in the light of structural changes in both economic phenomena and the fashions of economic thought.

Hayek's context

Any economic theory requires the specification of a domain of applicability. If we are to take that theory as a worthy basis for either description or prescription, then this domain needs to be clearly identified. Hayek insisted that theories recognize some of the important features of the economic context – complexity, widely dispersed information, adaptation, discovery and persistent change – and he left sufficient room for individual economists to express their judgement. Thus he combined direct observation and institutional awareness with acts of faith or intuition in determining the appropriateness of particular advice. Both of these elements, influenced by his personal experiences, led him to see economic phenomena as governed by rational processes rather than by static aspects of choice. His persistent advocacy of less governmental interference and greater competition (but not perfect competition) reflected a practical concern with actual markets as he saw them and not with some fictional entity. Thus the focus of his economic theories, when rejecting the conceit of socialism and superficiality or when advocating moderation and more freedom, was always firmly centred in 'his world' and in his moral assessment of the relative efficiency of alternative economic structures, perhaps influenced by a professional youth spent in Vienna (Levitt and Mendell, 1988) and much polished by subsequent disturbances in Europe.

Hayek's context for economic theory identifies 'rationality' with a continual process which contains a number of significant constituents. It begins with the presumptions that the individual participants in economic markets have the capacity to think, that they wish to maintain themselves in the market, and that they are responsive both to general (unanticipated) information and to the actions of other participants. Competition, imitative behaviour, conventional rules and traditions are then considered to encourage the emergence of rational outcomes. This simple vision is markedly different from alternative visions that view individual rationality as part of an abstract system involving formal optimization (of utility, profits or costs), omniscience, widespread separability and equilibrium. Rational processes for Hayek were subjective, individualistic and evolutionary. These particular attributes, and the hypotheses to be derived from their use, are regarded as possible situations that 'for some reason we regard as specially relevant to conditions in the real world' (Hayek, 1937, p. 46). He kept Smith's metaphor of the 'invisible hand' for basic market processes, while he substantially added to our understanding of the underlying economic mechanisms; of the potential for congruent interests through the dissemination of information and imitation of the spontaneous nature of human actions and their inherent unpredictability; of the recognition of adaptive choice in the face of relative ignorance; and of the emergence of values and social institutions. This contribution does not mean that we must share his deep faith in the relative efficiency of freer markets, rather than in their contrariness. But it does encourage us to be more attentive to the tentative, often understated, relationship between our formal theories and 'what happens in the real world' (Hayek, 1937, p. 33).

Methodological individualism is now recognized by economists as 'the method which seeks to explain human action in terms of plans conceived before action is actually taken' (Lachmann, 1969, p. 306) in an uncertain situation with divergent expectations and unexpected changes. Taking this particular method as his basis, Hayek (1937) was preoccupied with individual mental states and with the frequent emergence of spontaneous order through some indirect combination of the 'fragments of knowledge existing in different minds' (p. 52). In particular, he was much concerned with the rationality problem of 'how the spontaneous interaction of a number of people, each possessing only bits of knowledge, brings about a state of affairs in which prices correspond to costs ... and which could be brought about by deliberate direction only by someone who possessed the combined knowledge of all these individuals' (p. 49). In the common presence of systemic complexity (or uncertainty) and temporary unique opportunities, the individual decision makers can progress through active learning (or 'discovery'). They use simple rules of adaptive behaviour to reduce just peripheral uncertainty (Hayek, 1976, p. 38); they seldom elucidate probabilities of any kind (the evolving economic environment is, perhaps, incompatible with our notions of stationarity and ergodicity, as well as with the stable existence of subjective 'odds'); and their competitive experience will permit them to learn how to learn. Here most data used to guide decisions are not objective and thus may not be replicable, either by participants or by external observers!

This picture of behaviour in an uncertain environment, clearly not one of purely random noise, is challenging. The reliance on complete and stable probability distributions (so common in later theories of information and search, which stem from the influence of Stigler over the last 30 years) is precluded. We are left with incomplete alternatives such as Shackle's surprise, heuristics and *ad hoc* devices – less elegant but, perhaps, also less misleading. Anticipations are thus not confused with mathematical expectations, while rational processes are remote from the normality, simplicity and linearity of our fashionable ARIMA processes for 'rational expectation' models. Obviously, following Hayek's route means we must give up much of what we have grown to accept in fashionable economic modelling. Simple inspection of many recent graduate textbooks (such as, for example, those of Sargent, 1979; 1987 or McCallum, 1989) reveals the wide gap between Hayek's perspective and the analytical focus of the economic models which are typically presented to our students as illustrations of the standard bases for theoretical exercises.

The removal of any excessive precision from economic theory (termed 'the pretence of knowledge' by Hayek in his Nobel Address) also brings with it a sharp lowering of the demands to be placed on theory and a reassessment of the procedures derived from other disciplines. Our recognition of essential complexity and imperfect knowledge means that valid theoretical predictions are severely limited, for they can only refer to general economic patterns; they are just 'predictions of some of the general attributes of the structures that will form themselves, but not containing specific statements about the individual elements of which the structures will be made up' (Hayek, 1974, p. 27). Obviously, we might hope for more than this limited role that is 'a second best with which one does not like to be content' (Hayek, 1974, p. 33), especially if we are reluctant to discard the pull of our familiar econometric rituals (Paqué, 1990); or if we are unduly attracted by the rapid expansion of computational facilities. Theoretical plurality is not banished by Hayek. However, from his own modest appraisal of economics, 'we possess a fairly good "quantitative" knowledge of the forces by which a correspondence between demand and supply in the different sectors of the economic system is brought about, of the conditions under which it will be achieved, and of the factors likely to prevent such an adjustment' (Hayek, 1974, p. 25) – but how much else?

With respect to appropriate techniques for economic theories, Hayek disliked the thoughtless imitation of successful methods used in the physical sciences, including both algebraic and empirical methods, for several reasons: the association with mechanical or uncritical habits of thought, the potential problem of quantitative bias (which may distort the validation of rival theories), the need for sufficient humility to deflect any striving to control society, and the danger of misunderstanding due to any neglect of the main interactions that significantly link the constituent elements of economic structures. The strength of such objections stemmed from the way in which he chose to describe the economic environment, from his belief in the relative efficacy of competition, and from the severe limitations on the knowledge of external observers that we have already cited. To some extent, his perspective seems closer to evolutionary biology (Georgescu-Roegen, 1979; Campbell, 1988), where the flow of transitory qualitative changes or 'novelties' may also weaken the usefulness of most analytical similes and adversely affect quantitative predictions.

In presenting his views on theory and theorizing, Hayek never sought to be neutral. Indeed he insisted that 'the very selection of our problems for scientific examination implies valuations and that therefore the clear separation of scientific knowledge and valuations cannot be achieved by avoiding all valuations, but only by an unmistakable statement of the guiding values' (Hayek, 1967, p. 254). Thus neutrality or indifference were seen as merely more pretence, to be expressly avoided (especially by academic teachers) so that any audience is permitted to 'recognize the dependence of ... practical conclusions on value judgements.' Many collections of his papers (those appearing in 1948, 1967, 1978, 1988, 1991, for example) show that the strength of his own convictions or values was visible and was explicitly integrated in both the theoretical details and the choice of topics that he addressed throughout his career. This openness often encouraged him to go much beyond his material, and to make assertions such as 'no society which has not first developed a commercial group within which the improvement of the tools of thought has brought advantage to the individual has ever gained the advantage of systematic rational thinking' (Hayek, 1979, p. 76). Similarly, he frequently invoked some supplementary mechanisms, such as those by which the traditions of competition would progressively stimulate the gradual spread of more rational methods through imitation – without, it seems, ever feeling it was necessary to defend the real existence of such mechanisms. Thus Hayek's context was generally flexible, incompletely specified, and open to further adjustment by other economists (even by those with different attitudes).

Special concerns – what is it all about?

We began by suggesting that the career and liberal views of Hayek present several difficulties for historians of economic thought and for methodologists. Our desultory comments in the last section should establish that his views of economic theory and theorizing were not trite, too simple to deserve more attention, and unduly restrictive. Nor was his persistent discontent with the technical formalities of mathematics and statistics ill-considered for economic applications. Recently, his concerns with the hazards of excessive formalization and with the explication of scientific elements in economic research have been paralleled in the comments of other scholars.[1] In econometrics, during the last decade, formal inferential procedures have been subjected to some radical reappraisals associated with Hendry, Leamer and

Kalman (Hamouda and Rowley, 1988; Darnell and Evans, 1990), and the methodologies of validation, testing and specification remain troublesome, at least for some prominent econometricians and statisticians. Elsewhere in economics and in other disciplines (including law, medicine and psychology, for example), the new recognition of cognitive biases and limitations (Arkes and Hammond, 1986; Evans, 1989; Kahneman, Slovic and Tversky, 1982; and Gardner, 1985) has already stimulated considerable debates on mental states, heuristics and individual decision making. Thus many topics that reflect elements in the context earlier described and stressed by Hayek remain pertinent to scholarly endeavours.

We have selected three areas of current significance, which reflect our personal backgrounds and interests, to identify some of the issues that must be posed should we want to link (or to contrast) various current activities and attitudes of economists with Hayek's distinctive perspectives on theory and theorizing. The first of these areas is primarily concerned with the basic methodological issues, including some aspects of prediction and explanation, familiar philosophical connections between Hayek and Popper, evolutionary epistemology and the sociology of knowledge (Radnitzky and Bartley, 1987). A second area focuses on other empirical matters associated with econometrics, testing and data. Hayek (1988, p. 148) noted 'the crucial phenomena determining the formation of many highly complex structures of human interaction ... cannot be interpreted by simple causal or "nomothetic" theories, but require explanation in terms of a larger number of distinct elements than we can ever hope individually to observe or manipulate.' This view (of market prices and economic values, for instance) is hardly compatible with the limited size of econometric equations, their presumed stability, and the general neglect of measurement errors.

The final area deals with particular challenges to Hayek's subjective individualism and to an overoptimistic reliance on the 'invisible hand' of competition. These strong challenges stem from some important structural changes in advanced capitalist economies, which have 'internalized' knowledge within large conglomerates, reduced the regulatory role of prices (as discussed, for example, by Simon, 1991; Stigler, 1991; and Williamson, 1986), and also facilitated the sharing of information within extensive corporate groups, such as the Japanese *keiretsu* and the Korean *chaebol*. Here, coordination has become part of a visible planning process, which partially replaces competition with 'groupism' and seems to provide efficient, perhaps rational, outcomes. Furthermore, the members of such corporate groups often share economic resources (including their access to financial resources, through the direct involvement of banks) and market information to effectively reduce the incidence of bankruptcy and market failures, and to change markedly earlier patterns of investment behaviour. This collusive situation is far removed from the individualism, rational processes and spontaneous orders envisaged by Hayek – although its existence is surely based on major developments in the means of collecting, processing and transmitting basic economic intelligence.

Theory and theorizing, predictions and explanations

The emergence of evolutionary epistemology in economics and other social sciences is part of a general movement, within which evolutionary notions have been attached to long-term theories. One of the best known elements in this movement in recent years is the controversial promotion of sociobiology (Wilson, 1975). However, evolutionary epistemology seems to stem from earlier efforts by Popper and subsequent contributors (Radnitzky and Bartley, 1987; Campbell, 1974) to widen discussions of the philosophy of science towards more biological analogies and away from a myopic focus on the methods often associated with physics. A convenient background is provided by Bartley (1987), while Redman (1991) indicates some of the relevant connections within and around the Popperian school. Hayek's own treatment of knowledge, imitative behaviour, rational processes, long-term themes, and adaptation can easily fit into the twin evolutionary visions attached to actual economic processes, on the one hand, and to the progress of science, on the other.

Popper (1959, p. 15) suggested that 'the central problem of epistemology has always been and still is the problem of the growth of knowledge' and that 'the growth of knowledge can be studied best by studying the growth of scientific knowledge.' Indeed, he often noted the interaction between descriptive assessments of 'man as knower', or common-sense knowledge, and the emergence of scientific knowledge. Campbell (1974, 1977) took the interaction of these two types of knowledge even further for the social sciences. He argued that if evolution is comprehensively viewed as a knowledge process, then we should require that 'an evolutionary epistemology would be at minimum an epistemology taking cognizance of and compatible with man's status as a product of biological and social evolution' and that extension of the paradigm of natural selection to the changes in knowledge 'can be generalized to other epistemic activities, such as learning, thought, and science' (Campbell, 1974, p. 413). Simple illustrations of this twin evolutionary approach to such diverse areas as jurisprudence and statistics are provided by Beckstrom (1989) and Durbin (1985).

The evolutionary elements of Hayek's own approach to theory and theorizing are usually expressed in descriptive terms and in his support of supplemental dynamic and selective mechanisms, which seem to guide progress both for the common-sense knowledge of individual market participants and for scientific knowledge. An illustration is provided in his view of competi-

tion as a discovery process (Hayek, 1968, pp. 180–81), which was influenced
by both Polanyi and Popper:

> The peculiarity of competition – which it has in common with scientific method –
> is that its performance cannot be tested in particular instances where it is signifi-
> cant, but is shown by the fact that the market will prevail in comparison with
> alternative arrangements. The advantages of accepted scientific procedures cannot
> be proved scientifically, but only demonstrated by the common experience that,
> on the whole, they are better adapted to deliver the goods than alternative ap-
> proaches.

Much of Hayek's economic theory can be clearly identified with arguments
for the provision of a better environment, usually involving some restraints
on governments, so that competitive economic agents can efficiently adjust to
the transitory changes in their environment. Survival of the fittest economic
agents depends here on their tacit acquisition and use of relevant knowledge.
The advances of science, on the other hand, are achieved by the search for,
and the discovery of, general non-transitory regularities. This simple distinction between basic adjustments to transitory reactions and searches for long-
term facts also affects the relative predictive content of economic theory and
of other scientific areas, with the former limited to general patterns.

Hayek's emphasis of tacit 'know-how' (Gray, 1984, p. 14) as the 'well-
spring' of our knowledge, although beyond any individual powers of articu-
lation, also linked the practical and subjective observation of economic activities with the familiar hypothetico-deductive or conjectural methods of
science – the advocacy of which he generally shared with Popper (Gray,
1984, pp. 20–21). Among the (Popperian) assertions identified for these methods by Hayek are 'that the theoretical sciences are all essentially deductive,
that there can be no such logical procedure as "induction" which leads with
necessity from the observation of facts to the formulation of general rules,
and that the latter are products of creative acts of the mind which cannot be
formalized' (Hayek, 1955, pp. 4–5). From this perspective, he also concluded
that 'the advance of knowledge consists in the formulation of new statements
which often refer to events which cannot be directly observed and from
which, in combination with other statements about particulars, we derive
statements capable of disproof by observation.' Despite a few differences in
emphasis, Hayek seems to have accepted much of the familiar methodological apparatus which we now typically attribute to Popper.

It has been suggested that the predictive content of economic theory is
either absent or insufficient (McCloskey, 1986, pp. 15–16; Rosenberg, 1989,
pp. 52–5). Due to the essential complexity of economic phenomena and to
the limitations of their quantitative data, Hayek argued that economists are
confined to 'mere pattern predictions – predictions of some of the general

attributes of the structures that will form themselves, but not containing specific statements about the individual elements of which the structures will be made up' (Hayek, 1974, p. 27). He warned us that other firmer predictions involve a quantitative bias, which stems from the presumption that 'our theories must be formulated in such terms that they refer only to measurable magnitudes' and, also, from 'the fiction that the factors which they can measure are the only ones that are relevant' (p. 24). The presence of uncertainty, which is not amenable to representation by probability distributions, fits with an evolutionary perspective that restricts most quantitative predictions, for 'man is not and never will be the master of his fate; his very reason always progresses by leading him into the unknown and unforeseen where he learns new things' (Hayek, 1979, p. 176).

The continuous emergence of qualitative changes due to unpredictable novelties, each of which is unique in chronological time (Georgescu-Roegen, 1979, p. 321), will generate evolutionary economic structures. Any failure to recognize the potential impact of such irregular qualitative changes on prediction and scientific explanation – by continuing, uncritically, to require quantitative predictions as the primary form of 'scientific' evidence – opens the way for 'charlatanism and worse' and 'is likely to make us do much harm' (Hayek, 1978, p. 33). Overall, looking at the current practices of economists, it seems that any more acceptance of the methodological framework of Hayek is unlikely. He asked that we be satisfied with modest generic patterns, deductive conclusions, non-quantitative analyses and restraint. Unfortunately, as we have noted elsewhere, looking at the history of economics offers little support either to the notion that selective processes will weed out inadequacies, rather than reveal the persistence of our fashionable pursuits, or that our profession can generally exercise sufficient restraint! Natural selection might not be progressive, and we may indeed be condemned to repeat earlier mistakes by ignoring the sensible criticism of our methods and the clarification of most economic situations.

Data, testing and econometrics

Hayek's distrust of the statistical approach predated his move to London, and the distrust continued unabated throughout his long career. In the English version of *Monetary Theory and the Trade Cycle* (1932, pp. 30–31), for example, this approach is criticized for its inherent ambiguity and incompleteness. Specifically, he identified the statistical approach with a failure to determine conditions under which any 'established' economic relations might hold good, and he recognized the equivocal linkage between these conditions and particular economic objects. Furthermore, he stressed theoretical priorities and some potential corroborative woes for the approach. Thus, he insisted that the 'empirically established relations between various economic phenomena continue to present a problem to theory until the necessity for their interconnections can be demonstrated *independently* of any statistical evidence' and 'the corroboration of statistical evidence provides, in itself, no proof of correctness,' which led him to the dismissive limitation that 'a priori we cannot expect from statistics anything more than the stimulus provided by the indication of new problems.'

Some prominent econometricians accept similar constraints on the limited generalizability of empirical evidence for economic phenomena but, clearly, the common practice among many economists (especially in connection with their fashionable reliance on basic Neyman–Pearson statistical tests) is to ignore the theoretical bounds of the statistical approach to estimation and inference and, thus, to exaggerate both the relevance of particular findings and the nature of statistical evidence. In part, these economists are preoccupied with quantities rather than with qualitative features so that the numerical indicators of significance are given too much attention – substantive significance being often confused with its statistical counterpart. Perhaps Hayek's practical objections to the approach are most clearly expressed in his persistent rejection of Keynes's macroeconomic functions because of their structural instability, quantitative biases, and artificial simplification.

> There seems to me ... not only to exist no reason whatever to assume that these 'functions' will remain constant, but I believe that micro-theory had demonstrated long before Keynes that they cannot be constant but will change over time not only in quantity but even in direction. ... They may change very rapidly as a result of changes in the microeconomic structure, and conclusions that they are constant are bound to be misleading. (Hayek, 1966, p. 285)

In this context, Hayek suggests that the usual irresponsible reliance on measurable magnitudes achieves 'pseudo-exactness at the price of disregarding the relationships which govern the economic system' so the simplicity of macroeconomic theory 'tends to conceal nearly all that really matters' (p. 289). If we look at the recent reappraisals of econometrics by Hendry, Leamer, Kalman and the proponents of rational-expectations models, these objections of Hayek remain pertinent. Hendry's research programme calls for 'dynamic specification' and 'encompassing', while insisting that 'the three golden rules of econometrics are test, test and test.' He stresses an evolutionary research process, whereby the changes in acceptable economic theory are driven by successful performance in empirical tests. However, all applications of this programme have fitted only simple equations (with just a few explanatory, global influences), using the standard data which are routinely collected by governmental agencies, and using only the conventional statistical methods that generally require linearity, normality, stationarity, or asymptotic justification. Because of their preoccupation with statistical testing and the constraints of computational software, these empirical applications generally seem fatally flawed. For example, they neglect most socioeconomic institutions, direct contextual information, the irregular timing of economic decisions, the pre-test biases that occur in sequential research, many of the impacts of inherent sources of structural instability, the clear consequences of both spatial and temporal aggregation, the practical awkwardness of encompassing alternative and incommensurable theories, and a host of other relevant factors. (Modest attempts to deal with any 'complications' seem only to invoke statistical checks.) Overall, it is unclear what progress can emerge from the pursuit of this particular research programme. Without substantial modification, as Hayek would have insisted, the programme appears likely to be quite misleading, perhaps unhelpful, and remote from the economic context!

Leamer's reappraisal of econometrics began with an important recognition that the growth of econometrics, and the corresponding assimilation of the statistical approach, has been accompanied by the haphazard treatment of specification for fitted equations. Like Hayek, he pointed to the common imprecision and artificial or whimsical simplification of all econometric modelling. He also drew attention to the need for more effective investigation of sensitivity, robustness and (possibly, non-statistical) diagnostic procedures. Unlike Hayek, however, he retained the statistical framework as a simple basis for specification searches, while recasting it in a sceptical Bayesian form – without the excessive pretentiousness of Hendry's encompassing principle. In another recent appraisal, Kalman took a different approach in which system-science notions were prominent, the classical sampling paradigm was dismissed, and the questions to be addressed were reformed (away from identification and estimation, and toward calibration). Like Hayek, he rejected physics as a good role model for economics. But the substitution of an engineer's perspective, with its search for 'canonical realizations' (or objective law-like relations), for structural invariants, for clear ranges of parametric values, and for definitive choices among alternative theories, does not lead to the approaches advocated by Hayek. In particular, beyond some obvious differences in regard to mathematical modelling, Kalman's two suggestions that unanimity was feasible among economists and that the choice of models should be data-driven are fundamentally at odds with many comments by Hayek.

The final reappraisal of econometrics in recent years has come from the proponents of rational-expectation models, including some economists who stressed newer, equilibrium, business cycle theories and who focused their attention on the qualitative characteristics of a few stochastically disturbed, linear difference-equations. Here, most testing is based on calibration and on the tentative identification of model dynamics with 'stylized facts' (such as those derived from the NBER chronologies and referential data). Hayek (1978, p. 28), despite his clear resistance to mathematical formalism and its concomitants, argued that the great advantage of the mathematical technique was that 'it allows us to describe, by means of algebraic equations, the general character of a pattern even where we are ignorant of the numerical values which will determine its particular manifestation.' This comment, and the strong anti-Keynesian sentiments of many rational-expectations theorists (as reprinted in Lucas, 1981, and Lucas and Sargent, 1981, for example), seem to link the views of Hayek with those expressed by some such theorists over the last two decades. This common impression is also fostered by the re-emergence of interest in business cycles, the subordination of macroeconomics (Lucas, 1987, p. 107), and the premature dismissal of Keynesian notions (such as the liquidity trap). However, the contrast between these two sets of views is quite startling, once the thin veneer of apparent similarity has been pierced. Lucas (1987, p. 2), in an influential book on dynamic models of business cycles, observes that 'it is now entirely routine to analyze economic decision-makers as operating through time in a complex, probabilistic environment, trading in a rich array of contingent-claim securities, and to study agents situated in economies with wide possible technologies, information structures, and stochastic disturbances.' Furthermore, he suggests that these dynamic and probabilistic elements can be incorporated in economic theory 'at the same level of rigor on which we study the problem of a single decision-maker making a one-time choice at given prices.' His optimization models, somewhat remote from macroeconometric alternatives and the usual statistical approach, are quite distinct from the context of Hayek that we sketched in the section above. But Lucas's models (at the frontier of the rational-expectations literature) exhibit many of the deficiencies which Hayek often portrayed. Certainly, the models and their companions are far removed from the complexity, tacit knowledge, adaptive behaviour, and other features with which Hayek characterized economic markets – even though they settle for qualitative findings, rather than for quantitative predictions. On the other hand, these models are deductive and conjectural – still insufficient to put them with Hayek's efforts.

Information sharing, competition and agglomeration
Modern capitalist economies differ quite markedly from those which existed when Hayek first launched his views on knowledge and rational economic processes in the 1930s. Clearly the relevance of these views needs to be reassessed in the light of the significant changes which have occurred during the last 60 years. It has already been suggested that, with the exception of Hayek, 'modern liberals rarely confront those changes which, in modern times, have dissolved the linkage between capitalism and individualism,

namely, the dominance on non-individualistic, corporate capitalism, and autonomous developments within individualism' (Abercrombie, Hill and Turner, 1986, pp. 3–4). Changes here include some restrictions on individual property rights, the growing depersonalization of capital ownership in capitalist economies (which is reflected, for example, in the significant growth of large institutional investors and in the widespread substitution of debt for equity by corporate borrowers), and the rapid rise of giant corporations and economic concentration or 'agglomeration' (Abercrombie, et al., pp. 131–43). Also the recent success of the Japanese economy has produced some effective challenges to the traditional appraisals by economists of collusion, the economies of scope (in contrast to an earlier preoccupation with economies of scale), routine government–business interaction, and information sharing, so it is difficult to sustain individualism as a defining feature of modern capitalism.

While Hayek stressed the market's role in the aggregation of decentralized and asymmetric information, he could not foresee the successful exploitation of other means of aggregation beyond the market. As Hahn (1984, p. 347) points out in some reflections on the invisible hand, Hayek 'certainly did not clinch the case that only the market can aggregate it' but he led us to realize that 'something will have to have decentralised decision features if the information is to be gained and used.' The Japanese *keiretsu* solve the problem of economic coordination by systematically bringing the principal decision makers together – so they can share extensive information, form consistent plans, and be mutually supportive. This routine programme for the interactive sharing of information and plans provides a self-maintaining *and orderly system* (which, in important respects, has dramatically rejected myopic self-interest, accepted positional goods, and strengthened the internal 'social responsibility' among members of particular corporate groups) within an expansionary climate. Compare this current development of strategic alliances with the typical account of Hayek (1988, p. 47) which suggests that 'the market enabled each, within set limits, to use his own individual knowledge for his own individual purposes while being ignorant of most of the order into which he had to fit his actions.' To the contrary, the primary strength of new Asian corporate alliances is found in the deliberate awareness of their constituents' purposes and in their attempts to subordinate some market influences by joint activity.

Overall, the emergence of an information-driven society and of effective systems for electronic communication has transformed the spontaneous orders and complexity which were stressed so often by Hayek. The evolutionary transformation of economic markets has resulted in new conditions that are somewhat remote from those found in earlier decades. Accompanying this transformation, the nature of economic intelligence and the standard forms of social institutions have been radically revised. These developments mean that our treatment of knowledge should be recast to reflect a new reality. Whatever emerges in the future, we need to acknowledge the wisdom of Hayek (1937, p. 33) when he contended that 'the empirical element in economic theory ... consists of propositions about the acquisition of knowledge.'

Final comment

To some extent, Hayek's potential impact on the current states of both economic theory and econometric research is understated. Despite the reverence which has frequently been attached to his efforts by both neoconservatives and liberals, the contents of his vision of thoughtful economic agents, their evolutionary responses to qualitative shocks, and the complexity of economic phenomena need to be rediscovered. Similarly, the consequences of these elements for our methods of analysis should be reassessed in the light of current concerns, including those that reflect sensible doubts about the way in which the statistical approach has been pursued by economists. He always set high standards for clarity and consistency. Now we need to assess whether the views that he expressed can still be instructive for understanding our current economic conditions, fashionable models, and the means of guiding political choices.

Notes

1.   See, for example, contributions by McCloskey, Katzner, Caldwell and Solow to a special issue of *Methodus*, June 1991, on such concerns.

References

Abercrombie, N., S. Hill and B.S. Turner (1986), *Sovereign Individuals of Capitalism*, London: Allen and Unwin.

Arkes, H.R. and K.R. Hammond (eds) (1986), *Judgment and Decision Making*, Cambridge: Cambridge University Press.

Bartley, W.W. (1987), 'Philosophy of Biology Versus Philosophy of Physics', in Radnitzky and Bartley (1987), ch. 1.

Beckstrom, J.H. (1989), *Evolutionary Jurisprudence*, Urbana and Chicago: University of Illinois Press.

Blumenthal, S. (1986), *The Rise of the Counter-Establishment*, New York: Times Books.

Caldwell, B.J. (1988), 'Hayek's Transformation', *History of Political Economy*, **20**, 4, 513–41.

Caldwell, B.J. (1991), 'Has Formalization Gone Too Far in Economics: A Comment', *Methodus*, **3**, 1, 27–9.

Campbell, D.T. (1974), 'Evolutionary Epistemology', in P. Schilpp (ed.), *The Philosophy of Karl Popper*, La Salle, Illinois: Open Court, 413–63. Reprinted in Campbell (1988), ch. 16, and in Radnitzky and Bartley (1987), ch. 2.

Campbell, D.T. (1977), *Descriptive Epistemology: Psychological, Sociological, and Evolutionary*, The William James Lectures, Harvard University. Partially contained in Campbell (1988), chs 12, 17 and 18.

Campbell, D.T. (1988), *Methodology and Epistemology for Social Science. Selected Papers*, Chicago: The University of Chicago Press.

Darnell, A.C. and J.L. Evans (1990), *The Limits of Econometrics*, Aldershot: Edward Elgar.

Durbin, J. (1985), 'Evolutionary Origins of Statisticians and Statistics', in A.C. Atkinson and S.E. Fienberg (eds), *A Celebration of Statistics*, Berlin: Springer-Verlag, ch. 9.

Evans, J.S.T. (1989), *Bias in Human Reasoning: Causes and Consequences*, London: Lawrence Erlbaum Associates.

Friedman, M. (1976), 'Foreword', in F. Machlup (ed.), *Essays on Hayek*, New York: New York University Press.

Gardner, H. (1985), *The Mind's New Science*, New York: Basic Books.

Georgescu-Roegen, N. (1979), 'Methods in Economic Science', *Journal of Economic Issues*, **13**, 317–28.

Gray, J. (1984), *Hayek on Liberty*, Oxford: Basil Blackwell.

Hahn, F. (1984), 'Reflections on the Invisible Hand', *Equilibrium and Macroeconomics*, Oxford: Basil Blackwell, ch. 6.

Hamouda, O.F. and R. Rowley (1988), *Expectations, Equilibrium and Dynamics*, New York: St Martin's Press.

Hayek, F.A. von (1931), *Prices and Production*, London: Routledge and Kegan Paul.

Hayek, F.A. von (1933), 'The Trend of Economic Thinking', *Economica*, **13**, 121–37. Reprinted in Hayek (1991), ch. 1.

Hayek, F.A. von (1937), 'Economics and Knowledge', *Economica*, **4**, 33–54. Reprinted in Hayek (1948), ch. 2.

Hayek, F.A. von (1945), 'The Use of Knowledge in Society', *The American Economic Review*, **35**, 4, 519–30. Reprinted in Hayek (1948), ch. 4.

Hayek, F.A. von (1948), *Individualism and Economic Order*, Chicago: The University of Chicago Press.

Hayek, F.A. von (1955), 'Degrees of Explanation', *British Journal for the Philosophy of Science*, **6**. Reprinted in Hayek (1967), ch. 1

Hayek, F.A. von (1964), 'The Theory of Complex Phenomena', in M. Bunge (ed.), *The Critical Approach to Science and Philosophy. Essays in Honor of K.R. Popper*, New York: The Free Press. Reprinted in Hayek (1967), ch. 2.

Hayek, F.A. von (1966), 'Personal Recollections of Keynes and the "Keynesian Revolution"', *The Oriental Economist*. Reprinted in Hayek (1978), ch. 18.

Hayek, F.A. von (1967), *Studies in Philosophy, Politics and Economics*, Chicago: The University of Chicago Press.

Hayek, F.A. von (1968), *Competition as a Discovery Procedure*, Lecture to the Philadelphia Society, Chicago. Extended version published in Hayek (1978), ch. 12.

Hayek, F.A. von (1973, 1976, 1979), *Law, Legislation and Liberty*, 3 vols, Chicago: The University of Chicago Press.

Hayek, F.A. von (1974), *The Pretence of Knowledge*, Nobel Memorial Lecture, Stockholm. Reprinted in Hayek (1978), ch. 2, and in *The American Economic Review*, **79**, 6 (1989), 3–7.

Hayek, F.A. von (1978), *New Studies in Philosophy, Politics, Economics and the History of Ideas*, Chicago: The University of Chicago Press.

Hayek, F.A. von (1984), *Money, Capital, and Fluctuations: Early Essays*, Chicago: The University of Chicago Press.

Hayek, F.A. von (1988), *The Fatal Conceit. The Errors of Socialism*, Chicago: The University of Chicago Press.

Hayek, F.A. von (1991), *The Trend of Economic Thinking: Essays on Political Economists and Economic History*, London: Routledge.

Kahneman, D., P. Slovic and A. Tversky (eds) (1982), *Judgment Under Uncertainty: Heuristics and Biases*, Cambridge: Cambridge University Press.

Katzner, D.W. (1991), 'In Defense of Formalization in Economics', *Methodus*, **3**, 1, 17–24.

Lachmann, L.M. (1969), 'Methodological Individualism and the Market Economy', in E. Streissler, G. Haberler, F. Lutz and F. Machlup, *Roads to Freedom: Essays in Honour of F.A. von Hayek*, London: Routledge and Kegan Paul.

Levitt, K.P. and M. Mendell (1988), *Hayek in Vienna*, Working Paper 6/88, Department of Economics, McGill University.

Lucas, R.E. (1981), *Studies in Business-Cycle Theory*, Cambridge, Mass.: The MIT Press.

Lucas, R.E. (1987), *Models of Business Cycles*, Oxford: Basil Blackwell.

Lucas, R.E. and T.J. Sargent (eds) (1981), *Rational Expectations and Econometric Practice*, Minneapolis: The University of Minnesota Press.

McCallum, B. (1989), *Monetary Economics: Theory and Policy*, New York: Macmillan.

McCloskey, D.N. (1986), *The Rhetoric of Economics*, Brighton: Wheatsheaf Books.

McCloskey, D.N. (1991), 'Economic Science: A Search Through the Hyperspace of Assumptions?', *Methodus*, **3**, 1, 6–16.

Paqué, K.-H. (1990), 'Pattern Predictions in Economics: Hayek's Methodology of the Social Sciences Revisited', *History of Political Economy*, **22**, 2, 281–94.

Popper, K.R. (1959), *The Logic of Scientific Discovery*, London: Hutchison. Revised edition published in 1968.

Radnitzky, G. and W.W. Bartley (eds) (1987), *Evolutionary Epistemology, Rationality, and the Sociology of Knowledge*, La Salle, Illinois: Open Court.

Redman, D.A. (1991), *Economics and the Philosophy of Science*, Oxford: Oxford University Press.

Rosenberg, A. (1989), 'Are Generic Predictions Enough?', *Erkenntnis*, **30**, 43–68.

Sargent, T.J. (1979), *Macroeconomic Theory*, New York: Academic Press.

Sargent, T.J. (1987), *Dynamic Macroeconomic Theory*, Cambridge, Mass.: Harvard University Press.

Simon, H.A. (1991), 'Organizations and Markets', *Journal of Economic Perspectives*, **5**, 2, 25–44.

Smith, J.A. (1989), 'Think Tanks and the Politics of Ideas', in D.C. Colander and A.W. Coats (eds), *The Spread of Economic Ideas*, Cambridge: Cambridge University Press, ch. 15.

Solow, R.M. (1991), 'Discussion Notes on 'Formalism'', *Methodus*, **3**, 1, 30–31.

Stigler, J.E. (1991), 'Symposium on Organizations and Economics', *Journal of Economic Perspectives*, **5**, 2, 15–24.

Williamson, O.E. (1986), 'The Economics of Governance: Framework and Implications', in R.N. Langlois (ed.), *Economics as a Process: Essays in the New Institutional Economics*, Cambridge: Cambridge University Press, ch. 8.

Wilson, E.O. (1975), *Sociobiology: The New Synthesis*, Cambridge, Mass.: The Belknap Press.

Comment

*Riccardo Bellofiore**

> If there existed the universal mind that projected itself into the scientific fancy of
> Laplace ... such a mind could, of course, draw up *a priori* a faultless and an
> exhaustive economic plan, beginning with the number of hectares of wheat and
> down to the last button for a vest. In truth, the bureaucracy often conceives that
> just such a mind is at its disposal; that is why it so easily frees itself from the
> control of the market and of Soviet democracy. But in reality the bureaucracy errs
> frightfully in this appraisal of its spiritual resources... (Lev Trotsky, *Soviet Economy
> in Danger*, 1932, as quoted by Lange (1938), p. 138)

In the 1970s and the 1980s the Austrians have mounted an effective counter-
attack on the standard account of the socialist calculation debate (Vaughn,
1980; Lavoie, 1985). The paper by Streissler (Chapter 3, this volume), on
which my comments will focus, follows the same line of reasoning.

What these authors remind us is that Mises and Hayek were outside the
static equilibrium framework of mainstream economics, which Pareto, Barone
and Lange took as the starting-point for their reasoning. In fact, as Streissler
quite correctly points out, Mises wrongly assumed that even within the static
framework of general equilibrium theory it is impossible to mimic the market
by central planning. Thus he was easy to criticize. Hayek's argument, however, was different, and was not well understood at the time by its opponents.
According to Hayek, knowledge is dispersed, incomplete, tacit. Information
is incessantly *created* by *real* markets, and is most effectively communicated
by market prices; the problems posed by the collecting of existing knowledge
therefore constitute only a minor, and secondary, difficulty. The market is
superior to planning because it takes advantage of this 'division of knowledge'. *All* the relevant knowledge, including tacit knowledge – this is Hayek's
point – is contained in condensed form in prices, which are signals revealing
the constantly changing scarcities.

I find Streissler's paper a scholarly detour in the doctrinal history which
can be traced behind Hayek's argument. It is also a balanced evaluation of his
contribution both to the original debate and to the interpretation of the collapse of 'really existing socialism'. I almost totally agree with many of
Streissler's conclusions. In particular, Streissler is right to emphasize that

*Financial assistance from MURST – the Italian Ministry for the University and Scientific
Research – is gratefully acknowledged.

195

Hayek's 'information argument' is aimed at showing the difficulties of *any* interventionist economic policy – it should be remembered that 'planning' for a long time encompassed much more than the Soviet-type command economy, and that Keynes explicitly advocated it.[1] Hayek's more fundamental target was not so much centralized planning, but 'socialism' *within* the capitalist market system, which seemed to him an irreversible road to hell. So his attack was much more against Walras and Keynes than Marx. Though Moss's paper (Chapter 5, this volume) specifies more carefully what has often been seen as Hayek's 'disillusionment' with regard to general equilibrium tools of analysis, he agrees that Hayek (and Mises) saw the socialists as misusing the Walrasians' fictitious models as representative of the actual workings of a free market economy.[2]

In my opinion, Streissler's paper allows us to shift our focus from the issue of assessing the relevance of Hayek's argument for the socialist calculation debate in 'no longer existing socialism' to the more urgent task of asking ourselves if his reasoning is effective in dealing with actually existing capitalism. For the sake of clarity, I should say at once that I do not accept Streissler's conclusion that Hayek's information-theoretic approach is better in condemning planning in 'market' economies than in explaining the deterioration in the socialist systems in the last two decades. On the contrary, as I shall try to show by comparing Hayek with Schumpeter, it can be argued that there is an interdependence between 'central' planning and 'free' dynamic competition within capitalism. This Schumpeterian train of thought does not rest on any adherence to Walrasian general equilibrium theory, but rather on Schumpeter's own monetary analysis of the capitalist process; thus it is not subject to the Austrians' critiques against the socialist position in the calculation debate.

I shall also suggest that a reconsideration of the generally neglected Schumpeterian analysis of the role of the banks as the agents of planning within capitalism may cast a new, more positive, light on some strengths in Lange's 'socialist' model, and on some weaknesses in Hayek's critique – strengths and weaknesses which are generally overlooked by the contemporary Austrian reappraisal of the calculation debate, and also by Jossa's paper (Chapter 4, this volume).

The interest of looking at Schumpeter is that his view of capitalist development and of 'free' competition was, like Hayek's, far removed from Walrasian general equilibrium theory. There are, however, fundamental differences between Schumpeter and Hayek. According to Schumpeter, capitalism is characterized by three elements: private ownership of means of production; production for private profit; and bank credit. The first two features are also present in Hayek. It is the third, however, which is for Schumpeter the *differentia specifica* of capitalism, essential as it is for the functioning of the system. The incessant creation of new plant and equipment, the introduction of new technologies, i.e. innovations, requires a shift of resources from existing uses to new ones. Private ownership of capital and the equilibrium position of the market (i.e. circular flow) must be *violated* if entrepreneurial action, the prime mover of economic progress, is to take place. The role of bank credit, in fact, is to do just that: it brings about an inflation where the changes induced in relative prices squeeze the old purchasing power, i.e. the money held and spent by the administrators of old business.[3]

According to Schumpeter, money is a system of social accountancy, governed by a fundamental arbitrariness. In general, money acts as both a receipt voucher for productive contributions and a claim ticket to goods. What is essential to money, however, is not the first feature but the second; the newly created sums of money which the banks put at the disposal of the entrepreneur for future production is only a claim ticket, not a receipt voucher. Provided that bank loans finance innovations, and not just investments, they cooperate to bring about an increased flow of commodities; but they will do this only after a time lag, whereas in the meantime the new liquidity is emitted in the context of unchanged quantities of commodities. Now, let us look at what Schumpeter says about the shift in purchasing power among individuals which encourages the expansion of production:

> The obstacles are removed which private property places in the way of him who does not already have command over means of production. The banking world constitutes a central authority of the economy whose directives put the necessary means of production at the disposal of innovators in the productive organism. (Schumpeter 1917–18, pp. 205–6)

The theme is a recurring one in Schumpeter's books – from the *Theory of Economic Development* and his unpublished 'Treatise on Money' to the two volumes of *Business Cycles* – as well as in most of his articles. The role of the banks as 'screening devices' follows quite naturally from their aforementioned function of 'social accountants',[4] and falls within Hayek's definition of socialism: 'any administration with coercive power which tries to divert private people in their employment'. Banks succeed in shifting productive resources in favour of the entrepreneur because they can (indirectly, but effectively) manipulate the system of prices. Thus prices communicate information, but they do not reflect the 'true' relative scarcities of a pure, unhampered, market system. More than that, the banking institution, declaring to society the creditworthiness of a particular firm, assures and insures the credibility of information. Thus, prices do not reflect only relative scarcities: information is supplied by banks by means other than prices.

In 'Kreditkontrolle' Schumpeter wrote:

> If a central bureau of the socialist kind is thought impossible, or if one thinks that
> its time has not yet arrived and in the meantime wishes to be faithful to the
> capitalist system, one should not reject that part of the mechanism which is the
> vehicle of economic progress. (Schumpeter, 1925, p. 318)

One may wonder if Hayek was not committing precisely this error when
he failed to recognize the existence of an inbuilt element of planning within
capitalism as essential to the working of entrepreneurial competition. The
notion of a totally unplanned economy, an economy that dispenses with the
'central' planning by banks (and government), seems to be an impossible
dream, a Utopia which destroys actual capitalism.

It is interesting that in that same article, as also in a contemporary one on
the gold standard (Schumpeter 1927), Schumpeter acknowledges Keynes's
position at the time of the *Tract on Monetary Reform* as a viable basis for a
rational politics of socialization, for a feasible socialist planning constructed
around the institutional centrality of the banking system. Moreover, it is
striking how much of the economic policy blueprint put forward in
Schumpeter's writings of the 1920s – with his stress on credit rationing and
selection, industrial policy, state support in foreign competition – reminds us
of the Japanese and South Korean economic miracles (Amsden, 1989; Wade,
1990). Asia's first giant, and Asia's next giant, both owe much of their
success to interventionist states performing a central informational role, altering relative prices, and governing the market.

It is interesting to note that in Schumpeter's theory, unlike in Hayek's, we
do not find sovereignty of the consumer but sovereignty of the entrepreneur.
According to Schumpeter, the interest rate does not reflect individuals'
intertemporal choices on consumption; it is the price paid by borrowers on
money balances, and is fixed by banks. It is not determined by consumers'
time preferences: rather, the other way round. A similar point of view was
also put forward by other monetary theorists of the time: let me recall only
Dennis Robertson, in *Banking Policy and the Price Level* and John Maynard
Keynes, in the *Treatise on Money*.

Looked at from this point of view, the controversy between Hayek and
Lange takes another twist. In Lange's *Economic Theory of Socialism* (Lange,
1938) and in his lectures on 'The Economic Operation of a Socialist Society'
(Lange, 1942) the rate of accumulation is arbitrarily fixed from above by the
central planning bureau, and may depart from consumers' preferences. The
rate of net investment affects the estimation of future production, and thus
the structure of prices. Lange himself argued that 'the economist' might
object that 'a rate of accumulation which does not reflect the preferences of
the consumers as to the time-shape of the flow of income may be regarded as
a diminution of social welfare' (Lange, 1938, p. 108). Lange's reply was that

even in capitalism the rate of saving was only partly determined by pure utility considerations, and much more by the distribution of incomes (ibid.): the latter depends on the divergence between savings and investment, which is governed by the rate of interest charged by banks and by the amount of credit they want to give. There is not – and never can be – anything 'natural' in the rate of accumulation of a capitalist market economy: 'What portion of the national income is being saved and consumed, and what portion is being invested in the creation of new productive instruments is largely decided on in a haphazard way' (Lange, 1942, p. 16).

Lange's argument turns Hayek's critique completely upside down. In a decentralized, anarchic system like capitalism, firms' and banks' decisions determine real consumption, irrespective of the voluntary choices of individuals.[5] On the contrary, in a socialist system the central planning bureau, or the public banking system, *may* fix the interest rate so as to secure a balance between investments and the saving habits of individuals (Lange 1942, p. 18). Lange never seems to have changed his views about the fixing of the rate of interest 'from above', even in his model of 'market socialism' with autonomous firms.

While it may be admitted that in the 'socialist calculation debate', Lange and the socialists underplayed some fundamental aspects of the capitalist market – e.g. competition as entrepreneurial rivalry and 'discovery procedure'[6] – both older and more recent Austrians seem to forget how much those very features depend on elements of 'central' planning within the market, and how much they conflict with consumer sovereignty within capitalism.

Notes

1. In a letter to Hayek (28 June 1944) commenting favourably on the latter's *The Road to Serfdom*, Keynes wrote: "I should say that what we want is not no planning, or even less planning, indeed I should say that we almost certainly want more".
2. It should be noted that the pure competition economy of the neoclassicals is, according to Lange, an ideal system which may be more easily embodied by socialism than by real capitalist economies.
3. For a balanced view of Hayek's views on money and equilibrium see Colonna (1990).
4. For a recent revival of this approach see Stiglitz and Weiss (1988).
5. Though it falls outside the subject-matter of my present remarks, I cannot refrain from pointing out that Lange was clear, in his 1942 paper, that he rejected the Pigou effect in an economic system like capitalism, where the money stock was mainly endogenous: "... money in our present system is far from being constant. As you know, money in our present economy is not simply the gold or even the Federal Reserve Notes, but it is money created by banks. It is the deposit that counts, the demand deposits which banks open for their customers largely on a credit basis, and what happens usually when the prices fall is that the very value of these banks deposits shrink at the same time. In other words, that the quantity of money shrinks more or less in proportion to the fall in prices and in consequence, this additional source of demand, the dishoarding of money, does not come into play, and however much wages and other resource prices fall, there is no increase in employment. And however flexible wages and resource prices are, an excess of saving over investment causes unemployment and no amount of wage and price reductions can remove

it, because hand in hand with the reductions of costs goes an equal reduction in the money'. (Lange 1942, p. 18)

6. However, as the quote at the beginning of the paper shows, the "information argument" was not so foreign to the socialist tradition as the Austrians made out.

References

Amsden, A.H. (1989), *Asia's Next Giant: South Korea and Late Industrialization*, New York: Oxford University Press.

Colonna, M. (1990), 'Hayek on Money and Equilibrium', in *Contributions to Political Economy*, **IX**.

Lange, O. (1938), *On the Economic Theory of Socialism*, Minneapolis: Minneapolis University Press.

Lange, O. (1942), 'The Economic Operation of a Socialist Society', in *Contribution to Political Economy*, **VI**, 1987.

Lavoie, D. (1985), *Rivalry and Central Planning. The Socialist Calculation Debate Reconsidered*, Cambridge: Cambridge University Press.

Schumpeter, J.A. (1917–18), 'Das Sozialprodukt und die Rechenpfennige. Glossen und Beiträge zur geldtheorie von heute' (quoted from the translation 'Money and the Social Product', in *International Economic Papers*, 1956).

Schumpeter, J.A. (1925), 'Kreditkontrolle', in *Archiv für Sozialwissenschaft und Sozialpolitik*, **LIV** (reprinted in *Aufsätze zur Ökonomischen Theorie*, Tübingen: Mohr, 1952).

Schumpeter, J.A. (1927), 'Die Goldene Bremse an der Kreditmaschine. Kie Goldwährung und der Bankkredit, in *Kölner Vorträge*, I, *Die Kreditwirtschaft*, part 1 (reprinted in *Aufsätze zur Ökonomischen Theorie*, Tübingen: Mohr, 1952).

Stiglitz, Joseph E. and Andrew Weiss (1988), 'Banks as social accountants and screening devices for the allocation of credit', NBER working paper no. 2710.

Vaughn, K.I. (1980), 'Economic calculation under socialism: the Austrian contribution', in *Economic Inquiry*, **XVIII**, October.

Wade, R. (1990), *Governing the market. Economic theory and the role of government in East Asian Industrialization*, Princeton U.P., Princeton.

Comment

Jack Birner

Hayek's work spans almost seven decades, and shows clear signs of development. It forms a research programme, and it cannot be properly understood unless this be kept in mind. Research programmes are defined by problems and methodological principles, and it has become common practice among philosophers of science to use these elements for reconstructing episodes of intellectual history. The reconstruction of Hayek's research programme is helped by the fact that from his earliest publications he explicitly and repeatedly states the problems he intends to solve, the solutions that have been attempted so far, the methodological constraints that successful solutions have to satisfy, and the direction his own future research is to take. Various claims that have been made in the essays in this volume are false precisely because they disregard the historical and methodological aspects of Hayek's work. The methodological principles that Hayek applies in his economics are (1) methodological individualism, (2) subjectivism, (3) theoretical unification and (4) the method of increasing abstraction.

The theoretical background of Hayek's research programme is static general equilibrium theory. In order for a static theory of equilibrium conditions to explain an inherently dynamic disequilibrium phenomenon such as the business cycle, two problems have to be solved. One is the incorporation of time, the other the introduction of a factor or mechanism that causes the disturbances of equilibrium. In Hayek's economic research programme these two basic or global problems give rise to two branches or sub-programmes:

1. An individualist programme, which is defined by the problem of how all economic theories, and in Hayek's case especially the theory of the business cycle, are to be reduced to the individualistic theory of marginal value (or the pure logic of choice as Hayek called it). The working out of this reductionist programme occupied Hayek for most of the 1930s. It involved finding solutions to mainly technical problems.
2. A subjectivist programme, which gradually, as he was working his way towards a dynamic theory, gained momentum.

The famous essay 'Economics and Knowledge' of 1937 forms a link between the two branches of his research programme. The article addresses the methodological question of the empirical content of economic theory. The answer is given by a description of the logical structure of economic theory. Its core is the pure logic of choice, which is tautologous, and the empirical content resides in the propositions surrounding the core which describe how individuals acquire knowledge. This account is defective from a methodological point of view, but I will not criticize it here. What is more important for my present purpose is that the article is in large part a methodological progress report in which Hayek summarizes the state of affairs in the reductionist branch of his research programme. What he says about the coordination of dispersed knowledge is probably inspired by the socialism debate, and it sketches the further development of the subjectivist branch of the research programme. However, Hayek's contribution to this debate does not constitute a break in the development of his thought, as Caldwell argues (Chapter 6, this volume). The continuity is confirmed by the fact that Hayek later speaks of three senses of subjectivism (cf. Hayek, 1955, ch. III): the facts of the social sciences are the opinions of the actors; heterogeneous knowledge is present in a dispersed form and has to be coordinated; and social scientists can explain the behaviour of other people because their minds classify external stimuli according to the same principles as the minds of their objects of study. The emphasis on the way in which individuals perceive economic reality (the first sense) was present from Hayek's earliest writings in his theory of the monetary system. Individuals perceive money prices, and these are the data of individual plans. The discrepancy between this informational input and real relative scarcities causes coordination failures. With Hayek's largely methodological 1937 article as a catalyst, this subjectivist sub-programme was generalized to explain the process of coordination between individual plans (the second sense). Caldwell is also mistaken when he states that 'Hayek abandoned [the] position [that any adequate theory of business fluctuations had to build upon standard equilibrium theory] once he began to consider more seriously the problems arising from assumptions about knowledge, foresight, or in modern jargon, expectations formation' (Caldwell, 1988, p. 538). Laidler is subject to the same misconception when he writes that Hayek, beginning in 1937, '(...) began to propagate a very different view of market processes to the Walrasian equilibrium approach which underlay his business cycle theory (...).' (Chapter 1, Volume I, p. 20.) At no point in his career did Hayek abandon intertemporal general equilibrium theory as a foundation. To suggest otherwise is to misjudge the structure of Hayek's economic research programme.

The relation between the internal coordination of an individual's plan and its coordination with all the other plans can be shown as follows:

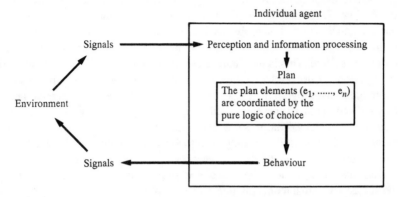

This scheme underlies Hayek, 1937, but it is already implicit in Hayek, 1928. The environment consists, *inter alia*, of all the other individual plans. In his methodologically most thoroughly systematic work, *The Pure Theory of Capital*, Hayek adopts a roundabout methodological ploy to get from an analysis of the internal coordination between the elements of the plan of a single individual to an analysis of the coordination between many different plans in an economy. First, he introduces the idealization of one economic dictator. Then he assumes the existence of more than one decision maker. On the next lower level of abstraction, he introduces competition, and finally money (see below, my discussion of the paper by Moss). When Caldwell says that in 1937 'Hayek first makes the claim that the coordination problem is the central problem, not just for economics, but for all of social science' (1988, p. 514) he strongly suggests that previously Hayek did not consider coordination problems as fundamental. However, the whole of Hayek, 1928 is addressed to the problem of intertemporal coordination and intertemporal coordination failures, and expectations. Equilibrium of the individual agent is defined as a situation in which the expectations on which his plan was based are not falsified. Expectations are the crux of Hayek's intertemporal general equilibrium theory, and therefore I cannot agree with Laidler's remark that 'Hayek ... systematically downplayed the significance of expectations in his work (...)' (Chapter 1, Volume I, p. 21).

The methodological structure of *The Pure Theory of Capital* reflects the different steps in the evolution of Hayek's research programme of the 1920s and 1930s, but then more systematically in accordance with the method of decreasing abstraction. It presents a systematized sequence of stills of the development of Hayek's programme. Hayek starts from a highly idealized model of the economy, which he subsequently factualizes by releasing one idealizing assumption after another.

The late introduction of money into the theory helps to explain why Hayek in *The Pure Theory of Capital* did not address in any detail the working of the market and coordination problems between individual agents. For him dynamic theory is tantamount to a theory that encompasses an analysis of the monetary system. This is only introduced on the last level of his methodological blueprint. However, by the time he had dealt with the technical problems of the reductionist programme of methodological individualism in capital theory, Keynes had captured the entire audience of economists, who lost interest in Hayek's economics. That was one of the reasons why he diverted his research to more general questions dealing with the stability of society as a whole. The momentum for this relatively new area was, however, provided by the work Hayek had already done in the field of economic coordination problems, that is, the subjectivist branch of economic research programmes.

The paper by Moss (Chapter 5, this volume) offers an example of the confusion that may arise if one does not take sufficient account of the fact that Hayek often introduces idealizing assumptions for a particular methodological purpose. Moss correctly observes that Hayek's analysis in *The Pure Theory of Capital* of an economy by means of an economic-dictator model derives from Wieser. However, when he states that 'within just a few years' time Hayek would find the approach misleading and obscuring a proper appreciation of the market process and its operation' (p. 103), he makes the fundamental mistake of confusing an idealization with a descriptive theory. Hayek never entertained the idea that a dictator model was descriptive of a real market economy. In *The Pure Theory of Capital* it has the specific (and explicitly specified) purpose of bringing out 'the various possible relationships between the organisation of production and the size of the product with special regard to the productivity of 'investment', that is, the use of different sorts of time-consuming methods of production' (Hayek, 1941, p. 97). This is part of the development of the technical apparatus which is preparatory to a full dynamic analysis of a market economy at a later stage of his research programme. Therefore, it is nonsense to say, as Moss does, that Hayek ever 'attempt[ed] to reconcile the household management model of the economy with the market system model' (p. 105). Because Moss has no eye for the fact that Hayek's economics is developed as a rather well-specified research programme, he gets so entangled in the confusion of his own making that he utters the historically false statement that 'sometime between 1944 and 1967 (...) Hayek had reached the conclusion that the household management model was fundamentally flawed as a representation of the market order' (p. 107). If Hayek ever held a different view, he had dispelled it at least as early as 1935, when he first contributed to the socialism debate.

Böhm criticizes Hayek's 1937 characterization of the central problem of all social sciences ('How the combination of fragments of knowledge existing in different minds can bring about a result which, if they were to be brought about deliberately, would require a knowledge on the part of the directing mind which no single person can possess') as 'running counter to distinctly Hayekian tenets' because it overlooks 'the notion of knowledge as being bound up with – that is, as not being available independently of – the social process of its generation' (pp. 161–2). Böhm also says that Hayek 'is mistaken to hold ... that the outcomes of competitive market transactions are independent of the processes generating them', and that Hayek seems to imply 'that the spontaneous ordering processes have a preassigned *telos*' (p. 162). By directly comparing two elements of Hayek's research programme as if they stood on the same level of analysis Böhm fails to recognize that Hayek's economics forms a programme, which, moreover, consists of two branches. The 'directing mind' in the quotation refers to the dictator, which belongs to the first branch of the programme, the one concerned with getting the technical details of the economic analysis right. For Hayek this means first of all doing static and stationary-state analysis. The idealizing assumption of the economic dictator is later released. After this, the dynamic element is introduced by paying attention to market processes and competition, in order to address the problem that informs the second branch of the programme, coordination failures. Individual agents equalize marginal rates of substitution by means of the pure logic of choice, and society 'does' the same through the price system. Of course, for a methodological individualist as Hayek then was, holistic entities such as societies 'do' nothing, which is why he says that the pure logic of choice elucidates the social allocation problem 'by analogy' (Hayek, 1949, p. 85). The methodological instrument for establishing the analogy is the fiction of the dictator.

The analysis of the way in which the price system works, the mechanism of competition and the diffusion of knowledge are held over till later, for the second volume of *The Pure Theory of Capital*. That volume was never written. What Hayek wrote instead are a number of separate articles on competition and coordination. Via *The Road to Serfdom* the argument was generalized so as to deal with the broader problem of how the coordination of individual behaviour in society, and still later the evolution of social institutions, can be explained. It is hard to see a discontinuity in this development of Hayek's thought, but Böhm is so intent on finding one that he gets the chronology wrong. He states that 'There is a noteworthy, important change of tack – no doubt under the impact of the socialist calculation debate – between the two "knowledge papers"' (p. 170). However, the calculation debate was published in 1935, two years before the first 'knowledge paper', and if Böhm is referring to Hayek, 1940, he has to show that that article is very different from Hayek's earlier contributions to the debate. Here, too, a methodological muddle leads to a falsification of history.

The essays in this volume have confirmed that the search for radical changes of direction in Hayek's work which was initiated by Hutchison has become a fashion. If Hayek's work is understood as a research programme in the way that was sketched above, I can find no reasons for seeing a discontinuity in 1935 or 1937. A more fundamental change of direction was taken by Hayek much later, when sometime during the 1960s he abandoned methodological individualism and adopted a holistic approach to social institutions in its stead. This has probably to do with the introduction of evolutionary arguments, which in the work of two other former staunch defenders of methodological individualism, Popper and Watkins, led to a similar change in methodology.

References

Caldwell, B. (1988), "Hayek's Transformation', *History of Political Economy*, **20** (4), Winter, 513–41.

Hayek, F.A. von (1928), 'Das intertemporale Gleichgewichtssystem der Preise und die Bewegungen des "Geldwertes"', *Weltwirtschaftliches Archiv*, **28** (2), 33–76.

Hayek, F.A. von (1937), 'Economics and Knowledge', in Hayek, 1949.

Hayek, F.A. von (1940), 'Socialist Calculation III: The Competitive "Solution"', in Hayek, 1949.

Hayek, F.A. von (1941), *The Pure Theory of Capital*, London: Routledge and Kegan Paul.

Hayek, F.A. von (1944), *The Road to Serfdom*, London: Routledge and Kegan Paul.

Hayek, F.A. von (1949), *Individualism and Economic Order*, London: Routledge and Kegan Paul.

Hayek, F.A. von (1955), *The Counterrevolution of Science*, Glencoe, Ill.: The Free Press.

Comment

Andrea Salanti

To deal with four papers in a single comment usually represents a difficult assignment. Here my task is made somewhat easier by the fact that three of them (those by Stephen Böhm, Tony Lawson, and Omar Hamouda and Robin Rowley) involve strictly related issues, so that I can start by commenting upon them jointly. Taken together, we may extract two important provisional conclusions about Hayek's methodology.

The first concerns the importance of the ontological dimension in understanding Hayek's conception of the proper object of economic theory. Note that some implications of such a conclusion are likely to prove to be less obvious than might appear at first sight, mainly because within current methodological discussions ontological questions are conspicuous by their absence. This is probably due both to what still remains of the legacy of logical positivism and to the fact that all the post-positivistic approaches in the philosophy of science (including the whole debate on the 'growth of knowledge') leave out ontology (and metaphysics, for that matter) from their research agenda.

Of course we remain with the (probably insoluble) problem of how to appraise different ontological perspectives. Take, for instance, Lawson's and Böhm's papers. If we are prepared to follow Lawson in his endorsement of Bhaskar's views on *transcendental realism*, then his critical reconstruction of Hayek's methodological vicissitude appears quite convincing and even fascinating. But, if we do not share the same ontological perspective, Lawson's 'external' critique loses almost all its strength and we remain with Böhm's observation that 'Perhaps Hayek's position [in the philosophy of science] is a full-blown Kantian one, combining *transcendental idealism* and *empirical realism*' (p. 173 in this volume, italics added).

Do not ask me, at this point, how it might be possible to choose between Böhm's and Lawson's different reconstructions! We do not have the right conceptual tools to guide us in such a choice. Although this may be discouraging, we must recognize that any choice between different ontological perspectives is doomed to remain a subjective matter of personal taste.

The second point to which I would like to draw some attention is suggested to me by the contributions presented by Böhm and Hamouda and Rowley. Both papers emphasize the huge difference between Hayek's penetrating vision of the importance of knowledge, as far as either the notion of economic rationality or the explanation of the functioning of a market economy is concerned, and the way such issues are commonly dealt with in more traditional approaches. As Böhm puts it,

> [W]hatever Hayek's notion of knowledge may be, it cannot ... be subsumed within 'information' as conceptualized in the economics of information literature. For Hayek, ... 'knowledge' is emphatically not [a] traded ... commodity which can be acquired at some specified resource cost. (p. 160 in this volume)

For their part Hamouda and Rowley point out that

> Hayek's context for economic theory identifies 'rationality' with a continual process which contains a number of significant constituents. [...] This simple vision is markedly different from alternative visions that view individual rationality as part of an abstract system involving formal optimization (of utility, profits or costs), omniscience, widespread separability, and equilibrium. Rational processes for Hayek were subjective, individualistic, and evolutionary. (pp. 180–81 in this volume)

In spite of the stimulating peculiarities of Hayek's views it can hardly be disputed, as noticed by Hamouda and Rowley at the outset of their paper, that Hayek 'shares with Adam Smith the dubious honour of being frequently cited but seldom read.' To the 'analytical' and 'theoretical' reasons for this state of affairs provided by Hamouda and Rowley I would add a consideration from the realm of the sociology of knowledge.

As we all know, the success of one author (or better, of his particular research programme) depends among other things on the opportunities he can offer to other, and especially younger, scholars to build up their careers by working within his research programme. Thus, if Hayek's theoretical insights are frequently praised but seldom pursued any more, one of the reasons is surely that his work does not satisfy this requirement; the problem with Hayek's theories is not so much that they are too simple (or too unorthodox) as that they are quite difficult to pursue further. In this respect it is ironic to have to acknowledge that Hayek is seldom read in these days for the same reasons that Keynes is seldom read either: because it has proved to be much too difficult to provide suitable microfoundations of the kind nowadays in fashion.[1]

Coming now to Bruce Caldwell's 'four theses on Hayek', first of all I must say that each one, if taken alone, seems to be quite sensible. My only comment in this respect is that it is not necessary to deny that Hayek's 'transformation' was concerned with the abandonment of Misesian *a priorism* (Caldwell's first thesis) in order to support the view that it actually involved the notion of equilibrium (his second thesis). Indeed the two moves, *per se* (that is, independently of textual evidence), might well have been consistently taken at the same time, because of the compatibility of *a priorism* with a theory of equilibrium (as Caldwell himself implicitly recognizes when he observes that the *a priorist* foundations of equilibrium theory would have fitted perfectly Hayek's claim that any adequate theory of cycle should be consistent with the 'equilibrium theory' result that all markets clear).

More generally, the problem I see in Caldwell's interpretation is that his four theses, if taken together, lead to the conclusion that Hayek's *ontological* perspective seems to hang in a *methodological* vacuum. Indeed, if we accept that Hayek never subscribed to *a priorism* as a foundationalist epistemology; that he paid only little more than lip service to Popperian falsificationism; and that due to his explicit rejection of methodological monism, we cannot interpret his hidden methodology by analogy with the then prevailing views on the structures of theories and the notion of explanation, then we are unable to reconstruct his methodology, in the sense that we are unable to specify Hayek's methodological stance concerning justification and appraisal of economic theories.

Of course, if we want to avoid retreating to the unconvincing story of Popper's falsificationism as Hayek's hidden source of methodological inspiration, it is far from easy to fill such a gap. The only hint I can offer here is that we might try to see if Hayek's methodological views can be reconstructed according to the Senior–Mill tradition. There are two possible indications, in my view, that seem to lead in that direction. First, Hayek's advocacy of more modest goals for economic analysis in his 'Scientism and the Study of Society' might suggest some parallels with the Millian thesis about the *inexactness* of economic 'laws'.[2]

Second, just because Hayek was not concerned with a pure logic of choice – as Caldwell points out towards the end of his paper – but with the more complex subject of 'knowledge and economics', his set of initial assumptions cannot be limited to the rationality principle and a description of somewhat *hypothetical* situations, but must include some statements about what he conceives to be really relevant for the explanation of actual economic behaviours. Thus we are likely to find in Hayek's premises something which, to use Nassau Senior's (1836) words, 'is a matter of consciousness' together with something else which 'is a matter of observation.'

In this last respect let me conclude by recalling that a fundamental concern with 'consciousness' and 'observation' rather than with axioms and formalization, as well as a clear awareness of the political implications of economic theories, also represent the common background against which the intellectual battle between Hayek and Keynes took place in the first half of this century. Why now those times seem so far away is a question which deserves further methodological reflection.

Notes

1. A similar point is raised by Richard Arena in the conclusions of his contribution (Chapter 10, Volume I of this series) when he notes the apparent paradox that unorthodox economists have perhaps more to learn from Hayek than their mainstream colleagues.
2. For a recent and detailed discussion of the Millian tradition in economic methodology (indeed a serious attempt to revive it), see Hausman (1992).

References

Hausman, D.M. (1992), *The Inexact and Separate Science of Economics*, Cambridge and New York: Cambridge University Press.

Senior, N.W. (1836), *An Outline of the Science of Political Economy*, New York: A. M. Kelley Reprints of Economic Classics, 1965.

Comment

Carlo Zappia

To begin my comment on the papers presented by Streissler and Jossa, I would like to thank the contributors for the profound insights they have shown in dealing with this subject, which, as they have brilliantly illustrated, can be considered fundamental not only as far as Hayek's thought is concerned but also in the more general context of comparing how different economic systems may work.

Streissler's and Jossa's papers deal with the 'socialist calculation debate' from two different perspectives. On the one hand, Streissler tries to emphasize Hayek's specific contribution to the subject by examining the topic in, let us say, a *positive manner*: he considers what Hayek did to increase understanding of the price system mechanism in a competitive economy, in particular by explaining why his contribution must be considered original even if the subject seemed to have been already dealt with in depth by his predecessors. Jossa, on the other hand, attempts to discuss Hayek's theory of socialism in, let us say, a *negative manner*: he gives careful consideration to what Hayek might have said, or discovered, had he studied a proper socialist economy, underlining the fact that Hayek studied socialism simply as a centrally planned organization and not as a specific economic organization, as Lange's theory of market socialism would require.

I shall comment on one particular point from each paper, starting with Jossa's, which I find more controversial. As Jossa suggests, Lange's first aim was to propose a system in which consumers and managers would take their decisions on the basis of prices adjusted in response to positive or negative excess demands by the central authority, in order to simulate the market. He substituted the authority of command of the planner for the discipline imposed by the market in the competitive economy.

What should be made clearer is in which sense Lange's market socialism, or 'socialism with autonomous firms', can be effectively distinguished from the planned economy to which Hayek (and Streissler) referred. Following Jossa's interpretation, I find it difficult to distinguish Lange's model from the model of centralized planning in which the well known results concerning the theoretical possibility of efficient economic calculation under socialism were first shown by Barone and Pareto, and which have been extensively restated in more recent times using duality theory, as Streissler reminds us.

To provide arguments in favour of the market system in the socialist calculation debate of the 1930s, Hayek tried to switch public attention from the parametric use of prices to the informational use. As Streissler emphasizes, this can be considered the main advance Hayek provided in following Mises's thought.

It is not clear, at least in my opinion, whether Lange understood the Austrian point about the informational role of prices as the essence of competition. It would be interesting to understand how, in Lange's model, prices could perform not only the ordinary allocative role but also the informative role that, in Hayek's view, they performed in the competitive economy.

Let us take an example. Jossa states that 'the economic policy advocated by Lange uses the levers of public intervention to channel the spontaneous market forces in a direction suited to bring about the intended results' (Chapter 4, this volume). Hence, he seems to advocate something like the redistribution of initial resources without distortion envisaged in general equilibrium theory by the second theorem of welfare economics. As is well known, this approach is essentially static and cannot account for the activity of discovery of new knowledge which characterizes Hayek's thought and explains his deep faith in the market mechanism.

In my opinion, it could be more useful to start the comparison between the two ways of interpreting market socialism from the perspective Hayek indicated, that is, by examining and comparing their respective informational efficiency.

Although one can disagree on the analytical point to stress, it is difficult to disagree with Jossa's general reflections on economic policy: Hayek's position seems to be difficult to defend. However, I think that Hayek's message might be interpreted in a slightly different way. The statement by Hayek that 'to control a spontaneous order is a contradiction in terms' is very difficult to interpret. Neither is it convincing, if seen from Jossa's perspective. In my view, this and other types of general statements made by Hayek might be seen not as normative assertions but as general warnings against massive policy intervention. In short, we could probably say that Hayek's contention is not necessarily that man must never control social evolution, but simply that he might not be able to do it correctly.

Let us now consider Streissler's paper. I would like to come back to the 'lack of incentive' argument he mentions, and try to examine this aspect in greater detail. Streissler finds it 'surprising how little Hayek used the ancient (lack of) incentive argument in his strictures on socialism' (Chapter 3, this volume), and doesn't suggest a clear answer to this lack of concentration on the problem. I think Hayek's approach can be partially explained and I shall propose an interpretation of it. For this purpose a brief analysis of his notion of private information is useful.

In Hayek's theory the properties of the achievable equilibrium depend strictly on the degree of knowledge which can be aggregated and transmitted by the price system. In fact, we would say that it is assumed that a certain degree of common knowledge is reached in the process of adjustment to equilibrium. This is why we must be precise in defining the features of Hayek's notion of private information. Please note that, in this context, I am considering private information and personal knowledge as synonyms.

The knowledge Hayek considered is 'the knowledge of the circumstances [which] ... never exists in concentrated or integrated form but solely as the dispersed bits of incomplete and frequently contradictory knowledge which all the separate individuals possess' (Hayek, 1976, p. 77). Even his aim of identifying a specific kind of information is clearly stated when he says: 'price expectations and even the knowledge of current prices are only a very small section of the problem of knowledge, as I see it. The wider aspect of the problem of knowledge with which I am concerned is the knowledge of the basic fact of how the different commodities can be obtained and used, and under what conditions they are actually obtained and used' (Hayek, 1976, p. 51).

Thus according to Hayek it is essential to stress 'the knowledge of the particular circumstances of time and place', on the basis of which 'practically every individual has some advantage over all others because he possesses unique information of which beneficial use might be made, but of which use can be made only if decisions depending on it are left to him or are made with his active cooperation' (Hayek, 1976, p. 80). Therefore, when he directly examined production, he firmly considered equally relevant both the knowledge of feasible alternative techniques and the knowledge which increases during production, namely the specific knowledge generated complementary to production.

As we have just seen, each agent's personal knowledge, or, as it is usually called today, each agent's private information, is precisely characterized, in Hayek's view. In particular, there are some properties of this notion which differentiate it from the kind of information used in a general equilibrium context with asymmetric information. First of all, the kind of information Hayek was considering was that which every agent operating in the system privately disposes of in connection with the specific activity in which he is involved, and thus that information does not relate to exogenous events. Second, this kind of information is not to be considered costly to the single agent, but might be sold at a price to a purchaser who is interested in it. Finally, the analysed information can be generated during the process of adjustment to equilibrium; so it cannot be precisely determined *ex ante,* because it depends upon the economic system's dynamic evolution.

As a result, we can say that Hayek's personal knowledge is something very similar to the private information examined in modern contract theory, at least as far as the first two properties highlighted are concerned (for a detailed analysis of this point, see Zappia, 1993).

Seen in this perspective, I don't think we can say that Hayek didn't realize how much incentive effects are connected with information dispersion in the market system. In my view, it is more likely that Hayek decided to eschew a deeper analysis of this topic, in order to concentrate on the analysis of information transmission. The reason that I would suggest for this is the following: Hayek didn't study incentive problems in depth because they are more related to the act of exchange between pairs of agents, and to the signing of contracts, than to the general interrelations emphasized in general equilibrium contexts. Therefore, the reason why he showed greater explicit interest in information transmission analysis might have been that it has more obvious relevance to the working of the entire economic system, which was his first concern in the socialist calculation debate.

Recent developments in information and contract theory would seem to confirm Hayek's attitude to this problem. In a general equilibrium context with asymmetric information, incentive problems deeply influence contracting activity. However, even if it has been shown that it is possible to write contracts which ensure incentive compatibility between two differently informed parties, one can surely state that an incentive compatible contract will not take the simple form postulated within the Arrow–Debreu model. Mainly for this reason it is extremely difficult to demonstrate the general equilibrium compatibility of many contracts of this kind.

In conclusion, I would like to relate my previous comments to a point stressed by some contributors to these volumes. The notion of private information I have discussed above has direct relevance for the properties of Hayek's equilibrium. The equilibrium Hayek thought to be actually achievable in a competitive economy is not characterized as Pareto-optimal. In my view, this can be explained through an 'information argument'. Defining private information as he did, Hayek was perfectly aware that, even in a competitive economy driven by the price system, there are pieces of dispersed information that cannot be 'extracted' by the market mechanism. This is why the attained equilibrium doesn't necessarily satisfy the informational efficiency property and its related normative standards – which some interpreters attributed to Hayek's equilibrium (see Grossman, 1989).

References

Grossman S. (1989), *The Informational Role of Prices*, Cambridge, Mass.: The MIT Press.
Hayek F.A. von (1976, 1948), *Individualism and Economic Order*, London: Routledge and Kegan Paul.

Zappia, C. (1993), 'The Notion of Private Information in a Modern Perspective: A Re-appraisal of Hayek's Contribution', *Quaderni del Dipartimento di Economia Politica*, **155**, Università di Siena.

Index